CAMBRIDGE

Brighter Thinking

The Making of a Superpower: USA, 1865–1975

A/AS Level History for AQA
Student Book

Tony McConnell and Adam I. P. Smith

Series Editors: Michael Fordham and David Smith

CAMBRIDGE
UNIVERSITY PRESS

University Printing House, Cambridge CB2 8BS, United Kingdom

Cambridge University Press is part of the University of Cambridge.

It furthers the University's mission by disseminating knowledge in the pursuit of education, learning and research at the highest international levels of excellence.

www.cambridge.org
Information on this title: www.cambridge.org/9781107530171 (Paperback)
www.cambridge.org/9781107530225 (Cambridge Elevate-enhanced Edition)

First published 2015

A catalogue record for this publication is available from the British Library

ISBN 978-1-107-53017-1 Paperback
ISBN 978-1-107-53022-5 Cambridge Elevate-enhanced Edition

Additional resources for this publication at www.cambridge.org/ukschools

Cambridge University Press has no responsibility for the persistence or accuracy of URLs for external or third-party internet websites referred to in this publication, and does not guarantee that any content on such websites is, or will remain, accurate or appropriate. Information regarding prices, travel timetables, and other factual information given in this work is correct at the time of first printing but Cambridge University Press does not guarantee the accuracy of such information thereafter.

Message from AQA

This textbook has been approved by AQA for use with our qualification. This means that we have checked that it broadly covers the specification and we are satisfied with the overall quality. Full details of our approval process can be found on our website.

We approve textbooks because we know how important it is for teachers and students to have the right resources to support their teaching and learning. However, the publisher is ultimately responsible for the editorial control and quality of this book.

Please note that when teaching the A/AS Level History (7041, 7042) course, you must refer to AQA's specification as your definitive source of information. While this book has been written to match the specification, it cannot provide complete coverage of every aspect of the course.

A wide range of other useful resources can be found on the relevant subject pages of our website: www.aqa.org.uk

Contents

About this Series

Cambridge A/AS Level History for AQA is an exciting new series designed to support students in their journey from GCSE to A Level and then on to possible further historical study. The books provide the knowledge, concepts and skills needed for the two-year AQA History A Level course, but it's our intention as series editors that students recognise that their A Level exams are just one step to a potential lifelong relationship with the discipline of history. This book has further readings, extracts from historians' works and links to wider questions and ideas that go beyond the scope of an A Level course. With this series, we have sought to ensure not only that the students are well prepared for their examinations, but also that they gain access to wider debate that characterises historical study.

The series is designed to provide clear and effective support for students as they make the adjustment from GCSE to A Level, and also for teachers, especially those who are not familiar with teaching a two-year linear course. The student books cover the AQA specifications for both A/AS Level. They are intended to appeal to the broadest range of students, and they offer challenge to stretch the top end and additional support for those who need it. Every author in this series is an experienced historian or history teacher, and all have great skill in conveying narratives to readers and asking the kinds of questions that pull those narratives apart.

In addition to high-quality prose, this series also makes extensive use of textual primary sources, maps, diagrams and images, and offers a wide range of activities to encourage students to address historical questions of cause, consequence, change and continuity. Throughout the books there are opportunities to criticise the interpretations of other historians, and to use those interpretations in the construction of students' own accounts of the past. The series aims to ease the transition for those students who move on from A Level to undergraduate study, and the books are written in an engaging style that will encourage those who want to explore the subject further.

Icons used within the series include:

 Key terms

 Developing concepts

 Speak like a historian

 Voices from the past/Hidden voices

 Practice essay questions

 Taking it further

 Thematic links

 Chapter summary

About Cambridge Elevate

Cambridge Elevate is the platform which hosts a digital version of this Student Book. If you have access to this digital version you can annotate different parts of the book, send and receive messages to and from your teacher and insert weblinks, among other things.

We hope that you enjoy your AS or A Level History course, as well as this book, and wish you well for the journey ahead.

Michael Fordham and David L Smith

Series editors

Introduction

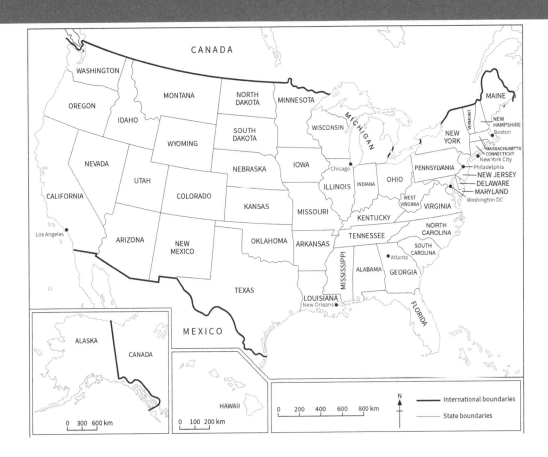

In November 1863, Abraham Lincoln, the 16th **president** of the United States of America, made a speech that would become famous. Known as the Gettysburg Address, his words were intended to mark the official dedication of a cemetery on the site of a battle, which had taken place four months earlier, between the two halves of his divided country. Lincoln saw the survival of his young nation in terms of the survival of constitutional, representative **democracy**: the Union had to survive, he argued, so that '*government of the people, by the people and for the people shall not perish from the Earth*'. Eighteen months later, with the American Civil War all but won, Lincoln became the first of four American presidents to lose his life to an assassin's bullet. The Union survived his death, and flourished.

In 1975, Lincoln's distant successor Gerald Ford, who had never won a national election but arrived at his high office through the resignation in disgrace of Richard Nixon, presided over one of the two world Superpowers, and prepared to celebrate, in 1976, the 200th anniversary of the signing of the **Declaration of Independence**. By 1990, with the collapse of the Soviet Union, the United States would stand alone as the only **Superpower** left.

This textbook is intended for the study of what happened between the firing of the bullet that killed Lincoln, the first Republican president, and the circumstances that brought Gerald Ford to the White House. There is an idea expressed by both these men – and by the many others who have held high office – that America has a special, privileged place as leader of the democratic world. This is the idea of **American Exceptionalism** – America as the 'last best hope of earth', as Lincoln put it, which often seems to dominate modern American politics and is rooted in history: the story of America is the story of becoming and remaining a force for good.

Historians should avoid the temptation to believe that American history is just the story of a country's rapid progress towards its natural or preordained position as the dominant nation in the world. By the turn of the millennium, America had the largest economy in the world. Its astronauts are the only men ever to have walked on the Moon. Its culture dominated that of many other countries, and its president assumed global leadership whenever possible. As is so often true in studying the past, the truth is far richer and more complex. How did America change in only a little over a hundred years from a fractured nation in danger of permanent collapse to become, if only briefly, the world's only surviving Superpower?

The origins of the United States of America

It was mostly northern Europeans who settled the land that would eventually become the United States. By the 18th century, the dominant force in the region was British. There were several reasons for the success of the British colonies in North America. There was plenty of space for production of cash crops. The institution of slavery made for even more profitable trade. The colonies also provided an attractive base for European, especially Scottish and English, dissidents. From their very earliest moments the colonies practised various forms of constitutional government based on political and religious liberty. By this they meant, roughly, that they proposed to create a political association of equals to govern their new land as part of the British Empire.

America is a big land, and it was underpopulated. Towns and cities were a European idea, and they were for the most part confined to areas within easy access of the Atlantic coast. Native American tribes were not often a problem, and if they were they could usually be played against one another.

A new country formed

Throughout the 18th century there were wars between Britain and France that spilled over into the Americas. In 1756 there began the conflict that would become known as the Seven Years' War in Europe and as the French and Indian War in America. The British sent a large force across the Atlantic and won a stunning victory in North America. Canada was theirs and France was forced out. Victory came at a price. The British, with far greater possessions now in America, embarked on a programme of reorganisation of their colonies, and decided that a frontier defence force was needed; it would have to be paid for by the colonists, and it would have to be a standing (permanent and professional) army. To the British this was all eminently sensible. For the colonists (who also saw themselves as British) it was a fundamental assault on their liberty. What the British saw as a necessary attempt to protect the colonies from further invasion became for the colonists a **tyranny**, and attitudes hardened on both sides of the Atlantic. All the colonies were affected by the new taxes and by the British reorganisation.

Key term

tyranny: the arbitrary and unconstrained use of power. It has become associated in American thought with any government action that deprives individuals of their rights.

The Thirteen Colonies, as the British colonies in America came to be known, are shown in Figure 0.1. Eighteenth-century Massachusetts included the area known now as Maine. West Virginia would not split off from Virginia itself until the American Civil War.

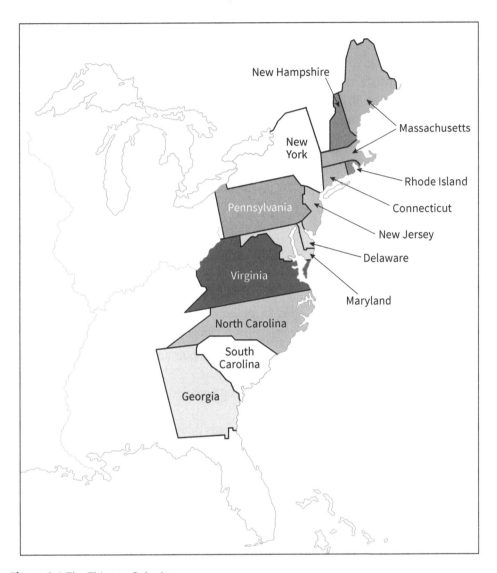

Figure 0.1 The Thirteen Colonies.

The sense of grievance that the colonists felt fed into 18th-century thinking about liberty. Key ideas that emerged among them, and remain crucial in modern American political thought, were:

- That there should be no taxation without representation – this meant that if the British Parliament demanded taxes, it could only do so from areas that elected MPs, which the colonies and other parts of the British Empire did not.
- That government was oppressive and, if left unchecked, would become tyrannical. This was particularly true of a monarchy.
- That power should be exerted locally and democratically, among an informed body of citizens with defined rights and responsibilities.

When conflict broke out in 1775, the Colonies raised an army for defence and put a general from Virginia in charge. His name was George Washington. Throughout 1775 it became clear that the British government would not deliver a version of liberty that the colonists were willing to accept; by 1776 it was evident that the ambitions of the colonial leaders could not be met while remaining within the British Empire. On 2 July 1776 the delegates to the colonial Congress declared independence; two days later they adopted a formal Declaration of Independence. This document was written chiefly by the Virginian Thomas Jefferson. The Declaration consists mostly of a list of grievances directed against the tyrannical British King George III; it also describes the inalienable **rights** of all men as being 'life, liberty, and the pursuit of happiness'.

How did the Americans get away with it by winning the war that followed? Essentially, the British found that they could not win a lengthy war on the other side of an ocean, in hostile territory – especially not once the French, seeking revenge for their humiliation 20 years earlier, became involved on the colonists' side. The British capitulated in 1781.

The Constitution of the United States of America

It was one thing to have won the war. The new nation had been led by the Continental Congress, when all the colonies were united in a common cause. To win the peace would be trickier. The former colonies had problems:

- Long borders with British Canada and Spanish Louisiana, and potentially hostile Native Americans.
- They had no money and large war debts, and needed to work together to borrow money.
- Competition between the former colonies was threatening to weaken all of them, even though it was clear that if they did not work together they would be vulnerable.

In 1787 a convention was called at Philadelphia to consider the problem. The **Constitution** it produced (see Figure 0.2) was designed specifically to strengthen the union between the states, and it was based upon various ideological principles that dated back in some cases to 17th-century England – where they had long-since ceased to operate. It has various key features:

- Separation of powers would ensure that no one branch of government – and no individual – could become too powerful.
- There would be a single executive, called a president, whose powers would be heavily limited by the legislature and by the judiciary, the **Supreme Court**.
- The Constitution would be federalist, which meant that the central government would have powers, and so would the individual states – the Constitution would outline which body had power over each particular issue. Sovereignty would lie with the people themselves, rather than with any governmental institution.
- The Constitution could be changed (by **amendment**) only when there was genuine general agreement that it should be.

Politics, economics and territory in the early USA

George Washington (Figure 0.3), the obvious choice for president, served for two 4-year terms. In neither election was he opposed. He was followed by John Adams,

Key term

Constitution: the set of ideas about how a country should be governed – its institutions, and the rights and responsibilities of its government and people.

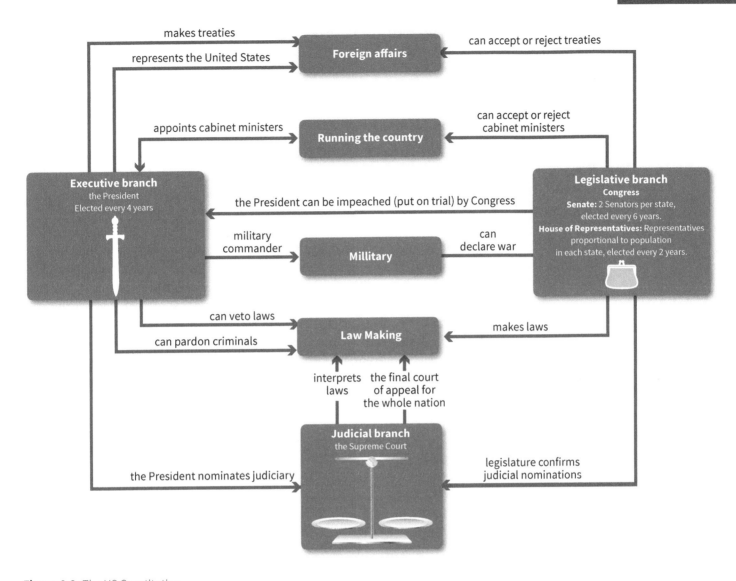

Figure 0.2: The US Constitution.

the political father of independence; then the primary author of the Declaration of Independence, Thomas Jefferson, became president in 1800. This marked the beginning of 24 years of consistency in American political assumptions. Government should be small. National debt was bad. The idea that national debt should be avoided persisted in American politics until the Second World War. Banks that were able to regulate the currency were dangerous – more dangerous, Jefferson is supposed to have said, than armies.

Westward expansion and war

The new nation born in 1776 already laid claim to most of the continent up to the Mississippi River, and this offered almost endless opportunities to expand. In 1803 President Jefferson negotiated a treaty with France to purchase the Louisiana Territory. This gave the USA complete control of navigation of the Mississippi and doubled its land area. It meant that new states could continue to be added to the Union. Further expansion came following the conclusion of the War of 1812, when President Madison encouraged Congress to declare war to prevent attacks on American possessions by the British in Canada and the Shawnee tribe in the

Figure 0.3: George Washington was the American commander-in-chief in the Revolutionary War, and the first president of the new country.

Mississippi Valley. The White House was burned down, but the Americans won the war. Or at least, they did not lose, fixing the border with Canada as well as making its significant territorial acquisitions, and gaining control of the navigation of the Mississippi River, meaning that they could exploit their new territories, and by the time the history of the war had entered the popular consciousness it was billed by some as a second revolution.

Steamboats carrying crops such as cotton sailed down the Mississippi, barges made their way along the network of canals, and in the 1830s and 1840s railroads would begin to cross the country. Americans came to see their domination of the continent as part of a 'manifest destiny'. The Monroe Doctrine of 1823, named after the president, stated that the USA would resist any further European attempts to intervene in Latin American countries. In a remarkable piece of chutzpah, this young nation, less than 50 years old, had effectively claimed an entire hemisphere as its sphere of influence. The idea was to prevent the European powers from bringing their own conflicts to the Americas, potentially dragging the Americans in. In later years the Monroe Doctrine (the term was first used a generation later) would be invoked to justify the idea that no European powers had the right to prevent Americans from intervening in the internal affairs of Latin American countries.

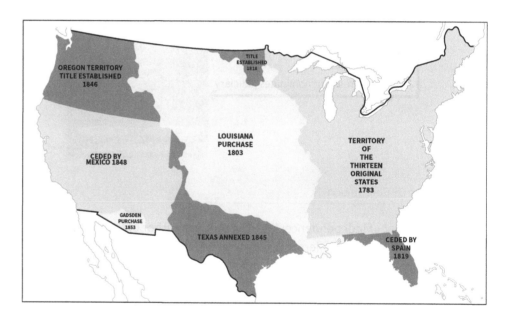

Figure 0.4: American territorial acquisitions, 1776–1865.

Sectional tension

In the South, cotton was rapidly becoming king. The invention of the cotton gin in 1793 had made it hugely profitable because the mass production of raw cotton was now possible; the expansion of the territory of the United States offered yet more opportunities to make profit. Existing states grew their populations, and sent pioneers to expand westwards and create new states following similar economic models. This expanding population gained extra representation in the **House of Representatives** in both North and South. The difference was that, thanks to a compromise in the US Constitution, slaves only counted as three-fifths of the value of non-slaves in determining congressional representation. Add a new state, though, and that meant two more senators.

This mattered because a sectional balance was evolving in Congress between north and south, free and slave. When Missouri applied for admission to the Union in 1820, as a slave state, a deal had to be done. The first part of the deal was that any future slave state had to be south of Missouri, thereby limiting the number of slave states that could be admitted. The second part of the deal was that the northern part of Massachusetts would be admitted as a separate, free, state, to balance the numbers – this was Maine. This was known as the Missouri Compromise.

Key term

manifest destiny: the idea that America was and is fated to dominate the continent of North America, the western hemisphere and the world. It drove expansion in the 19th century – see Figure 0.4.

The causes of the American Civil War

There is an episode of *The Simpsons* in which Apu, the Indian shopkeeper, is forced to take a citizenship test. He is asked about the causes of the American Civil War. He begins to explain the nuanced complexity of the issue and is interrupted and advised to give a shorter answer – 'Just say slavery'. Slavery was certainly the major cause of the American Civil War, but why slavery caused such a conflict is quite complicated.

Since the Missouri Compromise, new states had been admitted to the USA very carefully to avoid upsetting the North/South (free/slave) sectional balance. The annexation of much more territory from Mexico in 1848 looked set to cause problems; the discovery of gold in California made careful management of the new territory impossible. The area around San Francisco Bay became very popular for free immigrants in the 'Gold Rush' of 1849 and California was admitted as a large free state, upsetting the balance. In 1854 the Kansas–Nebraska Act established those two future states as territories, with the issue of slavery to be decided by popular sovereignty – that is, the people of the territories would vote on the issue. This was significant as neither of these territories was south of Missouri: the Missouri Compromise was over. The period from 1854–61 was known in Kansas as 'Bleeding Kansas', because of the violence and bloodshed that occurred between the pro- and anti-slavery factions there; this particular conflict was only stopped by the outbreak of the wider Civil War.

Sectional tension

Meanwhile the cultural battle lines were being drawn. Northern dislike of slavery had become active disgust, and northerners were disrupting the institution in an attack that was both cultural and economic. Harriet Beecher Stowe's novel *Uncle Tom's Cabin*, depicting a slave so cowed by his status that he was driven to accepting it, stirred up northern anger. There was a period of religious enthusiasm known as the Second Great Awakening, which directly attacked slavery in religious terms. Resistance movements such as the 'underground railroad', by which slaves were smuggled into free territories where they gained freedom, became effective enough to attract legal challenges.

In the North the anti-slavery movement comprised industrialists seeking to advantage their preferred form of economic activity over plantation agriculture, recent immigrants and those inspired by religious messages. In the South, meanwhile, affection grew for the 'peculiar institution' of slavery, even among those who were not themselves slave owners. 'Peculiar' in this sense means 'defining'. The South *was* slavery, and if the North did not like slavery, it seemed, then it did not like the South. Passions were stirred on both sides. In 1854, in response to the Kansas–Nebraska Act, a new political party – the Republican Party – was formed. It was pledged to oppose the expansion of slavery, and channelled the widespread anxiety in the North that (southern) slave owners were running the national government for their own ends. The Republican Party's vision was of small independent businesses, farms, entrepreneurs, people able to make their own opportunities in an economy in which all individuals could benefit from the fruits of their own labour.

In the 1860 presidential election, a former Whig named Abraham Lincoln was able to win the presidency for the Republican Party. He won the election by sweeping the free states, which, although he won less than half the national popular vote, gave him a majority in the Electoral College that decides the presidency. His name was not even on the ballot paper in most southern states: his free-state majority was based in the North. One month before the election, Lincoln's Democratic Party opponent Stephen A Douglas had conceded defeat and begun a tour of the South, the purpose of which was to try to persuade southerners not to leave the Union when Lincoln won.

Secession and war

The election of 1860 confirmed the South's worst fears. A candidate who was openly opposed to the expansion of slavery had won without any support from the southern section of the country. There was nobody left to negotiate a compromise. Secession – leaving the Union – seemed to be the only option. This was in place in seven of the eleven states that would go on to form the Confederate States of America before Lincoln had even been inaugurated. In April 1861 the Confederacy, as it was known, attacked the federal garrison of Fort Sumter in South Carolina. The Civil War had begun. The reasons for the Civil War are summarised in Figure 0.5.

The American Civil War

Why did the North win? It was more industrialised. The South recognised the need for European support, but President Lincoln was able to prevent this from coming to pass. The North, unlike the South, was able to enlist its working classes in its army – until March 1865, in desperation, southern politicians had little stomach for the mass arming of slaves, which would have been a recognition that their entire racial theory was wrong, as well as giving weapons to those whom they had oppressed. Both sides exhausted themselves but the damage was worse for the side that was the poorer, which was the South. It's also noteworthy that the vast majority of the fighting happened in the southern states. Virginia, Tennessee and Mississippi were particularly devastated. Of the states that had remained loyal to the Union only Missouri and Kentucky, both slaveholding states on the border, were subject to repeated fighting.

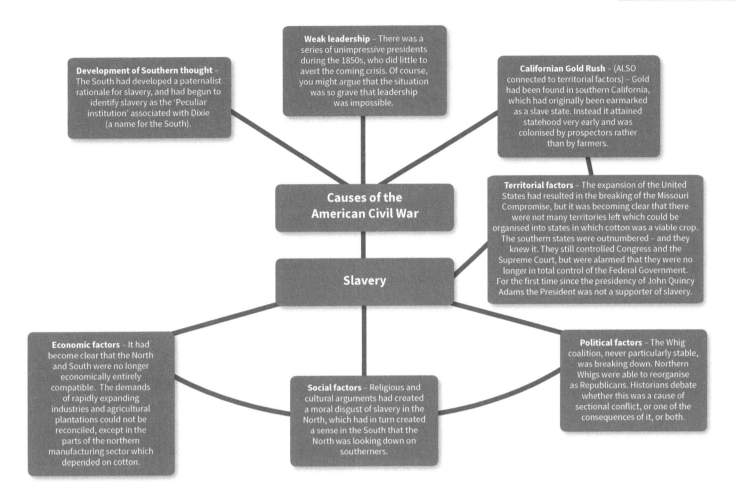

Figure 0.5: The causes of the American Civil War.

The Emancipation Proclamation

In order to maintain the loyalty of border states that might otherwise have considered leaving the Union, Lincoln had emphasised early in the war that the reason for fighting was to preserve the Union, not to abolish slavery. In 1862 he let it be known in the Emancipation Proclamation that he would free the slaves in rebel states – but only if they did not surrender first. Any state that surrendered by 1863 could keep its slaves. His freeing of the slaves was not, at first, a matter of high principle. It was an economic attack. The entire system of credit of the South was based upon slaveholding. If a southern plantation owner wished to borrow money, he might take out a mortgage using as security not his land but his slaves. By abolishing slavery, Lincoln abolished the wealth of the South. In the 1850s the value of slaves held in the United States was almost equal to its **gross domestic product (GDP)**. That is, the total amount produced by the whole country in a year would only just have paid for all the slaves in one of its sections.

The assassination of Abraham Lincoln

American presidents had died in office before, but Lincoln was the first to be assassinated. His assassin, John Wilkes Booth, apparently saw his actions in terms of revenge. His diary reveals that he knew the 'cause' – that is, the cause of the Confederacy – was lost. There was a wider plot to kill Vice President Johnson and **Secretary of State** Seward, and perhaps the Union general Ulysses S. Grant, on the same night. The aim was to decapitate the US government, and perhaps allow the Confederacy to recover following the surrender a few days earlier of its great general Robert E. Lee. It's one of the great ironies of US history that Booth, in killing the skilled conciliator Lincoln, arguably made things far worse for the South in the period immediately after the war, which is where our studies begin in earnest.

Themes in American history

As you read this textbook, you will be able to build a narrative – in fact several narratives, should you choose – of American history. One narrative will be of how the USA became a Superpower – were Americans working towards this change in status? Were they even willing for it to happen? How united was the USA, and to what extent did all its citizens share in its successes and failures? Who were the major players, the key individuals, in the story of America?

There are also certain themes to draw out. You should attempt to trace these themes, where appropriate, throughout your studies.

How did government, political authority and political parties change and develop?

The presidents who followed him were less powerful as Congress reasserted its power to set the agenda for the country following Lincoln's death. Over time, the American presidency would develop into the most powerful office in the world, shaped by some remarkable personalities, economic crisis and war. The Republican Party, based in the North (although with by no means universal support there), and the Democrats, with their power base in the South, have survived to this day, although they take their support from different areas of the country. It was certainly not predetermined that they would survive; many contemporaries did not think that they would, assuming in particular that once the issue of slavery was sorted out the Republican Party would not need to exist.

 Thematic link: government and politics

In what ways did the economy and society of the USA change and develop?

The America of Washington, Adams and Jefferson had been a simpler place than that inherited by President Johnson when he was sworn in, and as its population increased its demographics changed. Over the years following the Civil War the nature of the workforce would be altered. In the South, the newly freed black people entered the free labour market; some of them, and their descendants, would, over time, move to the North. European immigrants came seeking opportunity in America, establishing communities that were distinguished by their national origins. What would life be like for the poor immigrants and the ex-slaves? For a large number of Americans in the 19th century, freedom effectively meant ownership of land or other productive property. After 1865, freedom would be redefined as the right to participate in the wage labour market coupled with the right to vote. Over time the American economy came to rely on immigration and brutal capitalism; it would have booms caused by automobiles, and crashes, one of which was so severe that it shook the world. By 1975, most Americans would live in the suburbs, which did not even exist in 1865.

Thematic link: economy and society

How did the role of the USA in world affairs change?

The USA grew up fast. By 1865 it had taken its place as one of the world powers, and its **Monroe Doctrine** asserted (against little opposition) its pre-eminent position in the western hemisphere. The idea of American Exceptionalism, which had been tied up with its manifest destiny to expand itself across a continent bringing ideas of liberty and freedom, began to take on a worldwide aspect. Lincoln had expressed the idea that America was a beacon of democracy for the world. The USA would go through periods of isolationism and periods of international engagement before President Kennedy, in 1961, expressly claimed leadership of the 'free world' and sought to manage and indeed undertake its defence.

Thematic link: world affairs

How important were ideas and ideology?

The historian Richard Hofstadter, working during the early Cold War, said, 'It has been our fate as a nation not to have ideologies but to be one.' What it meant to be an American was ideologically and culturally defined. It had to be – the massive immigration that has been a key feature of American history meant that it was difficult to find any ethnic definition, although this has not stopped politicians and historians from trying. A key theme of American history is how the concept of Americanism has been defined and used in political battles, and how attainable the idea of 'being American' has been to different kinds of people in the country. We might also trace the ways in which social and fiscal conservatism have developed, and the different ways in which religious ideas have influenced American political thought.

Thematic link: ideas and ideology

How united was the USA during this period?

A great success of the Civil War was that it has not happened again. Indeed, the United States has arguably not faced a threat to its very existence since then (except, perhaps, for the Cuban Missile Crisis of 1962). If there is a core of 'Americanism' running through US society, how deep does it run? In many ways the scars of the Civil War – segregation and the impoverishment of the South – are still visible. Despite the best rhetoric of politicians such as Barack Obama, who said before he became president that, '*There's not a liberal America and a conservative America; there's the United States of America*', electoral maps reveal consistent political divisions between states.

 Thematic link: unity

How important was the role of key individuals and groups and how were they affected by developments?

The history of America, like the history of any society, is populated by individuals who appear to bestride the events in which they are involved like a Colossus. How influential were presidents such as the Roosevelts, Kennedy or Nixon? Civil rights campaigners such as Malcolm X and Martin Luther King Jr.? Or were they merely the public face of an ongoing process? What about the different groups in America – immigrants from Ireland, Italy, China or Mexico; women struggling for equality; the poor struggling to make good? What has affected their progress within American society?

 Thematic link: individuals and groups

How to use this book

This book is intended to provide a chronological and thematic overview of American history from 1865 to 1975. Inevitably, some topics and events are left out, or given slightly less weight than others. The authors hope that this book will be a starting point for your study, rather than its end. We would encourage you to look at the past from different perspectives. In particular, you should remember that the vast majority of Americans who lived during the hundred years you are studying were not presidents or members of Congress. Although leaders can be very important, particularly in times of crisis, the culture and prosperity of any country are built upon its ordinary people.

As you read, remember that we, as authors, are historians like any other. We present a version of the past that we believe to be accurate. Because we are writing a textbook, we also present alternative views of American history, and try to give you a flavour of the additional reading you might find, and what it might tell you. If we present something as a fact, it means that we have checked it and believe it to be true. If we present something as an opinion, it's just that: our opinion and it's no more or less valid than anyone else's opinion simply because we have put it in a textbook.

The individual chapters of the textbook occupy 25- and 30-year time periods. They are then further arranged into thematic sections about politics, economics, international relations, etc. Many of the themes of American history transcend particular periods; the six themes outlined in the section headed 'Themes in American history' are identified when they occur in the textbook, to help you to build up your own picture of how much America changed from 1865 to 1975, and what caused that change.

Although candidates for the AS examination need only work through this book to the end of Chapter 2, they are encouraged to read through Chapter 3 as well to gain some idea of what happened next; they should take care though to base their answers only on events up to the end of 1920.

Part 1: From Civil War to World War, 1865–1920

Introduction

In 1865 America was emerging from the long national nightmare of civil war, which had cost it greatly in terms of population and production. Its development over the next half century was uneven, but vigorous. By 1920 President Wilson had a claim to global leadership – he was arguably more effective by that stage as a world leader than as the leader of his own country – and America had established itself as a dominant power not merely in the western hemisphere but in the world as a whole. Wilson's predecessors had included some remarkable but contradictory men. Theodore Roosevelt, known as a progressive politician, lost the only election in which he campaigned on the Progressive ticket. William Howard Taft had given every appearance of not wishing to be president, but had also managed his career carefully to ensure that he attained that office. Lincoln's successors were unpopular, incapable or corrupt – in the minds of many of their contemporaries, at least. There is a common narrative of this period as an era where the power of the presidency was weakened, and then strengthened again.

America also developed economically. The new corporations that sprang up in America were largely unregulated at first, and part of the story of these years is the story of how limits were placed on the activities of tycoons and their companies. We will also see the ways in which change occurred, and explore the reasons why a richer country did not mean a better life for most Americans, and why the labour movement did not take hold in America in the way it did in some European countries. American economic expansion helped to create different ways of being American. The massive immigration that was required to provide labour for the growing economy transformed the character of American life, ultimately producing a reaction from the white Anglo-Saxon Protestants who had come to see themselves as indigenous Americans. In the West, independent American communities developed, far from the government in the East, but dependent upon it for capital.

We will see how liberation from slavery did not spell the end of African Americans' struggle. The period of Reconstruction that forms the first part of our narrative has been characterised as an utter failure (because so many of its reforms were later undone) and as a great success (because so many of its reforms were successful). Among African Americans themselves, different strategies evolved for improving their position. Among white people – in the South in particular – hostility against black people grew rapidly into lawlessness.

Finally, we will see how Americans acquired an accidental empire, and were ultimately persuaded to give up their international isolationism, although only on a temporary basis, to fight in the First World War.

1 The Era of Reconstruction and the Gilded Age, 1865–1890

In this section, we will examine the way in which Americans rebuilt after the Civil War. This was a period in which Republicans competed over how the South should be run, and northerners and black and white southerners vied for control of southern state governments. In Washington, DC, presidential authority seemed to be weakening. Meanwhile, America's economy grew rapidly but unevenly. We will look into:

- The weaknesses of federal government: Johnson, Grant and the failure of Radical Reconstruction.
- The politics of the Gilded Age and the era of weak presidents; political corruption.
- Social, regional and ethnic divisions: divisions within and between North, South and West; the position of African Americans.
- Economic growth and the rise of corporations: railways; oil; developments in agriculture; urbanisation.
- Laissez-faire dominance and consequences; the impact of the ending of the frontier.
- The limits of foreign engagement and continuation of isolationism: the continuation of the Monroe Doctrine; territorial consolidation (Alaska) and tensions over Canada.

With Lincoln's death in April 1865, Vice President Andrew Johnson was elevated to the presidency. His task would be a difficult one: he would have to reunite a country that had recently turned on itself in war. During that war, half of the country had seen economic development and improvement, while the other half, the South, had been devastated in myriad ways. The victorious Union had to find some way to reintegrate its rebel states – whose inhabitants did not see themselves as rebels at all – while dealing with the social upheaval caused by the elimination of slavery.

The period known as **Reconstruction** would set the stage for much that would define later economic development, political discourse and social conflict within the southern states. It was ended by a messy compromise in 1877. It gave way to an era known in the author Mark Twain's terminology as the 'Gilded Age' – an era of massive economic growth that certainly enabled the rich to get richer, and allowed some of the poor to become richer too.

By 1890 the South was politically, if not quite economically or socially, reintegrated into the Union; the position of African Americans had not changed substantially since Emancipation. Some Americans were united by a desire to gain and retain wealth. For many, America had become more than ever a land of opportunity; for many others, very little had changed. White Americans were united in a way that had not been true in the 1860s, but the dream some had had of racial integration had been lost.

Key term

Reconstruction: the process by which rebellious southern states would be readmitted to the Union and have their political rights restored and their economies and societies stabilised. It was begun in 1863 by President Lincoln, although it stalled in 1864 because of Congressional opposition. Most historians believe that it ended in 1877 when President Hayes was inaugurated, although some believe that it lasted until the 1880s or 1890s.

The weaknesses of federal government

Some historians blame the failure of Reconstruction on weaknesses in the federal government – that is, that Presidents Johnson and Grant, and the Congresses that served from 1865 to 1877, were not strong enough to make it happen. There are two main problems with this view. The first is that it makes an assumption that the **federal government** worked together as a single entity – and that is not true. The second is that it suggests that the federal government was itself responsible for Reconstruction. It was, but so were the individual states being reconstructed, and in seeking reasons for the failure of Reconstruction (if, indeed, failure it was) we should not discount the fact that many southern whites simply did not want their states to be reconstructed, and that resistance was simply too strong to be easily overcome.

Lincoln's early attempts to plan for the readmission of southern states had successfully stressed that African Americans should have a measure of legal equality – although when he proposed giving them the vote he was unenthusiastic, never proposing more than a very limited suffrage. He seems to have intended that states should be allowed to re-enter into political union, by which he meant send senators and representatives to Washington and vote in presidential elections, when their slaves had been emancipated and 10% of their citizens had sworn a loyalty oath. Lincoln, the Great Emancipator, himself had had no illusions about how easy the process of social integration would be, and he had openly discussed and attempted to implement plans by which America's African American population might voluntarily remove itself to Africa, the Caribbean, Latin America or the West. Lincoln's various schemes to achieve this came to nothing.

By 1864 Lincoln was sure that the Union would win the war, and was planning for the peace. He navigated the 13th Amendment through Congress in 1865, banning slavery across the United States, with deliberate haste as he knew that it would be easier to achieve this before the rebellious southern states were defeated and readmitted to the Union: their senators and representatives might, he feared, object. Lincoln's last great political victory showed all his strengths. He has been called the great conciliator, able to draw disparate groups together. A genial man, he built good personal relationships and used them to broker compromise whenever he could. And so, the story goes, Lincoln might have been able to impose Reconstruction without upsetting anyone, by persuading and cajoling them. He might have been able somehow to convince both Congressmen and southern white society to pull together for the good of the Union. He might have been able to oversee the quiet dissolution of the Republican Party, its purpose served, after the war. If we are to blame the weakness of the federal government for the failure of Reconstruction, we must remember that the task might have been beyond even a Lincoln who survived an assassin's bullet.

 Thematic link: individuals and groups

Reconstruction under Andrew Johnson

President Johnson (Figure 1.1) had been selected as Lincoln's running mate in the election of 1864 because it made it more likely that Lincoln would win. Johnson was a southerner, and a former Democrat; he matched well with the northern (officially former) Republican on the National Unity Party's ticket. Johnson was the only southern senator to have remained loyal when his state, Tennessee, had seceded. He'd gone on to become its military governor following its partial reconquest in 1862. His only notable achievement as vice president had been to invite public ridicule following the drunken speech that he gave at his own inauguration.

Johnson did not really believe in Reconstruction. He referred to the process that he had to undertake after the formal end of the war as restoration. For him, the rebel states had never really left the Union; there was no basis for keeping them out of political life once they had formed loyal governments. On 29 May he issued a general pardon to those prepared to take an oath of loyalty, and recognised the government of Virginia. This was one of the governments set up by Lincoln towards the end of his life following the Ten Percent Plan, which stated that once 10 percent of voters in a state had taken that oath of loyalty to the Union those loyalists might form a government. Lincoln had vetoed a previous Congressional plan that had placed the bar at 50 percent; Congress, however, had been adjourned at the time of Lincoln's death and was not due to reconvene until December 1865. Johnson was governing on his own.

It may seem remarkable that defeated southerners were treated as leniently as they were. There was clearly no appetite at all in the South for further fighting; equally clearly, the North had won, and the Union would be preserved. There seemed little need for revenge. The rebel president, Jefferson Davis, was

Figure 1.1: Andrew Johnson, Lincoln's second vice president and then his successor as president.

imprisoned for only two years. Their iconic general, Robert E. Lee, lost his estate at Arlington, Virginia (a plantation that stood on a hill overlooking Washington, DC) but lived the remainder of his life a free man, with honour. The South, it seemed to many in the North, had suffered enough, and if the point of the war had been to preserve the Union and perhaps, eventually, to end slavery – well, then, the war was won. In the South itself there was little will to carry on with the war, which led to a greater acceptance of the peace. The entire South, with the exception of Texas, was devastated. In 1865 there were few southern objections to Johnson's plan, which was to bring southern states back to their rightful place in the Union as quickly as possible, while trying to prevent further deaths through dislocation and poverty. Slavery was gone, but the basics of southern life, its struggle to preserve its unique identity – 'The Cause', as it was known – was still active in the South, particularly among women.

The North, meanwhile, was divided on the issue of how radically to reconstruct the South. To Johnson, and many of those who had supported Lincoln in 1864, the only remaining questions to be settled were ratification of the 13th Amendment banning slavery and the repudiation of **Confederate debt**. The first was a done deal. The second – which meant that the rebellious states would pay for the debts incurred by the Confederacy – was accepted as inevitable by the southern states. At the time northerners referred to these as the 'fruits of victory'. Johnson, never a Republican, may well have thought that with slavery gone and free labour established as the economic model for the whole of the United States, the sectional Republican Party would be no more, and a conservative unionist party would emerge – a party he expected to lead. Meanwhile, the Radical Republicans in Congress were becoming increasingly alienated by the policies that Johnson was implementing during the Congressional recess: those who had hoped for more substantial fruits than these could see their opportunity to impose **Radical Reconstruction** drifting away.

The rights of black people in the South were protected to a certain extent by the Freedmen's Bureau. Set up by Lincoln in March 1865, the Bureau was intended to manage the dislocated newly emancipated African American populations of the South in the first year following the war. It provided legal services, advice for those who had never worked for wages before, help to find lost families and the like. The Bureau provoked considerable opposition within the South, the meagre resources of which were already stretched beyond breaking point. The newly elected governments of the southern states issued legislation that has become known collectively as the Black Codes (see Figure 1.2). This legislation was aimed at minimising the disruption caused to plantation owners by the abolition of slavery – that is, ensuring that the practical working conditions of free African Americans were not substantially different from those of the slaves they had been.

The southern reaction to Johnson's moderate Reconstruction, or restoration, was positive. Southern leaders' public position on the Black Codes was that they provided freedmen with the discipline they would need in their newly free lives – an echo of the old paternalist justifications for slavery. They also seemed to serve a further function: by far the easiest way for black southerners to earn a living would be by working in plantation agriculture – that is, doing exactly the same work as they had during the time of slavery. No wonder one former slave claimed

Key terms

Confederate debt: The significance of the Confederate debt issue was that to honour the debt would be to recognise the legitimacy of the governments that had taken on the debt in the first place. The North, of course, had always refused to do this – hence the Civil War. It might seem strange that southern states were anxious to take on more debt. The reason is that the creditors (those to whom the debt was owed) were themselves southerners. They had lent their own money to their government during the war. The southern leaders who had financed the war would lose a lot of money unless they were able to get it back from the southern states afterwards.

Radical Reconstruction: refers to the specific set of plans for Reconstruction put forward by Republicans in Congress in the years from 1867. This programme, also known as Congressional Reconstruction, was almost entirely opposed by President Johnson. Congressional leaders went far further than President Johnson in supporting the rights of African Americans in the South.

that there were 'two snakes – one pointing South and named Slavery, and the other pointing North and named Freedom', and both were 'full of poison'.

Many in the North saw these Black Codes for what they were – the old Slave Codes, modified. They saw that the newly passed stiff penalties for crimes such as murder, rape and arson in many of the states, including Tennessee, were being applied only to black criminals. They saw that southern politicians were beginning to argue about precisely how much of the war debt they should take on. They also saw the nature of the politicians whom southerners had elected to form their governments. Whether through defiance or because there were very few southern leaders who had not been prominent supporters of the Confederacy, southern voters elected prominent Confederates. Most notably, one of the new senators from Georgia would be Alexander H. Stephens, until recently the vice president of the Confederacy. By the time the Congress reassembled in 1865, a significant proportion of its members was in no mood to support the South – or President Johnson.

Congressional reactions to Johnson

Johnson's time governing without Congress was unsuccessful. Johnson himself was arrogant and either unable or unwilling to compromise: he was certainly not willing to recall Congress, which he could have done, in order to consult them. He was an alcoholic given to intemperate, rambling speeches. He claimed for himself a view of presidential power that was equivalent to Lincoln's, but he had neither Lincoln's gift for creating and maintaining consensus nor the ability to see the urgency of his situation as commander-in-chief in a war. It was also clear to Radical Republicans in Congress that Johnson expected that the Republican Party would turn out to have been a single- or dual-issue party – preservation of the Union and the ending of slavery – and that a new configuration of parties was in the making. In this he was aided and abetted by some members of the **Cabinet**, such as William Seward, the secretary of state who had also been Lincoln's closest advisor. During 1865 they had watched as Johnson rode roughshod over radical members of his Cabinet and surrounded himself with the kinds of advisors who, it was noted, might have been expected to inhabit the White House had the Democrats won the presidency.

The Radical Republican opposition to Johnson is best exemplified in the reactions of the Congressional leaders Senator Charles Sumner of Massachusetts, and Senator Benjamin Wade (who saw himself as the real Republican leader) and Representative Thaddeus Stevens of Pennsylvania: see Table 1.1.

 Thematic link: individuals and groups.

The alienation of moderate Republicans, 1866

The Radicals were not in the majority among Congressional Republicans in 1865. By 1867, they were. The reasons for this can be found in Johnson's conduct in 1866, when he proved entirely incapable of managing his relations with Congress. His attack on Stevens and Sumner as traitors in a possibly drunken speech he

ACTIVITY 1.1

Read the section headed 'The causes of the American Civil War' in the Introduction. Use this information to make a list of what seem to you to be the most significant causes of the American Civil War.

How many of those causes had been resolved by the outcome of the war in 1865? For each of the causes you have selected, explain whether the issue was resolved, and why.

Compare your explanations with those of others in your class. What more might people in the North have wanted to be done in 1865 and 1866?

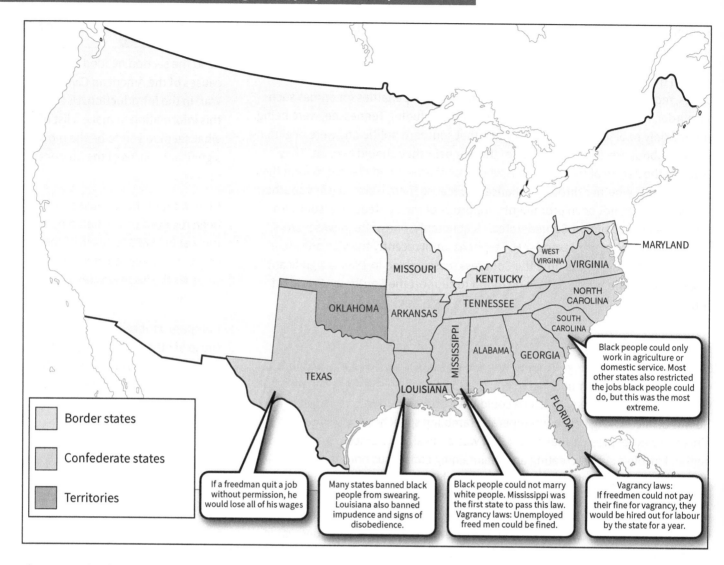

Figure 1.2: The Black Codes of 1865–66 varied from state to state. They were all aimed at ensuring that the newly emancipated freedmen were not able to make much further social or economic progress.

gave on the anniversary of Washington's birthday in February was one thing, but his decision to imply that they had been responsible for Lincoln's assassination seemed to go beyond the pale. He also vetoed two Congressional bills, making it clear that he had been disappointed not to have had the chance to veto more.

The first measure he vetoed, a week before that speech, was the Freedmen's Bureau Bill, passed in February 1866 to extend the Freedmen's Bureau's life beyond its deadline of one year after the end of the war. Johnson's veto, calling the bill unconstitutional and unnecessary, came as a surprise to the bill's sponsor, Senator Lyman Trumbull, a moderate Republican who had taken the time to check with Johnson that the contents of the bill would be acceptable.

A month later Johnson vetoed the Civil Rights Bill, also sponsored by Trumbull. This bill gave citizenship to all black Americans. Johnson vetoed it on the grounds that it was not compatible with the right of every state to determine its own citizenship, that it was unwise to determine such a measure with 11 states unable to vote on it in Congress and that it was discriminatory against white people. This

Leader	Charles Sumner	Benjamin Wade	Thaddeus Stevens
Position on Reconstruction	States that had seceded had committed 'state suicide' and would not be allowed to return until Congress agreed. Full voting rights for freed slaves would be a condition of return.	Reconstruction had to be completed before southern states were readmitted, because otherwise southern votes in Congress might make the process less radical.	Southern plantation owners were the enemy. Their estates should be confiscated and given to freed slaves.

Table 1.1: Radical Republicans and their opposition to Johnson.

time, the president's **veto** was overridden and the Civil Rights Bill became an Act. For this to happen to a president whose own supposed party controlled both houses of Congress, on a major bill, was unprecedented.

Johnson was not in control of the Republican Party. Still, Congressional Republicans attempted to work with him. Unable to pass bills for fear of his veto, and recognising that it would not necessarily be beneficial for there to be a series of veto overrides, they sought to change United States law in the only way over which a president has no formal influence: a constitutional amendment. The 14th Amendment is one of the key achievements of the Reconstruction period. It defined citizenship for the first time, although without mentioning race. Instead, citizenship was conferred on anyone born in the United States. It also encouraged black suffrage by reducing representation in Congress for states that denied male citizens the right to vote. It specifically set out that equal rights would not be denied to people on grounds of race or of having been a slave. Johnson was not appeased. He advised the South not to ratify the 14th Amendment, and the amendment failed in the summer of 1866.

The **mid-term elections** loomed. President Johnson actively campaigned against the Republicans, going on a campaigning tour known as the 'Swing Around the Circle' – the first time a sitting president had done this. It was a disaster. Moderate Republicans failed to come around to his notion of a National Union Party, so he was left with very few supporters, drawn from Democratic ranks. His campaign stops were ill-conceived, his audiences hostile and his speeches vulgar and sometimes incoherent and drunken. He was booed and jeered. Meanwhile outbreaks of violence were beginning around the South, which seemed to suggest that the Radicals' predictions that stronger measures were needed might be true.

Key term

veto: the president is entitled to veto legislation of which he disapproves, which prevents it from becoming law. He can be overridden by a vote of two-thirds of both the House and the Senate.

21

1. Look carefully at the section on 'The alienation of moderate Republicans, 1866'. Highlight all the words and phrases that suggest that the split between Johnson and Congress was Johnson's fault.

2. What do you think was the most important reason for Johnson's split with Congress? You might wish to consider the clash of personalities between Johnson and congressional leaders, the different ideological positions that the two sides took, their different attitudes to the South and Johnson's actions during 1866, but do not lose sight of the fact that it was the Radical leaders who ultimately created the split.

The worst example of violence was in New Orleans, Louisiana, in July 1866. The mid-term elections, when they came, confirmed that the Radicals were in the ascendancy. Stevens was in effective control of the House, and Senator Wade of the **Senate**.

Radical Reconstruction and the impeachment of President Johnson

In 1867, led by Wade and Stevens, the Radicals began their own process of Reconstruction by passing a series of Reconstruction Acts. They were designed to enforce the provisions of the 14th Amendment and to ensure that the southern states would be reorganised along lines acceptable to the North. The first of these Acts, passed on 2 March, organised the ten remaining excluded states (Tennessee had been fully readmitted in 1866) into military districts. They would have to call constitutional conventions to produce new constitutional documents granting African American people the vote, and ratify the 14th Amendment before readmission. The remaining Reconstruction Acts represented Congress's response to the various attempts by southern states to wriggle out of this, by refusing to call constitutional conventions, or by organising voter boycotts. Johnson's vetoes were overridden.

Congressional leaders also faced opposition from the US Supreme Court, which was supposedly the guarantor of the constitutionality of the actions of the other two branches of the US government. In the case known as *ex parte Milligan* (December 1866), the Court had held that when the civil courts were open, martial law could not be imposed. This had the effect of threatening the operation of the military courts, which were part of the Freedmen's Bureau. Congress threatened to close the Court. The Supreme Court was suitably intimidated until 1868 when it accepted a case known as *ex parte McCardle*, which was about military tribunals. Congress promptly passed a law banning the Court from hearing appeals in that sort of case, on 27 March 1868. The Court could not do anything about this.

During this period, ex-Confederate states were run by Republican parties consisting of black people allied with three main types of white voters:

- Poor white farmers, who had never been slaveowners and had often been opposed to secession in the first place.
- Planters who thought that these changes were inevitable, and wanted both to modernise and to show themselves willing to embrace the new order. These were the so-called '**scalawags**' – southerners who were viewed as betraying their class and section.
- '**Carpetbaggers**' – northern politicians who moved South (in the popular image, with their belongings slung over their shoulders in a bag made of carpet) to seek political office there.

These governments established state-supported schools to try to educate their devastated populations, many of whom had no formal education at all. They invested in railroads in an attempt to modernise the South, and sometimes they even managed to redistribute land from white planters to black people, especially in South Carolina. However, they were faced with tremendous opposition as they were seen as tyrannical, and were vulnerable because they lacked support and were seen by many white people as illegitimate.

This picture was encouraged by Johnson. The Reconstruction efforts were mostly based on the military occupation of the South, and Johnson was commander-in-chief. He dismissed Radical military leaders. He obstructed efforts to remove the vote from Confederate sympathisers by encouraging them to go to court, and he tried to set up opportunities for them to swear their allegiance, which were clearly illegitimate. Congress was forced to frame new legislation to oppose him. But by June 1868 all the states apart from Mississippi, Texas and Virginia were back in the Union, and the 14th Amendment had been ratified. Georgia was then put under military rule again in 1869 and was readmitted in 1870.

Johnson's vetoes, his proclamations and his rhetoric were not making the Radical reformers' job any easier. They devised a plan to be rid of him. There was no vice president and, by the rules of the time, Johnson would have been replaced by the most senior senator – Benjamin Wade. The only way in which they could do this was by impeaching and convicting him of bribery, treason or high crimes and misdemeanours. Irritating though they found him, he did not seem to be guilty of any of these.

At his **impeachment** trial (March to May 1868), Johnson's lawyers convincingly demonstrated that he had not in fact breached the terms of the Tenure of Office Act in dismissing Secretary of War Edward Stanton (who had barricaded himself in his office for months), and that even if he had, this was not a high crime or misdemeanour and was not an impeachable offence. Nor had he violated the terms of Congress's Command of the Army Act, which attempted to restrict him to commanding the army only by direct communication with its leading general Ulysses S. Grant. The final accusation against him was that he had made 'intemperate harangues' designed to bring Congress into disrespect. This was undeniably true, but hardly a high crime. Even so he only just survived. To be convicted by the Senate would have taken 36 votes; in the end, there were 35 votes against him. Seven of the votes in his favour came from moderate (or liberal) Republicans, who were perhaps uncomfortable with the obvious unconstitutionality of what seemed like a revolution against presidential power, or who perhaps did not wish to see a President Wade who may have seemed to be equally as intransigent as Johnson. One of those seven Republicans was Lyman Trumbull. Neither he, nor any of the others, held federal office again. There were widespread allegations that at least some of the Republicans who supported Johnson had been bribed to do so.

Grant and the failure of Radical Reconstruction

It was no surprise that the Republicans refused to nominate Johnson for the presidential election of 1868 (in fact, Johnson attempted unsuccessfully to persuade the Democrats to nominate him instead). The Republicans nominated Ulysses S. Grant (see Figure 1.3), the commanding general of the US army, who seemed absolutely perfect. He was highly popular, a war hero and had no discernible political opinions. Congressional Republicans expected that they would have a malleable candidate who would not obstruct them. Grant won the

Figure 1.3: Ulysses S. Grant was a very successful commander in the US Civil War, but a less successful president.

election easily. His support in the South came mostly from newly enfranchised African Americans. This was noted by hostile white southerners who started to think about how to stop black people from voting. Republicans in Congress came up with the 15th Amendment to the Constitution, which expressly forbade the banning of the right to vote on the grounds of race or having been a slave. This was eventually passed in 1870, and would be creatively ignored for most the next 100 years, in ways detailed in several sections of this textbook. Grant supported Republican governments in the South with military force if necessary, for example in Louisiana in 1872, when he sent federal troops to support the claim of the Republican candidate for governor, William Pitt Kellogg, in a dispute among members of the Louisiana elections returning board over who had actually won the election; his opponent, John McEnery, had been an officer in the Confederate army.

Radical Reconstruction: the position in the South

There are two narratives of Radical Reconstruction. One of them happened in the North, among Republicans, as politicians argued about what should be done, and Republicans' ideas about what do to in the South became confused with ideas about who should be president, and about whether Congress should have greater power than the other branches of the federal government. Do not forget, though, that this was a dispute over how to treat a defeated enemy upon whom a solution had to be imposed (or perhaps, how to treat an honoured but misguided friend who should be a partner in negotiation). Johnson's impeachment did not succeed in removing him, but it did settle for the moment the issue of who should run the process of Reconstruction. With Johnson sidelined, and then with Grant in the White House, the Radicals had won. So what, then, happened in the South?

In 1865 the South had suffered a quarter of a million dead, an economy in ruins and a political class either utterly defeated or utterly inexperienced. By 1877, for a variety of reasons, the Reconstruction governments of the South had failed. There were economic and social components to this failure that were reflected in the structure of southern society in the post-Reconstruction age.

What *might* southern society have looked like, had Radical Reconstruction worked as intended? We might have expected to see some of the following:

 Voices from the past: Lyman Trumbull

Lyman Trumbull was a United States senator from Illinois. As Chair of the Senate Judiciary Committee, he wrote the 13th Amendment and the 1866 Civil Rights Act. His legislation therefore had a profound impact on the lives of African Americans. He lost his Senate seat in 1873 as a direct result of his failure to convict Andrew Johnson. Trumbull spent the rest of his life campaigning against the corruption of the period known as the 'Gilded Age'.

Trumbull started life as a Democrat, joining the Republican Party in the wake of the Kansas–Nebraska Act. In 1872 he supported the Liberal Republicans, and then became a Democrat again. He would end his life as a Populist. His political trajectory was not entirely uncommon.

- Land, not slaves, now used for collateral and security in the South for those wishing to borrow money.
- Black landownership.
- Equality of opportunity for black people (education, jobs, etc.).
- Equal civil rights and suffrage for black people.
- Black political officeholders.

There were stunning successes in terms of black office holding – a black majority in the legislature of South Carolina, where black voters outnumbered whites (as they did from Louisiana to Florida); there were also a couple of black US senators from Mississippi. In 1870 there were more black officeholders in the United States than at any time in the next 100 years. Across the South in the late 1860s white voters joined with black voters to elect Republican governments and federal representatives. It was not all, or even most, white voters who did this. Poor white voters, it seems, had joined forces with poor black voters to stand behind the Republican ticket.

The early 1870s would sometimes be called 'Black Reconstruction' by those writing from a (hostile) southern perspective, although it's only in South Carolina that black people came even close to running the Republican Party in a state. Across the South, black people who participated in government tended to be northerners moving back South, or ministers, businessmen and academics. There were examples of semi-literate former slaves taking office a few years after emancipation, but not many. The majority of southern African American politicians of the 1870s were already established figures, and most had been born free.

Radical Reconstruction had many achievements. Southerners (white and black) went to school in great numbers for the first time. The Freedmen's Bureau, southern governments (especially that of South Carolina, where the Speaker of the House, and the majority of the representatives, were black) and northern charities collaborated to make this happen. Meanwhile, taxes went up for three main reasons:

- The social programmes introduced by Radical Reconstruction governments in, for example, education, were expensive. Six times more South Carolina children were in school in 1870 than in 1860; in North Carolina four generations of the same family studied the same books together in order to learn how to read.
- The damage done to the South during the Civil War needed to be repaired.
- The tax base of the South had been severely damaged during the Civil War, so the income of southern governments was diminished anyway.

There were also examples of governmental waste and corruption – South Carolina had some very modern issues of fraudulently claimed legislative expenses and poorly negotiated expensive government contracts (one year the legislature spent half a million dollars on printing). None of this looked like anything much more than teething trouble for the new administrations.

The efforts of southern Radical governments to establish themselves, and of African Americans to gain advancement, met serious resistance in other ways. The Freedmen's Bureau, the operation (or not) of which had formed part of the argument between Johnson and Congress, has been criticised by historians for failing to push forward the land reforms suggested by Radicals such as Thaddeus Stevens. A few plantations were confiscated and redistributed to African Americans – in South Carolina, of course – but the major effect of suggestions of land reform was to antagonise southern white landowners, who tended to be influential and wealthy. Instead, the Bureau backed down, helping white plantation owners to manage black farmers working on their land. The more charitable explanation is that the Freedmen's Bureau made it a lot easier for black farmers (mostly ex-slaves) to find work in the jobs that needed doing, which were of course very similar to the jobs they had always done. It also helped them to find homes near those jobs.

There are compelling examples of positive African American efforts to improve life in the Reconstruction-era South. Here is one. A northerner, Jonathan Clarkson Gibbs, from Pennsylvania, moved to South Carolina at the end of the war to tend to the African American population in the devastated South. His motivation was partly humanitarian and partly corrective – he was concerned that the religious knowledge of southern blacks was inaccurate. He came to believe that peace in the South, and racial harmony, could be maintained simply enough – by the provision of rudimentary education, clean clothes and personal hygiene equipment such as toothbrushes. By 1867 he had moved to Florida and opened a school; by 1868 he was Florida's Secretary of State – a position that the influential historian Eric Foner[1] has argued was largely ceremonial. That is, black people were made secretary of state, but white people took the decisions. In the Floridia constitutional convention of which he had been part, Gibbs and his faction had pushed the creation of a state-run public school system; as secretary of state, Gibbs used his position on the State Education Board to make this happen. When he ceased to be secretary of state in 1873 (the last full year of his life) he became Superintendent of Public Instruction, keeping his seat on the Board of Education. He claimed that he was, genuinely, second in power only to the governor during his tenure as secretary of state; in reality, he was allowed to build and direct schools, and to investigate the violence and fraud that was a feature of southern society.

To white southerners, the whole period seemed fraught with danger. Their new governments were imperfect; there was no magical solution to the South's economic problems; no doubt the sight of emancipated, educated and assertive African Americans was alarming to many southerners brought up on the racial theory of white supremacy, especially as under Radical rule ex-Confederate officers could not vote (these pillars of white society were denied the vote, while their former slaves could cast their own ballots!). Perhaps, if there had been more money, and if the governments had not been corrupt (it should be noted that Grant's government, and northern state governments, were just as corrupt themselves – but they could afford to lose more money), Radical Reconstruction might have been pushed through in the South.

Among the various other rifle clubs and protest groups that grew up in the Reconstruction era, the most significant was perhaps the Mississippi Plan. This involved Red Shirts – the local white paramilitary group – openly attacking black people, **scalawags** and carpetbaggers. The group was part of the Democratic

Party, and had first come to prominence in 1874 in Vicksburg, Mississippi, in a conflict that had resulted in the black sheriff being shot by his own white deputy. White Republicans fled the state; black people found themselves economically isolated. The Red Shirts ensured that black people largely did not vote in the statewide elections in 1875. President Grant, who had intervened in Louisiana in 1872, refused to intervene for political reasons, as he was concerned about how it would look to send in federal (northern) troops to attack white southerners on behalf of the black community, just 10 years after the end of the Civil War. The plan was so successful that it was exported to the Carolinas in 1876. In all three states, the Radical governments fell.

The slow failure of Radical Reconstruction

As problems mounted in the South, northern enthusiasm for Reconstruction began to wane. It became clear that the object of 'maintaining Republican government' was at least as important to some northern Radicals as was building stable political societies in the South. The southerners who participated in government were outnumbered by those who did not. Republican regimes in the South were supported largely by northern members of the Union League, who were widely and often correctly suspected of encouraging compliance to the Radical platform rather than creating self-sustaining local parties. The Radicals were also running out of leaders. Grant was no radical, and he surrounded himself with his friends rather than with people of particular political gifts or beliefs. Stevens had died in 1868, and Wade, blamed for having undermined attempts to convict Johnson because he was so unattractive as a successor, lost his Senate seat in 1869. Sumner would die in 1874. There were no great leaders to take their place. The most high-profile Radical remaining was Grant's vice president Schuyler Colfax, who had comparatively little influence and no ability to initiate any action. In the South there was active opposition to Radical Reconstruction; in the North there was simply diminishing support.

In 1869 the federal government had failed to deal properly with attempts to corner the market in gold. American businesses had lost money, and Grant, then a new president, had seemed unequal to the task of ensuring financial and economic stability. Then came a financial crash, which Grant was also unable to deal with. The Panic of 1873 was inconvenient in the North but in the still-impoverished South, it was a disaster. The revenue base of southern governments was undermined. The Freedmen's Savings Bank went bust, meaning that hundreds of thousands of black investors were sent back into poverty. Meanwhile the North, with labour unrest on the railroads, a crisis of credit and rising unemployment, realised that sorting out the South might no longer be its priority.

The end of Radical Reconstruction must not be blamed squarely on economic factors connected to the Panic. In 1872, an Amnesty Act had restored political rights to almost all the ex-Confederates, and the Freedmen's Bureau that Johnson had so disliked was allowed by Congress to lapse. The rhetoric of the 1872 election campaign – fought between two Republicans from the North, one of whom, Horace Greeley, was unenthusiastically endorsed by the Democrats, who saw no hope of winning a national election – had been of reconciliation. By the time of the next election campaign the regimes of the carpetbaggers and scalawags had failed

Read the section on Radical Reconstruction: the position in the South. Isolate the reasons for the stagnation of Radical Reconstruction during Grant's presidency. How many of them could have been blamed on Grant?

Key term

electoral college: where each state is assigned a number of electors based on its population. To win election as president, a candidate needs to win more votes in the electoral college – which means a few big states, or lots of small states. Most states award their votes on an all-or-nothing basis. Winning a state worth 10 electoral college votes (ECVs) by a narrow margin is more useful to a presidential candidate than winning three states worth three ECVs each by huge margins. It's possible to win fewer states, and fewer votes, and still to win the presidency.

in every state but Louisiana, South Carolina and Florida. The South was once again run by the same political class that had run it in the 1850s.

The Compromise of 1877

The reasons for the failure of Radical Reconstruction can be summed up in three ways. First, resistance in the South grew too great to be contained. Whether this took the form of violent resistance against black participation in leadership, or non-violent resistance against perceived black domination, or simply of growing resentment against carpetbaggers and scalawags, southern society did not as a whole change its worldview and embrace the new order. Second, the North ran out of leadership and energy in its pursuit of Radical Reconstruction. The battles of the Johnson era had nearly caused a revolution – and what had the North to show for it? A ragtag bunch of governments that needed constant support and showed no signs of being able to look after themselves. For both of these reasons, it had become clear by the mid-1870s that the political class of the South could not have been be entirely replaced even if there had been the will to do so. Third, the economic difficulties caused by the Panic of 1873 caused the North, and the US government as a whole, to divert its focus from the South, while also undermining the economic progress made by former slaves and allowing white people to reassert their dominance in yet another way.

The 'official' failure, though, came in the murky circumstances known as the Compromise of 1877. The presidential election of 1876 had produced a clear popular majority for the Democratic candidate Samuel J. Tilden of New York over Rutherford B. Hayes of Ohio, the Republican candidate for the presidency. A majority of votes is not, however, what is needed to win the presidency. Instead, each state is assigned a number of votes in an **electoral college**. In 1876, Tilden achieved 184 votes and Hayes 166; 185 were needed for a majority. The remaining 19 votes belonged to South Carolina, Louisiana and Florida, and therein lay the problem. They were still controlled by carpetbaggers, although not securely, and each of these states had submitted two sets of election results and two sets of electors. Give all three states to Hayes, allowing the submissions from the carpetbag electors, and he would win. Give even one of those states to the Democrats, and Tilden would be president.

It appears that neither side was innocent. The Democrats, it seems, had tried to prevent people from voting as they wished; the Republicans had tried to prevent officials from counting accurately. The issue ultimately came down to Florida – not for the last time in a presidential election – and a Congressional committee awarded the votes to Hayes. Their decision had been along party lines. Congressional Democrats threatened to disrupt the formal process by which the votes were received; this would have left the country with no president at all. In return for the votes he needed, Hayes offered the following compromise:

- He would appoint a southerner to the Cabinet.
- He would subsidise southern railroads.
- He would withdraw federal troops from the South. This would mean the collapse of the carpetbag governments that relied upon federal troops for protection.

The carpetbag governments of the South thereby sacrificed their own existence in order to win the White House for their party. The Union had been preserved, and various constitutional amendments were in place to protect the rights of black people in the South. In one way or another, those amendments would be largely ignored – but the Republicans held the White House. It remained to be seen whether this was a prize worth having.

One big question about Reconstruction that has been debated by historians since the 1960s is this: is it better to think of it as amazing because of how far it went, or as a tragic wasted opportunity to heal the racial divide in America? Kenneth Stampp[2] argued that the Radical Republicans had noble aims and substantial achievements, such as the 14th Amendment. Michael Les Benedict[3] stressed the ways in which Congress was reluctant to intervene directly, preferring to respect the principle of states' rights even for those states that had recently seceded. Eric Foner[4] combines these two strands of thought.

Historians writing about Reconstruction at the moment tend to focus on the reasons for its failure, which begs the question: what were its aims? Since different constituencies had such different aims, Reconstruction was either a failure or a success, and everything in between, depending on what people thought it might achieve. Also, if you think that it's amazing how far the country went in the direction of equal rights, given the massive opposition, and institutional obstacles, then 'failure' is hardly the right term. Can something be fairly judged a failure if its aims were never attainable?

If failure is an appropriate term, why did Reconstruction fail? One explanation is that southern whites were unutterably violently opposed, and so cohesive that they were bound to come out on top. Sarah Anne Rubin[5] grounds this in their emotional attachment to the Confederacy. Others focus on internal divisions within the non-white population. Michael Fitzgerald[6] suggests that the programme of land redistribution that was part of Radical Reconstruction was fatally stalled by objections from mixed-race and free black landowners whose sympathies lay with other landowners, rather than with other African Americans.

David Blight[7] makes the point that in the popular imagination the Civil War became a noble struggle between two sets of white men who fought bravely for what each believed to be key to the American tradition. One set fought for freedom – by which they meant the freedom of states to order their own social affairs – and the other for the Union. Over the 1870s each side came to understand the other's point of view – the North conceded the South's view on race, and the South conceded the North's view on secession. A Civil War that had claimed nearly 700 000 lives became a national patriotic event about white Americans. Black Americans dropped out of the narrative.

The politics of the Gilded Age and the era of weak presidents and political corruption

In 1873 Mark Twain (who two years later would publish *The Adventures of Tom Sawyer*, the first novel produced on the new-fangled typewriter) coined the term the 'Gilded Age' to describe the America of his day. He was referring not just to

---

ACTIVITY 1.4

1. Why did Radical Reconstruction fail?

   Some reasons why Radical Reconstruction failed might be:
   - The actions and failings of presidents.
   - The failure of Radical Republican leadership.
   - Opposition in the South.
   - The Panic of 1873.

2. Construct a mind map of these reasons for the failure of Radical Reconstruction. Write a conclusion to an essay 'Why did Radical Reconstruction fail?'.

the new taste for lavish interior design, but to the state of American politics and society in his day. America's prosperity, at least partly based on the farming of golden wheat and the mining of golden minerals, was perhaps only skin deep. Scratch the surface, and real suffering might be revealed.

Presidents Grant, Hayes, Garfield, Arthur, Cleveland (twice) and Harrison are often thought of as being 'weak', as to a certain extent is President McKinley (1897–1901). Certainly none of them was a Lincoln or a Roosevelt, and certainly much of the important political action of the era was Congressional (much, in fact, was not even federal). If the presidency declined in power, though, then most Americans would have thought this a good thing. Lincoln had suspended *habeas corpus* (the right to avoid arbitrary arrest) as a Civil War measure, and had entirely ignored the Supreme Court's order that he reinstate it. The most powerful president in the history of the Republic up to that point, he had also faced the gravest emergency. It seemed right, perhaps, that his successors return running the country to the states, and running the federal government to the Congress. Besides, and the key point: these men believed that Congress should run the country.

These presidents had all seen what had happened to Andrew Johnson. His battles with Congress had resulted in his near-impeachment, and he was widely known to have been saved only by a combination of corruption, reluctance to undermine the rule of law and fear of elevating Benjamin Wade to the presidency. There was a clear message for his successors – and for the party leaders who would nominate them for election.

The Stalwarts and the Spoils System

Ulysses S. Grant, the great general, had proved compliant but also not particularly competent. His administration was discredited from the start. The corruption scandals that surrounded him never touched him personally and only served to underline his out-of-touch irrelevance, and that of his office. His successor Rutherford B. Hayes (Figure 1.4) had come to office in such murky circumstances in the election of 1876 that he was known as His Fraudulency. He had no clear mandate because he had lost the popular vote and seemed to have lost the electoral college vote too. He was allowed to get on with the business of undoing the remaining parts of Radical Reconstruction – the deal that had seen him elected – but was immediately blocked when he tried to do anything else.

This took the form of an attempt to reform the **spoils system** – the idea that winning an election gave the newly elected politicians the right to appoint people to (lucrative) public offices as civil servants. He dismissed the candidates of Senator Roscoe Conkling of New York from their positions in the New York Customs House in 1878. The Senate simply refused to confirm his nominated replacements. Conkling was a major leader of the Republican Party, and when it came to 1880 he and his Stalwart faction had their revenge upon Hayes when they refused to renominate him. Without major-party backing, he would not be able to hold on to the White House.

Hayes's failure did become a success of sorts – one of the few achievements of the presidents of the Gilded Age was indeed to begin some kind of reform of the civil service. The **Stalwarts** were able to remove Hayes, but not win the battle

Key terms

Stalwarts: led by men such as Roscoe Conkling of New York, favoured a system whereby the president (and the party machine that selected him, and which they controlled) had freedom to make whatever civil service appointments he wished.

Key terms

Mugwumps: who supported Grover Cleveland, a Democrat, in the presidential election of 1884, were anti-corruption candidates who felt unable to support Senator James G Blaine for president, although they otherwise joined the **Half-breeds** in opposing the Stalwarts.

Half-breeds: including James G Blaine, supported reform of the civil service to make it more professional and less dependent on patronage.

Both Stalwarts and Half-breeds worked on the assumption that the Democrats were not able, in the 1880s, to win the presidency (which, without the help of the Mugwumps, they were probably not).

over who should succeed him. The candidate, James Garfield, was balanced by Chester A. Arthur – a dedicated Stalwart, and one of the New York Customs House officials dismissed by Hayes in 1878 – as vice president. Garfield won the election, and asserted his right to appoint the replacement officials in 1881, much to the disgust of Conkling who, relying on the doctrine of **senatorial courtesy**, objected. Conkling resigned from the Senate to make his point – but the New York legislature refused to re-elect him. The Stalwarts appeared to have lost, until Garfield was assassinated by a Stalwart supporter hoping, as he said at the time, to elevate Vice President Arthur to the presidency. Garfield took three months to die from his wounds. When he did die, in September 1881, the Stalwart Arthur proved surprisingly (and disappointingly to his former comrades) happy to reform the civil service, in the 1883 Pendleton Act. This Act introduced competitive examination as an entry requirement for the civil service, eliminating at least in theory some of the corruption. Arthur, meanwhile, suffered the same fate as Hayes, when his nomination was refused by his own party (this time in 1884) following an argument about the spoils system.

Thematic link: government and politics

Grover Cleveland – a strong weak president?

The Democrat Grover Cleveland came to office as the Republican Party argued about the spoils system. Cleveland had been supported by some anti-Stalwart reforming Republicans (who called themselves **Mugwumps**). Cleveland's victory in the presidential election depended upon his winning New York, and the decision of the Mugwumps to vote for him there was probably decisive. Nevertheless, after some apparent initial hesitation, he divided the spoils of his office among Democrats, which was precisely what the Mugwumps had not wanted him to do. From Cleveland's point of view it was entirely understandable. He was the first Democratic president since 1861, and his party members expected to hold office. He did continue to attempt civil service reform, but only after sharing out the spoils.

Cleveland was faced with two areas in which he sought to limit the disorder that had built up over the previous 20 years. He encouraged states to sort out the considerable land ownership issues that had grown up in the West, where new residents had a habit of putting their fences up whether they had a title to the land or not, and there was growing tension between settlers. He also sought to limit the large number of claims for Civil War pensions, many of which appeared fraudulent. By the standards of the 1880s he was an energetic president. He was brought down by an argument over **tariff** reform. Party lines had broken down in the 1888 election. The question was: how high should the tariff be? The higher it was, the better for big business. Local parties were thrown into chaos over this question.

Although he won more states and more votes than his opponent Benjamin Harrison of Indiana, the Northeast voted against him en masse in 1888 and Cleveland was ejected from office. Harrison had been nominated by the Republicans as a deliberately weak figure from a swing state, which duly voted for

Figure 1.4: The presidency of Rutherford B Hayes started in controversy. He was not an effective president.

Key term

senatorial courtesy: the doctrine, broadly accepted in American politics, that senators of the president's party should be allowed to choose civil servants working in federal roles within their own states. At the very least, they should be consulted.

Key term

tariff: a tax placed upon the importation or exportation of goods. Higher tariffs are usually seen as good for industrialists, and lower tariffs as good for consumers.

him, providing crucial votes to contribute to Cleveland's defeat. The tariff, when it was passed in 1890, was known as the McKinley Tariff after William McKinley, the chairman of the House Ways and Means Committee, to popular dismay. The Republicans of the Billion Dollar Congress, as it was known, were soundly defeated in the 1890 mid-term elections. Two years later, President Harrison followed them out of office – to be replaced by the vindicated former President Cleveland, the only person to have held the presidency in non-consecutive terms.

Non-presidential politics

As the saying of the time went, an honest man is one who, when bought, stays bought. Even by these unexacting standards, many of the politicians of the Gilded Age were not honest. Many congressmen followed the interests of big business slavishly, seeking to improve the United States by expanding them. Speakers of the House and senior senators, often ex-war heroes, dominated proceedings. Senators, in particular, answered to their state legislatures, and state legislatures answered to their party machines. They promoted states' rights and small central government. The Supreme Court, still smarting from Lincoln's conduct during the war, tended to support them.

America's rapid industrial and demographic growth led to a clearly defined role for the federal government: stay out of the way, regulate interstate commerce (although what, precisely, that meant, was ill-defined), and ensure the safety of Americans, which essentially meant safety from Native Americans who objected to the expansion. Local – city or municipal – governments, meanwhile, flourished. The new immigrants needed housing, feeding and work, and the party machines needed votes. The rapidly expanding party organisations became powerful, and corrupt. In New York City the Democrats centred their organisation around William M. Tweed (widely known as 'Boss' Tweed), who was also associated with the Fraternal Association at Tammany Hall (see Figure 1.5). In Philadelphia, the Gas Ring grew up – originally formed in the 1840s to provide power, by the 1880s they were an entirely corrupt cabal running the city. If corruption seemed to be

Voices from the past: Grover Cleveland

The idea that the 1880s was the era of weak presidents and corruption has taken a real hold in the American imagination. Grover Cleveland, perhaps, is an exception to this picture. His unique status as the only ex-president to win the presidency can be explained in this way: he lost the presidency in the first place by standing up to powerful interests, and won it back when he had been proven right. The eight years of his presidencies were the only years a Democrat held the White House between 1861 and 1913.

It's difficult to criticise Cleveland for implementing the spoils system when he became president. He had watched a series of presidencies destroyed by

Republican Party infighting, and did not wish to provoke similar among his own Democrats. The issues on which he chose to take a stand were important ones, which risked his own popularity. He could have left the states to sort out land rights in the West (alienating farmers), and he could certainly have continued to ignore the issue of war pensions. He then lost an election that he could have won, in 1888, by refusing to take the principled stand on the tariff that alienated big business.

Discussion point

If Cleveland was, in fact, a strong weak president, does it mean that the so-called era of weak presidents is misnamed? Might we call it instead the era of weak Republican presidents?

hard-wired into politics in the Gilded Age, it was at a local level as well as on the national stage.

There were more positive aspects to state and local governments too. They were, after all, doing most of the governing. Most federal employees in the 1880s worked in the Post Office or in customs: the most impressive achievement of the federal government at the time was perhaps the wholesale delivery of pensions to civil war veterans, but this level of endeavour was the exception rather than the rule. William Novak[8] argues forcibly that late 19th-century American governance was very effective. Instead of comparing an authoritative European-style national bureaucracy with a supposedly powerless American government, we need to consider the many diverse forms of **state capacity**. In particular, we must not be distracted by the laissez-faire nature of American politics from the many deliberate things that state and local governments did to shape politics, society and the economy. Novak cites the work of Albert Shaw, who wrote *The American State and the American Man* in 1887 explicitly to confront the idea that American government was weak. Shaw looked at the actions of the state of Minnesota in producing regulatory legislation, and argued that the American public was in danger of believing its own publicity about how little government did for it. Shaw, who had also worked on laws in Illinois, cited among other legislation the Granger Laws – laws passed across the Midwest under pressure from the interest group the National Grange of the Patrons of Husbandry. These laws regulated charges for grain storage and short-haul railroad freight, both of which were otherwise set by eastern corporations to the disadvantage of Midwestern farmers.

Elisabeth Clemens[9] has written an especially good book about how women, farmers and workers were able to mobilise as interest groups – giving considerable power to mass-based private (non-party, non-union) organisations. Such organisations inevitably sought to exert pressure initially at local levels.

1. The labels historians give to periods should be the starting point of historical debate, not the end of it. This period is sometimes referred to as the 'era of weak presidents'.

   • Create a graph with time on the *x*-axis and presidential power on the *y*-axis. Mark the *x*-axis from 1865 to 1890.

   • Now draw a line on the graph to represent how presidential power rose and fell over time. Annotate key turning points.

   Does this period deserve the name 'the era of weak presidents'?

   Come back to this activity when you have completed the course. Were future presidents much stronger?

2. 'The most important political decisions of the 1880s were taken at a local, not a national, level.' Explain why you agree or disagree with this view.

Figure 1.5: Tammany Hall, the powerful unofficial centre of the Democratic Party's organisation in New York City.

Social, regional and ethnic divisions

During the Gilded Age, the economy was regionalised. The Northeast, centred on New York City, was the home of banking and commerce. The Midwestern Ohio Valley was the home of the industrial belt. The South and the West provided raw materials and crops. The South, and immigration from Europe and China, provided cheap labour. The key to this was the system of railroads. This helped the integration of the economy while also holding back the South, which found it cheaper to import consumer goods rather than develop manufacturing capacity at home. This meant that there were different tensions apparent within and between the northern, western and southern regions of the United States, but at their heart these tensions were all economic.

This was an era of massive immigration. Immigrants to the USA, with the exception of some Chinese landing on the Pacific coast, tended to enter at Castle Clinton, the southernmost point of Manhattan Island, New York City. What happened next was a matter of either luck or good management. Some immigrants were expected, and met by their families. Others were met by members of their own ethnic communities, who organised themselves to support new arrivals from the old country. Some were alone, sometimes because they were pioneers and there was as yet no community to welcome them. They might well fall prey to unscrupulous welcoming committees and find their luggage stolen, or lodgings in an expensive guesthouse with no guarantee of work.

Many immigrants stayed in New York City or the nearby towns of New Jersey. Others boarded a train. Some went all the way to California. Those with families rarely went west of the Mississippi. Scandinavians settled Minnesota and Wisconsin. Germans also headed to the Midwest. The Irish settled in Boston and

Chicago as well as New York. The origins and destinations of immigrants to the USA in this period can been seen in Figure 1.6.

Divisions within and between North, South and West

In 1861 sectional tension – that is, a feeling that the different geographic regions of the United States also had different political, economic and cultural priorities – had caused a civil war that even those pleased with the abolition of slavery regretted for its violence and destructive consequences. The option of secession – that is, of leaving the United States and thereby demonstrating that the Union was no longer forever – was off the table: hundreds of thousands of Americans had died to protect it. Relations between North and South were only part of the equation. There was also, in America, the West – meaning, roughly, the area beyond the Mississippi River in which there was a mixture of new states and proto-state colonies.

There are some basic distinctions that can be drawn between the three sections – North, South and West. The North had more industry and commerce than the others (although in 1865 it was still more agricultural than anything else). Slavery was confined to the South (including Texas, a state with characteristics of both South and West). Related to this, cash crops such as cotton (the kinds of crops that relied upon intensive agriculture) grew almost exclusively in the South. The West was a land of wide-open spaces with pioneers, cowboys and Native Americans, some of whom were understandably hostile. It was still, just about, the land of the buffalo – although pioneers from out East were rapidly killing them off. In the run up to the Civil War the West had been the scene of conflict between North and South over the expansion of slavery.

Slavery in the antebellum (pre-Civil War) period had been both the symbol and the substance of the divisions between North and South. It was the symbol because it seemed to characterise the South (it became known as the 'peculiar institution' – peculiar in the sense of 'distinctive' rather than 'strange'). After the war tension remained between North and South, which was partially resolved (arguably to the detriment of the African American population of the South) by 1890. The tensions between the North and the South, and the way they progressed, are illustrated in Figure 1.7.

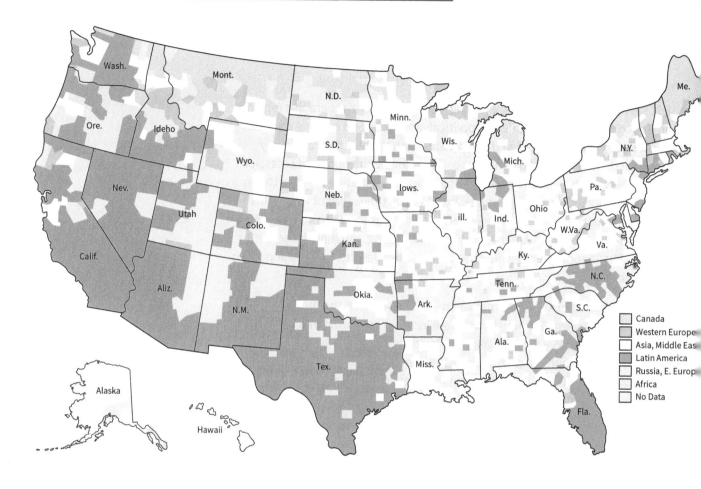

Figure 1.6: Immigration to the USA in the late 19th century. The colour shows the most numerous immigrant group in each county.

1865 – 1866: Moderate tension over the nature of the peace

There was no doubt that the North had won, or that emancipation would occur. The conspiracy that claimed the life of Abraham Lincoln (and would also have taken Andrew Johnson and Secretary of State Seward) was at least partly conceived by John Wilkes Booth, Lincoln's assassin, in order to cause such chaos that the South might escape relatively unscathed from its defeat; Johnson's policy of moderate Reconstruction appeared to confirm that this was so. The South appeared, however, to be pushing its luck when it began to introduce Black Codes and gave political office to high-ranking Confederates such as Alexander H. Stephens (the Confederate Vice President, elected as senator for Georgia).

1866 – 1887: Extreme tension, which then fell away, over the nature of Reconstruction.

Undoubtedly some of the northern Radicals in Congress – Stevens and Wade, for example – had a punitive agenda towards the South. Black southerners on the whole were fully behind northern efforts to reconstruct the South; many influential white southerners were opposed to the nature of northern interference (hence the particular insult of 'carpetbagger' levelled at politicians who moved from North to South to impose what seemed like the northern way of life upon the South. When in 1872 it started to become clear that the northern-dominated federal government no longer viewed radical Reconstruction as its major priority, opposed white southerners became reconciled to the North. This all came to a head in the compromise of 1877; the new president, Rutherford B. Hayes, removed federal troops from the South and supported federal subsidies for southern railroads. He had meant to do this anyway, but the policies were sold as a concession by the North and the South was suitably greatful.

1877 – 1890: The picture of the South as a distinct section co-existing with, but different from, the North – peculiar even without its institution – began to grow.

The Civil War seemed now like a distant nightmare; the northern federal government let the South get on with running its own affairs (northern states also saw little interference). The Old South became a romantic, almost tragic, figure, with war memorials and vetrans' reunions and nostalgic books such as Thomas Page's collection of short stories *In Ole Virginia* (1887). When there was tension in this period, it was because northern corporations were expanding into the South in a vigorous and largely unregulated way, invited in by southerners who held a series of industrial fairs (such as that in Atlanta, Georgia, in 1881). There was tension in the textile industry caused by the obvious advantages of the new southern textiles mills which were, unlike the northern mills they had copied, very close to the raw materials and therefore incurred fewer costs.

Figure 1.7: Tensions between North and South, 1865–1890.

The West had been an outlet for the tension between the North and the South in the antebellum period, and the key characteristics of its sectional culture had developed: by 1890 it had a distinct political culture. Formed in the late 1880s, western farmers' movements would ultimately become Populism, the history of which is more fully documented in the section on Political tensions and divisions in Chapter 2. In terms of western relations with the North and the South, though, the key points are:

- In the 1870s and early 1880s there was an assumption that western and northern economic interests were so fully aligned that northern capital (based in New York City, and actually expressed as 'out East') would come to the rescue of western pioneering and agricultural production, should that become necessary. When crises did begin to hit – there was an agricultural depression in the 1880s – the financiers out East were unsympathetic.

- Early in this period the South existed as a rival to the West, at least in the sense that both sought northern investment (for example, involving the expansion of railroads). Later on, as the West became disillusioned with the North, western agricultural interests sought to make common cause with southern farmers, in opposition to northern capital.

Tensions in the North

The population of the United States doubled from around 31 million to around 63 million from 1860 to 1890, despite a Civil War that had claimed nearly 1% of the total population among its dead. In 1890 one in seven – nine million – Americans were foreign born. Add to this the number of second-generation immigrants, and trouble might be expected, especially in the North, where immigrants tended to be concentrated. There was in fact remarkably little tension between communities: there were so many immigrants from so many different groups, and so much work, that tension did not really have time to arise. Anti-Catholicism had been a feature of relations in the big cities of the North in the 1850s – the Know-Nothing Party, a forerunner of the Republicans, had certainly been anti-Catholic – but it subsided.

One source of tension in the North was what should be done about railroads. The heart of the problem was 'freight rates' – the amount charged by the railroad corporations to move goods. This contributed to tensions between North and South, and North and West (and Midwest – the area centred on Chicago, which was a railroad hub itself) – but also created tension in the North itself, especially in Massachusetts. Boston, Massachusetts, played second fiddle on the East Coast to New York City as a transport and commercial hub, and found its influence diminishing. This ultimately resulted in the Interstate Commerce Act of 1887, which enabled Congress to regulate the railroads and therefore the freight rates; the case that precipitated the passing of the act originated in Illinois, and the context in which it was passed was the growing dissatisfaction of western farmers with state-based attempts (called 'Granger Laws') to deal with the various issues surrounding railroad charges (their charges were unclear, too high and anti-competitive). The impetus behind its passing, however, came from northern businessmen in Boston and New York.

The section on Urbanisation later in this chapter outlines the urbanisation that occurred in the North, which was fuelled by industrial expansion. In this period, the new urban citizens were most often immigrants and the children of immigrants. For the first time large numbers of immigrants to the North were neither Protestant nor English-speaking; inevitably, tensions began to arise not so much between the different communities as between the new communities and the original population, which had the money and power that the newcomers lacked. This helps to explain why American trade unionism failed to take off. It was not that northern workers were entirely satisfied with the unrestrained capitalism of the Gilded Age; instead the capitalist bosses were able to keep the working classes from uniting.

The pattern in Europe was clear. In the 1840s Marx and Engels had formulated the idea of revolutionary socialism, which predicted that the working classes would unite and seize power from the bosses who owned the land and the means of production; by the 1880s the processes were well underway, which would lead to the rise of viable socialist parties in western Europe and the Russian Revolution in the east. In America there was no moment when the working classes banded together; American labour could not sustain anything more than a very moderate trade union movement. There was a radical fringe – the Haymarket riot of 1886 in Chicago, inspired by a German anarchist named August Spies and Samuel Fielden, a radical socialist and Methodist lay preacher from Lancashire, is the best example of this. The social tensions of the North were, however, constrained by a number of factors:

- The availability of both a ready supply of labour and a ready supply of jobs (if not in the North, then out West).
- The disunity of the working class.
- The booming American economy.

Perhaps the social tensions of the North were also moderated by the example of the South; it became clearer and clearer throughout the 1880s that the white immigrant labourers of the North were not the worst off of all Americans.

The Haymarket Affair, 1886

Police were attempting to disperse a protest in favour of an eight-hour working day in Haymarket Square, Chicago, on 4 May 1886. The previous day, several workers had been killed by police; this protest, though, was peaceful. A bomb was thrown at the police, and in the ensuing chaos many people were wounded and at least 11 killed, seven of them police officers. Although the bomb-thrower was not caught, the bomb-makers were; they were anarchists, and foreign-born. Eight men were convicted, four of whom were hanged. The juries, and the judge, were clearly biased against the defendants.

There were doubts expressed at the time about whether the men were guilty of this particular bombing; some of them were certainly 'guilty' of being anarchists, or perhaps revolutionary socialists. Three would later be pardoned. This would not be the first time that fear of revolutionary socialism would come to America.

Amidst the controversy, the cause of those promoting an eight-hour working day was, of course, seriously damaged.

Thematic link: economy and society

The West

How should we tell the story of the West? Should we start with the deaths of Wild Bill Hickok and Billy the Kid, stories of saloon bars and cowboys? Should we focus on the last stands of the **Native Americans** and the final battles to expand? Should we focus instead on the pioneering settlers homesteading their way across the new nation, walking across the endless landscape in search of the home they would find just over the horizon?

The story of the West is, of course, the story of all of these things. It has been romanticised in print (the American 'Dime novels' began in the 1860s) and on film, in children's games of cowboys and indians, and in the view of the pioneers as the 'real' Americans, hardy survivors, rugged individualists. The reality is complex.

Let's begin with the story of the final destruction of the Native Americans as independent peoples. By the 1860s the remaining tribes were mutually antagonistic. The white Americans faced their biggest problems in the Plains area – the vast area between the Mississippi and the Rockies. The Sioux War in 1865–67 was all about American efforts to build infrastructure into the northwest across Montana, through buffalo hunting grounds. The Sioux, like other Plains tribes, were reliant on buffalo for everything. In Wyoming in 1866, 81 American soldiers were killed by a band of around 1000 Native Americans, including some Sioux under Crazy Horse. This incident has become known as Fetterman's Massacre after the defeated US commander. The federal government, with little stomach for a fight against the warlike Sioux, negotiated plans for reservations for Native Americans in the West. These were areas that would not be open for American settlement and railroads. These Dakota settlements were immediately violated

Voices from the past: *Adventures of Buffalo Bill*

This is part of the prologue to *Adventures of Buffalo Bill*, an American Dime novel from 1882.

'The land of America is full of romance, and tales that stir the blood can be told over and over again of bold Privateers and reckless Buccaneers who have swept along the coasts; of fierce naval battles, sea chases, daring smugglers; and on shore of brave deeds in the saddle and afoot; of red trails followed to the bitter end and savage encounters in forest wilds.

'And it is beyond the pale of civilization I find the hero of these pages which tell of thrilling adventures, fierce combats, deadly feuds and wild rides, that, one and all, are true to the letter, as hundreds now living can testify.

'Who has not heard the name of Buffalo Bill – a magic name, seemingly, to every boy's heart?

…

'A child of the prairie, as it were, Buffalo Bill will go down to history as one of America's strange heroes who has loved the trackless wilds, rolling plains and mountain solitudes of our land, far more than the bustle and turmoil, the busy life and joys of our cities, and who has stood as a barrier between civilization and savagery, risking his own life to save the lives of others.

…

'Knowing the man well, having seen him amid the greatest dangers, shared with him his blanket and his camp-fire's warmth, I feel entitled to write of him as a hero of heroes, and in the following pages sketch his remarkable career from boyhood to manhood.

'Born in the State of Iowa in 1843, Buffalo Bill, or Will Cody, was inured to scenes of hardship and danger ere he reached his tenth year, and being a precocious youth, his adventurous spirit led him into all sorts of deeds of mischief and daring, which well served to lay the foundation for the later acts of his life.'

Source: Colonel Prentiss Ingraham, *Adventures of Buffalo Bill from Boyhood to Manhood. Deeds of Daring, Scenes of Thrilling, Peril, and Romantic Incidents In the Early Life of W. F. Cody, the Monarch of Bordermen.*[10]

Discussion point
What can this extract about Buffalo Bill tell a historian about the way in which Americans viewed the Frontier West by the 1880s?

in 1875 when gold was found in the Black Hills. General George Armstrong Custer famously fought an ill-advised battle there in 1876, at Little Big Horn. Custer's Last Stand, as it's known, was the last victory for the Sioux, who had been defeated by the end of 1877. There were other battles but in the end men armed with rifles and supplied by railroads, and with a unity of purpose, were able to defeat fractured tribesmen who in the words of the chief of the Nez Perce, surrendering in Oregon in 1877, had become, '… tired; my heart is sick and sad … I will fight no more forever'. The effect of the final defeat of the Native Americans was to enable Americans to 'close' the frontier. This meant that there would be no more westward expansion, and the consequences of that are discussed in the section on the impact of the ending of the frontier towards the end of this chapter.

The popular image of the Wild West is either lawless, or of a single sheriff bravely upholding law and order. The fact is that in many areas the states' and federal governments' writs did not entirely reach. The Plains were vast and new communities sprang up where there seemed to be good farmland, or a river, or a junction of routes on the Cow Roads along which cowboys drove their cattle. In farming communities there was plenty of space and a pioneering spirit, and the settlers were armed to protect themselves from Native Americans. In Cow Towns – staging posts on their routes – there might be sporadic violence caused by a combination of stir-crazy armed cowboys and alcohol – think of a thousand Westerns with swinging saloon doors. In Deadwood, in the Black Hills of South Dakota, and Tombstone, Arizona – both notoriously lawless places in the 1870s – the problem was caused by the fact that these were gold and silver towns and there was more to steal. Law was provided by the local sheriff and whatever firepower he could muster on his side.

The West attracted cowboys because it had excellent land on which cattle could be grazed (Figure 1.8). The reality of life as a cowboy was that it was long, hard and badly paid. Cows had to be driven to market, which meant the East. In 1866 the Long Drive began, as cowboys realised that rather than driving cows all the way East they could be driven to the railroad in Missouri – just 600 miles from Texas. Cow Towns such as Abilene, Texas, sprang up on the route to provide overnight services for the cowboys. In 1875 the invention of the refrigerated railcar made this more efficient. The cow business boomed until 1886–87, when a late spring led to disaster. There was too little pasture to provide food on all the ranches, and cattle died in unseasonable snowdrifts. In 1887 there was a summer drought, and there were droughts on and off for ten years.

Figure 1.8: This poster illustrates the appeal of taking land in the West.

The range was ultimately replaced by the ranch. Cowboys fenced in land, perhaps using the relatively newly invented barbed wire. They did not take any particular steps to purchase the land beforehand. This ultimately led to tension with the sheep farmers who came West in the 1880s – tension heightened by various unscientific assertions that sheep dung poisoned the water for cattle, and such like. It was these tensions that President Cleveland sought to ameliorate, alienating the West in the election of 1888.

Although it's right that large areas of the West were effectively lawless in the famous Wild West way, and the dominant myth of the West was of individualism, it's also true that the federal government had vastly more influence in the development of the trans-Mississippi West than it ever has done anywhere else in the USA. Land policy, which was the fundamental political issue in the West, was always pre-eminently a federal issue. The federal government was by far the biggest landowner and even the second biggest – the railroads – owed their land, and their ability to enforce their ownership of it, to the federal government. Late 19th-century California, for example, was dominated by the Southern Pacific Railroad and its powerful owners, including Leland Stanford and Samuel P.

Huntington. The Railroad's monopolistic power and dominant position as a land owner gave it huge power to shape settlement patterns, and stimulated massive resistance, as did New York City's financial domination; the droughts had made it clear that neither the railroads nor the bankers were willing to help the farmers when times were hard.

The post-Reconstruction society of the South

The Old South had been defeated in 1865 and some form of Reconstruction was clearly necessary; the abolition of slavery meant a major change to the nature of the southern economy and society. Only the most radical of the Radicals were aiming at immediate and full black equality. The failure of Radical Reconstruction is outlined in the section on Grant and the failure of Radical Reconstruction. Even the changes that had occurred by 1877 were not permanent. Why not? We have already seen the political reasons for the unpopularity of the new southern governments, led by scalawags and carpetbaggers and by some African American leaders. There were some fundamental structural problems, too.

The post-Reconstruction governments were often known as Redeemers, or Bourbons. Their reputations were better than those of the scalawag governments, which they had replaced, and their focus was at first largely on providing industrial expansion. They would not begin to enact social legislation – enshrining **segregation** in law – until the 1890s. Writing in 1955, in the wake of the Supreme Court decision that concluded that segregation was unconstitutional, C. Vann Woodward[11] argued that segregation was not inevitable, immutable or natural, but that it was the result of contingent political decisions made a decade or so beyond the end of Reconstruction. This idea has been the basis of all historical discussion of the origins of segregation ever since.

Socially, what was to be done with southern society? Actual racial integration was the aim of only a few northern Radicals, such as Thaddeus Stevens. Most had no such plans. If black people were to take leadership roles in southern society then they would have to be landowners, and by definition all southern landowners in 1865 were white. The interests of the large landowners were sufficient to prevent any serious effort at land redistribution, and land remained largely in the hands of white plantation owners and smallholders. They, and only they, had access to whatever credit there was.

Finally, how were black people to participate en masse in the leadership of a society? Black leaders emerged, but this was rare. The vast majority of the black population had no education – and government-provided education was one of the first elements of Radical Reconstruction to fail when the money ran out. In this regard, they were little different to the poor white population.

Class divisions in the South

There was racism in the Gilded Age in the South. There was racism in the North as well. In terms of describing the southern economy, it's possible to make the claim that race is not the most important factor. Class is.

The southern economic model had always included white yeoman farmers on their smallholdings, and this is of course what the majority of white southerners had always done. There were mineral deposits, especially in the Appalachians,

ACTIVITY 1.6

The idea of 'redemption' referred to saving the South from radicals, carpetbaggers and scalawags. 'Bourbonism' referred to the period after the fall of Napoleon in France, when there was an ultra-conservative monarchy. Why did post-Reconstruction southern governments happily call themselves 'Redeemers' and 'Bourbons'?

which encouraged mining. After the war the railroads began to expand into the South giving industry a chance to grow. Floridians started to cultivate fruit and vegetables. The real money, though, was made by doing what the South did best: growing cash crops such as cotton. Other crops were grown, such as rice and tobacco, but cotton was king. This, therefore, was the model to which the South turned after the Civil War, and much of the industrialisation was directed at the cotton industry. Textile factories in the South, often using female labour, had an advantage over textile factories in the North as they were closer to the supply of cotton and had fewer raw material transport costs.

Circumstances were more difficult. The South had always supplied cotton both to the North and to the British, but the British had made other arrangements during the Civil War and the USA's market share in 1867 was smaller than it had been in 1857. But cotton it was – and cotton was best grown on a large plantation with numerous unskilled manual labourers, whose payment was in something other than cash, which was scarce. Anyone trying to break up the large plantations into smallholdings found it very difficult to manage their finances and their risk. In fact, the original smallholders found themselves less and less profitable over time. The model that emerged, tenant-farming, is explained in Figure 1.9. The arrangement was to the advantage of the landlords, who owned the land and had by far the best access to credit. The tenants bore the risk of catastrophe should the crop fail (the boll weevil did serious damage to cotton crops in the 1880s) or reduce in price (cotton in 1890 sold for half its 1860 price). Storekeepers could exact tremendous penalties on those who failed to meet their loan repayments. The absence of cash in the economy made it difficult for tenants to build up any capital of their own: they were trapped.

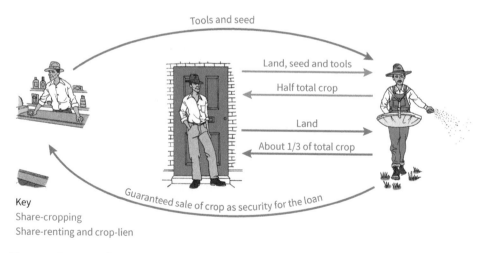

Key
Share-cropping
Share-renting and crop-lien

Figure 1.9: Tenant-farming in the South.

There was very little land redistribution in the Reconstruction period. In the South, land (and therefore access to the best credit), was generally owned by the major landowners whose identity had not substantially changed since before the Civil War. This meant that black people, and poor white people, had to farm as tenants. The precise economic arrangements made between landlords and tenants varied, but depended on three essential questions:

1. Who provided the seed?
2. Who provided the tools?
3. How did the tenant pay for the land, the seed, and the tools, given that there was not much cash available in the economy?

 Thematic link: economy and society

The position of African Americans

The section on the Radical Reconstruction: the position in the South tells the story of the South in the late 1860s and early 1870s. The most intractable legal consequence of this era was the Reconstruction Amendments (the 13th, 14th and 15th Amendments), which did not fare well in the Gilded Age. The latter two were in particular creatively ignored as black people found themselves prevented in various ways from voting and civic participation. Even if they had been able to vote, for whom would they have voted? Certainly not the Democrats, but not the post-1877 Republicans, either. Only in South Carolina, and only for a short time in the 1870s, were there viable black candidates to vote for in any numbers at all.

The Supreme Court also made its presence felt. In the Slaughterhouse Cases of 1873 it confirmed that the 14th Amendment did not prevent the states from setting their own rules for citizens' rights, including the right to vote. In 1875, in the case of *US vs Cruikshank*, the Court confirmed that while the state was not allowed to infringe anyone's (by which they meant black people's) rights, nor did it have a positive duty to prevent anyone else from doing so. In an era of small government, this meant that discrimination was largely legal. In 1883 the Court struck down the 1875 Civil Rights Act, holding that discrimination in public was legal. Private individuals could do what they wanted, wherever they were. By implication, this might also be permissible for the governments of the states.

There were social, political and economic attacks on African Americans. By 1887, the railroad company in Georgia had coined the phrase 'separate but equal' to describe its railroad provision, which segregated black from white customers. Florida also introduced segregation. Three years later, the Louisiana legislature made segregation on railroads compulsory. This was the beginning of the so-called 'Jim Crow' laws (Jim Crow was the name of a supposedly comical black character, and had become an insult directed at any black American). Meanwhile, voting rights were eroded by the Redeemer governments. Mississippi introduced a poll tax in 1890 to prevent black people from voting, prompting Massachusetts Senator Henry Cabot Lodge to attempt to introduce a Force Bill to force elections to be fair: it failed. Violence against black people began to resurface. The rise of Populism in the West and South brought with it a reaction from the Redeemers, who began to focus on race in order to hold onto the support of working-class southern whites – hence the introduction of Jim Crow laws, and the toleration of the practice of employers attempting to tie their black workers to unfair contracts that effectively re-enslaved them. In a series of cases in Georgia, employees found themselves signing contracts they could not read, and that committed them to debts they could not afford to pay, and therefore had to work off. The police and courts assisted in this process.

ACTIVITY 1.7

Read the section on 'The post-Reconstruction society of the South'. How would you argue against the claim that class was more important than race in the southern economy during this period?

ACTIVITY 1.8

Identify **three** key problems faced by the South in the period 1865–90. Evaluate how well the South coped with these problems, and identify anything that Southern governments might have done differently to create better conditions by 1890.

Do you think it's fair to criticise the post-Reconstruction governments of the South?

ACTIVITY 1.9

Create a mind map of 'American society' in 1890. Consider whether your links should be sectional, racial, class-based, religious – or can you think of any other potential links?

Use your mind maps as a basis for a discussion of what it meant to be American by 1890.

Was life entirely negative for African Americans? Black people formed their own churches, banks and insurance mutuals (insurance companies jointly owned by those they insured) – they had felt unwelcome from, excluded from or cheated by the white alternatives. The schools of the era of Radical Reconstruction were no longer funded, but northern charities provided some of the money needed and educational progress continued. In many cases, the schools that were formed were entirely African American. The best-known example is the Institute, in Alabama. Its head, Booker T. Washington, would become an influential black leader who sought an accommodation with white people in the South. That accommodation was needed was a sign that the very highest-minded goals of Radical Reconstruction had failed.

Economic growth and the rise of corporations

In 1890, the United States overtook Great Britain as the world's most productive economy. At the heart of this economic growth were capitalism and a more-or-less unrestrained free market. The centre of this world was Wall Street, New York City, the home of the New York Stock Exchange. It's no accident that most of the individual capitalists introduced in this section have names that are familiar to anyone who has been to New York City and spent time in the Guggenheim Museum or the Frick Collection, enjoyed ice-skating at the Rockefeller Center or gone to Carnegie Hall. The Gilded Age was the era of the ruthless capitalist who was also a philanthropist.

What were the ingredients for this apparent economic miracle? Economic expansion requires:

- A good source of raw materials to produce something.
- A market in which to sell whatever you produce.
- A plentiful supply of labour to make it.
- A source of power.
- Protection from serious threat of invasion or disruption.
- Sound infrastructure with which to transport your raw materials to factories and your goods to market, and raw materials with which to expand that infrastructure.
- Individuals willing to take the risks needed to innovate and build businesses – and to suffer the consequences of these risks should their plans go wrong.
- Room to expand (this minimises the opportunity cost of failed ventures: you can open as many failing businesses as you like and they do not take up space that could otherwise have been taken up by successful businesses).
- A helpful government, which often means simply a government that does not get in the way.

This set of criteria describes reasonably precisely the United States after the Civil War. The United States had its own supplies of coal and iron, and underwent an industrial revolution overseen by a government that was neither willing nor able to restrain it. If there was lawlessness in the mining towns of the frontier, that was a small price to pay for expansion. If the Plains Indians had to be given territory, the pioneers knew that there was for the time being plenty to go around. The key American ideology of freedom came to mean something quite specific: it was the freedom to better oneself by taking whatever risks one wished. A businessman's risk might be financial; an immigrant might risk their own life.

 Thematic link: economy and society

The role of Congress was to avoid getting in the way. A major problem was the money supply. The economy was booming until the Panic of 1873, when controversies over the paper currency introduced during the Civil War when there was a shortage of specie (coinage) became very serious. The key issue was that paper currency is not inherently valuable; it's representative (so, these days, are coins) because it has an inherent value much less than the 'promise to pay the bearer on demand' written it. Paper currency only works if it's guaranteed by a bank sufficiently large that its promises are believed – that meant the Federal Reserve in the USA, and it ultimately meant the federal government. The Greenback Party, which participated in the presidential elections of the Gilded Age, argued unsuccessfully for a looser relationship between the money available and notes printed. The federal government instead raised money to buy up gold bullion. It confirmed that money definitely had some kind of meaning, ensuring that inflation could not run out of control. This dampened economic growth.

Meanwhile, corporations grew up to extract and move wealth. The great corporate tycoons of the late 19th century were utterly cutthroat in business, fixed in rivalry with one another, and perfectly happy to bribe or otherwise persuade politicians to let them have their own way. They were responsible for miserable working conditions, and suppressed the unions that tried to improve them. At the same time, though, they had cordial personal relations – the only obviously personal animosity was between the railroad magnate Cornelius Vanderbilt and the financier Jay Gould, who had tried to bring him down in 1873. They also hired public relations experts, and many of them were noted philanthropists who made vast endowments, often to purchase art, and gave huge amounts to charity. They sometimes enjoyed their exalted positions through genuine innovation. Carnegie and Frick were American pioneers of the Bessemer process, which made for the more efficient production of better steel. Sometimes a few early successes made the big tycoons better able than others to absorb unsuccessful ventures (in mining, especially, many ventures failed). The trend was towards monopolies and cartels. Some of the corporations, and some of the relationships between them, can be seen in Figure 1.10.

Railroads

Congress saw the role of the federal government as to facilitate, but not to speculate. Rather than building railroads, the government instead made land grants to railroad companies along the proposed routes. These land grants were traded between companies and used to raise finance, some of which went back to the Treasury, and formed a powerful part of the economy. The railroads served to bind the interests of the Northeast, the Midwest and the West very firmly together, with Wall Street at the geographic periphery of the system but the figurative heart. When the Congress did try to make railroad charges reasonable and just,

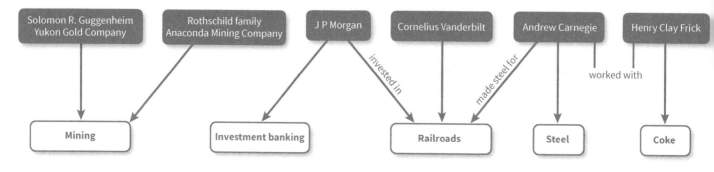

Figure 1.10: Magnates and corporations in late 19th-century America.

in the 1887 Interstate Commerce Act, it did so because it realised that railroads ran between states and were therefore definitely the federal government's responsibility. Initially, the railroads found creative ways around the legislation, although ultimately the act paved the way for J.P. Morgan, the investment banker, to organise ('Morganize') the railroads in the 1890s.

Oil

John D. and William Rockefeller controlled Standard Oil, incorporated in Ohio but formed to extract 'black gold' newly discovered in the West, most obviously in Texas. Standard Oil was established in 1882 as a trust – a new corporate device designed to split up a business that was a monopoly so that it did not look like a monopoly. This was a polite fiction. The Rockefellers, like so many of the businessmen of the era, had built up a dominant position by being very good at making money, and they were not willing to let it go. Standard Oil was remarkable for being the first trust created in America. It should not be assumed that it was necessarily a bad thing; the price of oil dropped as Standard Oil made its production more efficient, capitalising on its dominance of the market. It would regularly be one of the top five companies in the United States by wealth – United States Steel, the first billion-dollar company, was the wealthiest.

Rockefeller made his company more profitable in a number of ways. Some may seem to have been more 'ethical' than others; perhaps 'ethics' were not a particularly useful concept in the context of late 19th-century industrial capitalism. Standard Oil:

- Had deliberately efficient production.
- Controlled all stages of the process from extraction to warehousing of the final product.
- Used anti-competitive tactics such as price-slashing to force competitors out of business (this meant that he set his own prices deliberately low, forcing competitors who were less able to absorb a loss to do the same).
- Had systematised marketing.

Rockefeller was widely disliked; he was also very rich.

Developments in agriculture

Farmers were an important part of the American economy. Market relations penetrated further than ever before. Subsistence agriculture – the idea that small communities produced the food they needed for themselves – had been marginalised into the Appalachian Mountains and a few places in the West. The idea of agriculture as a cash business – always the idea of the southern plantations – became dominant. In the South, both cotton production and prices were down. Production bounced back to its 1860 level by 1880, but prices never recovered, and there was more land being farmed. The South was in truth barely able to feed itself, and the average condition of the southern farmer was to be mildly malnourished because he spent his time in debt to his landlord and the storekeeper, farming poorer land.

In the West, the land was poorer still. There was conflict between the two major types of pasture farmer – a function of land disputes, although expressed as sheep farmers accusing cattle ranchers of poisoning water supplies. Cattle farming, in particular, needed vast spaces in the West. Railroads helped, and so did barbed wire. Western arable farmers found life difficult. The land was poorer than in the Midwestern Mississippi Valley, and there was constant danger of tornados, grasshoppers, drought or economic crises making it difficult to transport goods across the country. No wonder that, by the late 1880s, poor western and southern farmers were beginning to find a common political cause: see the section on The ideas and influence of Bryan, Roosevelt and Taft in Chapter 2.

Urbanisation

The tension that grew up in the cities was based on class, and it was expressed at least sometimes in violence. The new urban class, often living in hastily erected slum conditions, found their routes to power blocked. There were partial solutions to this in the party machines that evolved to look after poor city dwellers. In order to win votes, party bosses such as those in Tammany Hall organised social activities such as baseball and singing. They helped with legal disputes, providing a translation and advice service and helping new members of the community to avoid being cheated by the legal system. If their case was weak, with any luck the judge was a member of the machine, but he could always be bribed if he was not.

 Hidden voices: Mussel Slough, California

On 11 May 1880 there was a gunfight at Mussel Slough, California. Seven men were killed. The fight was over land that had originally been granted to the Southern Pacific Railroad; the railroad company had used a different route, and the land had been settled by a group of settlers who now claimed 'squatters' rights'. The railroad company wanted to reclaim the now valuable settled land.

The settlers presented themselves as fighting not just for their homes but more than that, for a way of life – a vision of a cooperative community that was under threat from the rapacious forces of a monopolistic corporation that corruptly dominated California politics. They presented a petition to President Hayes in which they described themselves as 'respectable American citizens' not 'outlaws'. They had created 'a little Eden made by patience and endurance'. More than that the local newspaper, the *Fresno Republican Weekly*, compared life on the Frontier with life in the cities: 'While our large cities are filled with agitators, millions of acres of the richest land on earth is only awaiting a little intelligent labor'.

When he heard about the Mussel Slough killings, Karl Marx, who was in London, wrote that California was important because it showed how quickly capitalism was moving.

In return for this, the party bosses expected (and got) votes and party workers. These party machines did so much of the work of integrating and supporting urban workers that governments did not need to – and unions were not always wanted.

Still, labour unions began to be formed. Someone, it seemed, had to stand up for the ordinary person. Most labour unions failed quickly. One such was the Order of the Knights of Labor. This short-lived labour union had begun as a fraternal organisation and secret union during the Pennsylvania coal strike disputes of the 1870s. Its membership was deliberately cross-cultural (although heavily Catholic, perhaps inevitably as so many labourers were of Irish origin). It also accepted labourers of all types, expelling people such as bankers and lawyers and others engaged in professions that were not useful. Over time, the Knights had evolved into a union promoting higher wages and better safety at work. By 1886, with 700 000 members, they were campaigning for an eight-hour day. They lost control of their own protest at Haymarket in Chicago, which became violent. Their protest failed, and very soon so did their union. Similarly, attempts to organise workers on the railroad in Pittsburgh had failed in 1877, put down by the government amidst scenes of violence. It's worth noting that at least one reason why labour unions failed to take hold in the USA was that many of the workers were recent immigrants who had come to the country with the express intention of working very, very hard. The industrialisation of the United States had been very, very fast, and had occurred on a scale unknown in Britain, France or Germany. Wage labour was dramatically more common than before. Even where unions were wanted by the workers, and where the workers had the time and the wherewithal to organise themselves before the corporations simply found some new workers, unions were seen as undemocratic because they interfered with the absolute right of everyone to freedom of action in the market, which was becoming part of the definition of liberty. Labour conditions were poor. Government did not help and always backed the capitalists over the workers when it came down to it, either through an aggressive tariff policy or by force. The only union really to emerge from this period was the American Federation of Labor in 1886, founded by Chicago cigar makers in response to the Knights of Labors' failure to deal with wage cuts. The AFL survives to this day.

Beneath the thinnest of gold coatings lay a leaden world, where everything was judged by its price in the market. According to the interpretation of this period, which was dominant throughout most of the 20th century, issues and principles counted for little, parties were divided by nothing more than a fight for the spoils of office and most politicians were cynical and corrupt. In fact, the period from the end of the Civil War to the end of the 19th century saw the beginnings of a fundamental shift in the structures of political life. Rather than a stagnant thirty years between the excitement of the Civil War and the activism of the Progressive Era, interesting only because of the comic value of gross corruption, the late 19th century was in fact a crucial transformative period, which Mark W. Summers[12] has called an 'Age of Energy'. A fair case can be made that public life in the Gilded Age was not democratic politics at its worst, but the opposite: late 19th-century Americans participated in politics as never before and laid the foundations for the important structural changes that came later.

Laissez-faire dominance and consequences

The first major issue that you need to think about is this: how was it that capitalist relations came to be so embedded in American life? Capitalism may well be the great American revolutionary legacy. As a way of thinking about the world, and about organising social relations, it has swept all before it. Capitalism was not of universal benefit and yet, by the end of the 19th century it seemed that it was, and whether to be a capitalist society was, for Americans, no longer a question that seemed worth asking. Why should that be? Why were the obvious negatives of unregulated **laissez-faire** capitalism overlooked by American society as a whole? Note, of course, that the examples of the Granger Laws in the Midwest, and the regulatory efforts of 1880s Minnesota legislators, demonstrate that this oversight was not universal.

Laissez-faire capitalism: not the free market

There were two areas in which laissez-faire capitalism did not necessarily mean a free market. The first was that tariffs – the imposition of import and export duties governing the movement of goods and raw materials – were very common. In fact they were the federal government's major source of income. The second is that corporations were free to distort the market where they wished to, for example by forming uncompetitive trusts, or northern corporations using railroad pricing to try to force southern competitors out of business.

Unregulated capitalism is very difficult to predict. The success or failure of a business venture can depend on a number of factors. There was a lot of speculative investment and markets tended to overheat. The Panic of 1873 was caused by the bankruptcy of Jay Cooke, who had marketed the government loan book when it had been raising money during the Civil War. The message was clear: the government should be risk averse, and that meant staying out of direct involvement in capitalism. Besides, if something was worth doing it would continue to happen. In 1873, railroad stocks had crashed; the same would happen in 1893 but the railroads would continue to run and business would continue to be done. The cycle of boom and bust still had an upward trajectory, and everyone involved, it seemed, understood the risks.

The capitalist magnates understood how to make businesses run. They consolidated their businesses, buying each other out, rather than trying to cooperate – as they had realised quickly that cooperation did not work and hostile competition risked the future of the corporation. An interventionist government would have stopped this as the consolidated corporations and trusts formed effective monopolies and cartels – by driving out competition they could set their own prices. During the Gilded Age this did not much matter as the volume of business was so high that prices could be low. Of course, there were 'robber barons' but none seemed wholly bad – or very few. Jay Gould, who had attempted to corner the gold market in 1869 and then tried to bring down Vanderbilt in 1873, seemed the worst of them.

Key term

laissez-faire: a French phrase meaning, essentially, 'let it happen'. Laissez-faire capitalism is an economic system based on capital that is unregulated by the government.

The consequences of unregulated capitalism

Southerners who thought that the South needed to modernise saw an excellent model in the North. There was an asymmetrical relationship between the two. The northern railroad corporations, so admired by forward-thinking southerners, were in hostile competition with any southern challengers who might arise. Until the passing of the Interstate Commerce Act freight rates were certainly used to promote 'northern' rather than 'American' interests. Until 1886 the two systems even ran on a different gauge and so were incompatible. For their part, though, southern textile companies placed pressure on their northern counterparts. For some, this unregulated capitalism allowed the Old South – slavery and agriculture-based – to become modern. Birmingham, Alabama, became the centre of a thriving iron industry. 'Buck' Duke of North Carolina modernised the tobacco industry. His company, which he built up (so he said) with great personal effort, became the giant American Tobacco Company. Redeemer governments, for all their corruption (which led, for example, to the granting of contracts to those who offered the biggest kickbacks) were committed to industrialisation.

For the people actually working in the mines, the fields and the factories, and building the infrastructure, life was not quite so good. Abraham Lincoln had said that labour always came before capital, meaning essentially that it was more important to have people to do the work than it was to have work to be done. By the Gilded Age there was plenty of work to be done in the North and West, and plenty of people willing to do it. In some parts of the South the picture was slightly different – economic growth was coming more slowly and there was not quite enough work to go around. Even so, across the country, women began to enter the labour force in greater and greater numbers. Some were attracted by the opportunity, but others by necessity as prices went up and wages went down in a market with plenty of labour. For African-American women in the South this often meant working in domestic jobs.

Opposition to capitalism did occur. In the West, the unpleasant (but perhaps predictable) consequence of capitalism – that the corporations would seek to exploit rather than support workers – had led to opposition to the North (East) focused on railroad companies, and culminating in the late 1880s in the rise of Populism and support for the Interstate Commerce Act. In the South there was a certain amount of nostalgia for the past, reflected in literature such as Joel Chandler Harris's *Uncle Remus* (1880). This cultural pining for what had been lost was perhaps a response to the industrialisation that was changing the character of the South.

 Voices from the past: Henry W. Grady

'The old South rested everything on slavery and agriculture, unconscious that these could neither give nor maintain healthy growth. The new South presents a perfect democracy, the oligarchs leading in the popular movement – a social system compact and closely knitted, less splendid on the surface, but stronger at the core – a hundred farms for every plantation, 50 homes for every palace – and a diversified industry that meets the complex need of this complex age.'

Source: http://historymatters.gmu.edu/d/5745/[13]

In the North, there was opposition to capitalism itself from trade unions, but it was muted. How could it be otherwise, when so many of the workers had come to America specifically to participate in the capitalist system, to live the American Dream? Those who had come to America seeking refuge from the conservative governments of Europe – men such as August Spies, the German-born principal protagonist of the Haymarket Riot of 1886 – found libertarianism rather than socialism in America. In general, when there was criticism, the criticism was of the unregulated nature of capitalism rather than of capitalism itself. So the cartoonist Thomas Nast, who worked for *Harper's Weekly*, had been in the 1870s a major critic of the corrupt William 'Boss' Tweed, who controlled political patronage, railroads and a sizeable proportion of immigrant jobs in New York City; by 1886 he was criticising the Knights of Labor for demanding too much for the trade union movement.

There are further details in the section on Economic growth and the rise of corporations earlier in this chapter. In summary, the consequences of laissez-faire capitalism were:

- Unregulated and uneven, but extreme, expansion of the American economy, involving rapid industrialisation in North and South.
- A degradation of working conditions in North and South – wages were low and industrial accidents high.
- Economic realignment in the West, which became disillusioned (in the true sense of that word) as to the motivations of its partners back East.
- Opportunities for political corruption.
- A rise in immigration in the North, and consequent urbanisation creating slums (which would ultimately lead to the rise of Progressivism – see the section on The ideas and influence of Bryan, Roosevelt and Taft in Chapter 2).
- The creation and ultimate regulation (beginning with the Interstate Commerce Act) of new types of corporations in America.

The economist Henry George is now largely forgotten, but in the late 19th century he was probably the most famous American in the world. His books, especially *Poverty and Progress* (1879) sold millions of copies worldwide. George was born in Philadelphia in 1839 and emigrated to San Francisco as a young man. There he was struck by the apparent paradox that in the less developed West, the poor were relatively better off than in the highly developed eastern cities. He argued that landowners benefited immorally from economic and technological progress. By restricting access to natural resources, profiteering landowners profited from the improvements carried out by others, just as slaveowners lived off the work of their slaves. If wealth stayed with those who actually produced it, however, everyone could share in economic progress and poverty would be eliminated. George's solution was the Land Value Tax, which would make it unprofitable for landowners merely to possess land and charge rent for it. For George, this philosophy was a logical extension of the free labour ideology that had led him to support Lincoln and the abolition of slavery during the Civil War. He also saw it as a bulwark against communism. His system, known at the time as the 'single tax', provided that the resources of an area or country should be owned by all the people, but that individuals should be free to profit from the value that their own labour added to it. This idea would not have been necessary had there been an unlimited supply of land, but George recognised that the acquisition of land by one person denied another person an opportunity to create wealth on that land, and he thought this was unfair. George's critique of laissez-faire capitalism was that it was not free market enough, but he also had radically left-wing ideas about common ownership.

The laissez-faire nature of American capitalism in the Gilded Age was a necessary cause of America's rapid industrial expansion. That America did not have a 'socialist moment', remaining instead libertarian and laissez-faire for as long as it did, is perhaps explained by the safety valve allowed to American industrial expansion by its territorial expansion. There was always somewhere else to go. What might happen when this was closed off?

The impact of the ending of the frontier

In the West, anyone was free to move to another town (and they often did: everyone knew that in the 1880s an abandoned home with the letters GTT scrawled on the door meant that the occupants had Gone To Texas, with its vast open spaces). In the North, though, if workers disliked their job, they could leave it and find another. This might seem to indicate that working conditions should improve – surely, in an economy where there were plenty of jobs, only the best jobs would be done? This was not so. There was a ready supply of immigrants straight off the boat to do the unpleasant jobs (and dangerous: industrial accidents in the USA happened at a higher rate than anywhere else by 1890).

In 1883 Henry George had looked at the country filling up as immigration continued in the East and asked what was to be done with the 'human garbage' who would not be needed when the continent was full, except to be chased for their vote. Laissez-faire capitalism had thrived in an America in which further expansion was possible. In 1890 the final territory, Oklahoma, was opened up for expansion. Frederick Jackson Turner's paper, given in Chicago at the 1893 World's Columbian Exposition, argued that this would be the end of growth conditions. As often happens in prosperous conditions, these voices of doom were heard but not entirely understood. Turner also argued that the receding frontier explained both American democracy and the American moral character. Both, he thought, would be endangered by the closing of the frontier.

Was there even such a thing as the 'American moral character'? There were different ways of being American, and they have been detailed in this chapter. There was a (white) southern mode of thought – modernising while nostalgic for the lost past, vaguely resentful of northern (Yankee) success. There was a western pioneer spirit, tempered by 1890 by the realisation that northern capitalists would allow western ventures to fail in the free market. There was an increasingly complex northern society, not quite fully multicultural but more a succession of monocultures dominated by a white Protestant hierarchy. Turner and George between them raised three important questions:

- What would the closing of the frontier do to American notions of 'manifest destiny' now that America truly did have a continental empire? Would she seek an overseas empire too?

- How would the American economy function without the constant availability of new resources and new markets provided by the West?
- How would American politicians create an equitable democratic settlement for the maturing communities of the West and South?

To the various consequences of the end of laissez-faire capitalism would be added another: conservationism. The first national park had opened at Yellowstone, Wyoming, in 1872, with the aim of preserving the natural American wilderness for future generations, safeguarding it from development. In the decade after Turner, conservationist feeling would become even more important, not least as a conservationist would become president.

The limits of foreign engagement and continuation of isolationism

In foreign policy terms, what were the Americans up to at this time? Essentially they were defining the limits of their own expansion and paving the way for the ability to defend themselves. By 1890 they were building a fleet to defend their vast coastlines, and had established exclusive refitting rights in Pearl Harbor, Hawaii, 3000 miles off their western coast in a prime strategic location in the middle of the Pacific. Lincoln and Johnson's secretary of state, William Seward, had sought to annex Hawaii and been prevented from doing so by the Senate. By 1890 it would be very hard to sneak up on the USA, whose **isolationism** would, it hoped, mean that it would not need to defend itself again. However, in this era of weak presidents it had no ambition to take its place at the top table of world affairs, seeking only security in the western hemisphere.

Modern students are perhaps not used to the idea that America did not seek to participate on the world stage; this is the country that within 80 years would be asserting world leadership. Remember, though, that America was a very long way from any threatening nations. Only the British had the naval power truly to threaten America. They had been repelled twice in the past 100 years, and besides were now friendly enough and clearly unwilling to risk their entire empire in an American adventure. The American government sent few ambassadors abroad (throughout this period, rarely more than 30 at a time). Ambassadors are appointed by presidents, and the presidents of this era did not generally seek to assert their power.

Security concerns did not prevent American isolationist thought; nor did the need to ensure the availability of new markets. Americans provided their own new markets through westward expansion. The primary use of other countries to America in this period – and the area that provided flickers of international engagement, such as with China during Rutherford Hayes's presidency – was as a source of immigrants willing to provide labour.

The continuation of the Monroe Doctrine

From 1865 to 1890, America's foreign engagement took two forms. Americans defended their borders and reasserted the Monroe Doctrine, which stated that the European powers should not intervene in the Western hemisphere. America also expanded its own borders through the purchase of Alaska, and began to take an

ACTIVITY 1.10

1. What reasons might Frederick Jackson Turner have given for arguing that the ending of the frontier would be the end of growth conditions?

2. 'American lives were dominated by the frontier from 1865–1890.' Explain why you agree or disagree with this view. When you have come up with your ideas, look up what Turner actually said.

 Key term

isolationism: the idea that a country should not seek to involve itself diplomatically or politically with other countries or their disputes and wars.

interest in Hawaii. Why would the USA do anything else? There was no appetite for war with a powerful foe – there was barely appetite for the conflict with the Native Americans, which seemed necessary to secure westward expansion. They had plenty of internal demand to provide a market for the goods that they produced.

During the Civil War the Spanish had re-established their presence in Dominica and from 1864 to 1867 Mexico had been occupied by the French, who installed the Austrian Maximilian as Emperor. Neither sufficiently liberal to win popular support, nor sufficiently conservative to win the support of those Mexican nobles who had supported this French intervention, Maximilian found himself opposed by Johnson's government, and the French acceded to the Americans' request that he be removed. By 1867, with the US Civil War over for two years, they had very little choice. The Spanish, meanwhile, gave up on their presence in Dominica as a poor idea because of American opposition (this threatened American access from the Gulf of Mexico, and the mouth of the Mississippi, to the Atlantic Ocean). The yellow fever that affected the Spanish occupation force also helped to make up their minds to leave. The Americans did not seek anything further from the Spanish in the Caribbean. When the Cubans rebelled against Spanish rule in 1868, there were voices in America proposing support for them. These voices included the incoming President Grant, but wiser voices, including those of his secretary of state, prevailed. America was in no position for a foreign adventure. Ten years later, Rutherford Hayes sought to prevent French private citizens from building a canal across the Isthmus of Panama, invoking the Monroe Doctrine.

The Monroe Doctrine had originally been about preventing European powers from fighting their imperial wars in the western hemisphere and dragging America in. By the later 19th century it had become more assertive. Hayes opposed French plans to build a Panama canal because this would have given the French too much power in the region – control of a convenient crossing from the Atlantic to the Pacific. In the Caribbean the Spanish (and French) empires were tolerated, but Americans did not want them to expand. The Doctrine, explaining America's attitude towards European powers, had developed from 'don't fight in the western hemisphere' to 'don't expand in the western hemisphere'. The next logical stage in its development was clear enough: 'don't be in the western hemisphere'. The message from America was: send us your citizens, but leave us alone. The Monroe Doctrine, with its resonant naming after one of the earliest US presidents, the last to have been a Founding Father of the United States, was a convenient and patriotic shorthand for this message.

Territorial consolidation (Alaska) and tensions over Canada

In 1867, William Seward, Lincoln's and Johnson's secretary of state, had purchased Alaska from Russia. The deal became known as Seward's Folly, and the territory as Seward's Icebox. He had anticipated neither the gold nor the oil that were later found there: he viewed Alaska as the ideal base from which to annex at least part of Canada. Instead, the Canadian response was to form a federation – that is, to unite the various British colonies to form the modern nation of Canada as a dominion within the British Empire. The general air of tension along the northern border was not helped by the Fenian raids – raids from the US Northeast by American Irish communities designed to support calls for Irish Home Rule in Britain by attacking British possessions in Canada.

While the Fenian raids were not deliberate US policy, they were not unwelcome. The British had seemed unofficially to have supported the South in the Civil War, and some Americans wanted revenge for this. The issue that was uppermost in their mind was that the British had allowed the Confederate SS *Alabama* to refit without detaining her during the Civil War. In 1871, brought to the table by concerns over the US-Canadian border, the British signed the Treaty of Washington, which allowed an international tribunal to determine (by 1877) that they should pay $15.5 million in compensation to the United States. The British paid if not happily then happily enough, relations across the US-Canadian border were normalised and for the first time an international tribunal was allowed to settle a dispute between powerful nations.

 Thematic link: world affairs

 Practice essay questions

1. How far were the gains made by African Americans during Reconstruction (1865–1877) wiped out by 1890?
2. To what extent was life in the American West fundamentally different from life elsewhere in America 1865–1890?
3. 'The economic growth of America from 1865 to 1890 depended entirely upon the laissez-faire attitude of successive governments.' Assess the validity of this view.
4. Assess the validity of the view that Grover Cleveland was the only president from 1865 to 1890 with any serious accomplishments to his name.
5. Using your understanding of the historical context, assess how convincing the arguments in the following three extracts are in relation to the objectives of post-Civil War Reconstruction.

Extract A

'A desire to return to how things had been went to the heart of white northerners' ideal of "Reconstruction". Reunion would take reconciliation if it was to win over those whose allegiance had been lost. Any settlement that was going to last must come by mutual agreement, and the harsher the terms set on the Confederate states, the less prospect that the settlement would last very long. Northern Republicans saw the South as a different society, perverted from what democratic, dynamic society ought to be by its reliance on slave labor and its commitment to a caste system, but not even they could quite see white southerners as a different people. They shared too many traits to be anything but a variant strain of American, and the language of the southern states as wayward "sisters" or southern men as "brothers" in arms never wholly died out. The Union, then, was not meant to destroy the South so much as to save it, against its will.'

Source: Mark W. Summers, *The Ordeal of the Reunion: A New History of Reconstruction.*[14]

Extract B

'Uniting Stevens, Sumner and other Radicals in 1865 was the conviction that the Civil War constituted a "golden moment," an opportunity for far-reaching change that, if allowed to pass, will have escaped for years, if not forever. While some of their constituents demanded the execution of Southern leaders as punishment for treason, only a handful of Radical leaders echoed these calls. Rather than vengeance, the driving force of Radical ideology was the utopian vision of a nation whose citizens enjoyed equality of civil and political rights, secured by a powerful and beneficent national state. For decades … Stevens, Sumner and other Radicals had defended the unpopular cause of black suffrage and castigated the idea that America was a 'white man's government'. Although Stevens and Sumner were racial egalitarians, many Radicals could not free themselves entirely from the prejudices so pervasive their society. Yet even those who harbored doubts about blacks' innate capabilities insisted that that to limit on racial grounds the egalitarian commitments central to American political culture made a mockery of republican institutions.'

Source: Eric Foner, *Reconstruction: America's Unfinished Revolution.*[15]

Extract C

'Freed slaves and northern Republicans had their own ideas about what a new, free, postwar America should mean, and they had no intention of permitting white southerners to replicate the traditional South. With their strong connection to the government, ex-slaves and Republicans were willing to use federal power to establish free labor in the South; they turned to it increasingly as southern white withheld wages of hurt their black neighbors. While many former slaves rejected capitalism in favor of a amore communal economy, others immediately adopted some of the economic goals of free laborers. Following to its logical conclusion the idea that labor created value and that workers were entitled to the fruits of their labor, former field hands wanted the land and possession their work had paid for. And if they could not get land, freed people were determined at least to have wages and control over their own hours, and to live in households with a bread-winning husband and a domestic wife and daughters who could be protected from white sexual predators.'

Source: Heather Cox Richardson, *West from Appomattox: The Reconstruction of America after the Civil War.*[16]

Taking it further

'The surprising thing about the presidency of Andrew Johnson is not that he was impeached; it is that he was not convicted.' Do you agree?

Further reading

History has not been kind to the Grant regime. In truth, though, it should be noted that there was little he could have been done about the Panic of 1873, and that Panic did not cause the North to begin to lose interest in Reconstruction. There has been a recent move by historians to rehabilitate Grant as a politician – see Jean Edward Smith's *Grant* (New York, 2001), Brooks D. Simpson's *Let Us Have Peace: Ulysses S. Grant and the Politics of War and Reconstruction, 1861–1868* (Chapel Hill, 1991) and Frank J. Scaturro's *President Grant Reconsidered* (Lanham, MD, 1998).

Chapter summary

By the end of this chapter you should have gained a broad overview of the way in which American society developed between 1865 and 1890. You should also understand:

- the reasons for and extent of the Congressional reaction to presidential power, and whether presidential power was weakened during this time
- the extent to which the rapid expansion of the American economy, and the formation of new kinds of corporations, were good for all Americans
- the reasons why American foreign policy changed very little at this time, and why there was such an emphasis on securing America's borders
- the reasons for the romanticisation of the American West
- the extent to which the divisions between North and South had been healed, and the extent to which they had been replaced by new divisions
- the significance of immigration.

End notes

1 Foner E. *Reconstruction: America's Unfinished Revolution*. New York: Harper & Row; 1988.

2 Stampp K. *The Era of Reconstruction*. New York: Vintage; 1965.

3 Benedict ML. *A Compromise of Principle: Congressional Republicans and Reconstruction, 1863–1869*. New York: WW Norton & Co; 1974.

4 Foner E. *Reconstruction: America's Unfinished Revolution*. New York: Harper & Row; 1988.

5 Rubin SA. *A Shattered Nation: the Rise and Fall of the Confederacy, 1861–1868*. Chapel Hill: University of North Carolina Press; 2005.

6 Fitzgerald M. *Splendid Failure: Postwar Reconstruction in the American South*. Chicago: Chicago University Press; 2007.

7 Blight D. *Race and Reunion: the Civil War in American Memory*. Harvard: Harvard University Press; 2002.

8 Novak W. *The Myth of the 'Weak' American State. American Historical Review*. 2008; 113 (3) (June): 752–772.

9 Clemens E. *The People's Lobby: Organizational Innovation and the Rise of Interest Group Politics in the US, 1890–1925*. Chicago: Chicago University Press; 1997.

10 Ingraham Colonel P. *Adventures of Buffalo Bill from Boyhood to Manhood. Deeds of Daring, Scenes of Thrilling, Peril, and Romantic Incidents In the Early Life of W. F. Cody, the Monarch of Bordermen*. Beadle's Boy's Library of Sport, Story and Adventure, 1(1): New York: Beadle and Adams; 1882.

11 Vann Woodward C. *The Strange Career of Jim Crow*. New York: Oxford University Press; 1955.

12 Summers MW. *The Gilded Age, or the Hazard of New Functions*. New York: Prentice Hall; 1997.

13 http://historymatters.gmu.edu/d/5745/ [accessed 16 July 2015]

14 Summers MW. *The Ordeal of the Reunion: A New History of Reconstruction*. Chapel Hill: University of North Carolina Press; 2014.

15 Foner E. *Reconstruction: America's Unfinished Revolution*. New York: Harper & Row; 1988.

16 Heather Cox Richardson, *West from Appomattox: The Reconstruction of America after the Civil War* (New Haven: Yale University Press, 2007), pp. 47–48.

2 Populism, Progressivism and Imperialism, 1890–1920

In this section, we will examine how the USA became a global power, and the reasons why it decided to retreat from the global stage immediately afterwards. We will also examine the way in which American politicians, only to a certain extent led by their presidents, introduced progressive ideas into American politics. We will look into:

- Political tensions and divisions: the reaction against big business at national and state level.
- The ideas and influence of Bryan, Roosevelt and Taft; populism, progressivism and Wilson's New Freedom.
- Economic change and developments: the rise of US dominance as an economic and industrial power and the consequences of this.
- Social developments: mass immigration and urbanisation and their consequences; the position of African Americans.
- Foreign affairs: imperialism; engagement in international affairs; Spain and the Philippines; the Panama Canal; the First World War, neutrality and entry.
- The USA by 1920: economic power; social and ethnic divisions; political reaction and renewed isolationism.

By 1890 at least part of the USA was well on the way to recovery from the trauma of the Civil War. Although the South remained poor – devastated during the war and poorly rebuilt in Reconstruction, and with slavery, the foundation of its wealth and capital, abolished – the North was buzzing with industry and the West, although not booming as it had before the agricultural depression set in, had obvious potential in all that space. Presidents had reduced their roles as much as possible; Congress had often done little more than attempt to encourage growth; capitalists (or perhaps capitalism itself) had done the rest. In 1890 the USA faced a period of consolidation following the growth it had undergone in colonising the West. The Gilded Age of corruption gave way to the earnest attempts of the Progressives to improve matters, and the USA as a whole went from strength to strength. For the lower classes, the picture was less rosy – but still, people kept on coming, immigrants seeking to participate in the **American Dream**.

Political tensions and divisions

The politics of the Gilded Age were characterised by weak presidents, corruption (in the absence of orderly governmental regulation) and an inward-looking America whose expansion was driven by big business. The years that followed seemed, politically, a reaction against this. Big business found itself under increasing pressure, as the cycle of boom and panic driven by expansions and contractions in the availability of credit continued in America despite the attentions of the great industrialists and bankers, whose importance contemporaries overstated. Those who lost out created a cultural response, beginning a narrative analogous to today's 'Wall Street vs Main Street' debate – a not entirely accurate analysis of the different roles of small producers and big capital in creating economic success. And the weak presidents of the Gilded Age gave way to the three presidents of the progressive era – one who seemed to be a giant who redefined the presidency, another who seemed a pygmy who made his predecessor seem even greater, and another whose influence upon the world, and America's role in the world, promised and then failed to usher in a new age of American domination. The First World War should not distract; the real story of 1890–1920, politically, was in how politicians took control of capitalism.

Capitalism is essentially cyclical. If left unmanaged – laissez-faire capitalism – then it falls into a cycle of expansion and contraction, boom and bust. In the good times, when it is expanding, companies and corporations make money, meaning that more opportunities are created for workers to have jobs. When it is contracting, corporations close down – the weakest ones first. Those corporations that survive a contraction emerge stronger and leaner, with more profitable business practices, when the economy begins to expand again.

The major political tensions at the time were about how, and how far, governments should attempt to regulate or control capitalism. Should corporations be allowed to do what they wanted, allowing the market to decide which businesses worked and which did not? Or should the government say that some businesses were too important to be risked? A further tension of the progressive years was over how far workers should be protected from the personal consequences of capitalism, which might be poor working conditions and job insecurity.

Economic issues: what to do about unregulated capitalism	How far should capitalism be regulated? What, if anything, should be the responsibility of Federal and State Governments? See the section on Economic change and developments.
The power of the presidency	How powerful should the president be in providing national leadership and promoting legislation? Do presidents have a responsibility – or even the right – to take the initiative? See the section on The ideas and influence of Bryan, Roosevelt and Taft.
Tensions caused by the closing of the frontier	What should be the political response to the end of American expansion in continental North America? Should America seek imperial expansion? See the section on Foreign affairs.
Social issues	What should be done about the status of African Americans in the South? Note that there was as yet very little tension over the concept of states' rights to set their own policies: this was a series of state-level rather than national issues. See the section on Social developments.
How far should the state intervene to protect the poorest in modern America?	There was considerable tension about the extent to which governments should support populist and progressive policies. See the section on The ideas and influence of Bryan, Roosevelt and Taft.

Table 2.1: Political tensions 1890–1920.

There were further political tensions and divisions in this period. They are outlined in Table 2.1.

 Thematic link: economy and society

The reaction against big business at national and state level

By the end of the 1880s some sectional strains had begun to show in American capitalism as farmers in the West had realised that bankers and railroad operators in the East were not necessarily on their side. The western pioneer – the little guy – would have to stand up against big oil, or big finance. There was a further reaction against the apparently too cosy relationship between political and business elites. In 1894, in his book *Wealth Against Commonwealth*, Henry Demarest Lloyd attacked businesses like Standard Oil as destructive to democracy, and called for the government to take a larger role in the economy. The point was that democracy should have been about genuine economic opportunity – the ability to own productive property – and this was being denied to Americans as democracy was redefined merely as the right to vote. In 1899 Thorstein B. Veblen published *The Theory of the Leisure Class*, attacking businessmen as parasites who contributed nothing towards national prosperity. Meanwhile, in the East, western farmers began to be characterised as 'hicks' and 'hayseeds'. There was a cultural separation between increasingly urban eastern elites and ordinary farmers. It was no longer axiomatic that small-scale farmers were the essence of the Republic.

In 1890 the Sherman Anti-Trust Act was passed. The intention of the act was to allow the federal government to break up monopolies where they proved anti-competitive. It was easily circumvented. Thus in 1895 in the case of *US v Knight*, the Supreme Court held that the manufacture of sugar did not count as a trade, and refused to break up the sugar monopoly. The real point of the Sherman Act was that it required the president to take the initiative. If a president wished to, he might act to break up monopolies at a national level. Roosevelt would use the Sherman Act to break up the monopoly in banking in 1907, and he attacked Morgan's control of the oil industry in 1902. He used it in total more than 40 times. Taft, often characterised as a president who did very little, used it more in his four years than had Roosevelt in his seven. This key progressive tool had been in place since 1890.

In general, when there was an economic crash, the response of most Americans was to consider how to restore public confidence in big business, as if whatever had happened was somehow a failure of the public to realise how well things were *really* going. There were challenges to the precise nature of American industrial capitalism, but there were remarkably few challenges to the essence of capitalism itself (an economy based on private ownership and the market), except those from the Socialist Party whose leader, Eugene V. Debs, came a distant fourth in the presidential election of 1912. The Socialist Party of America was nevertheless thriving, far more so than the Labour Party in Britain. Still the major challenges came not to capitalism itself but to the mode of capitalism – Populism and William Jennings Bryan would challenge the precise mode of industrial capitalism that prevailed in the United States.

How did this play out in specific states and localities? One way was through the growth in powers and status of powerful mayors such as Tom L. Johnson in Cleveland, Ohio, who enacted progressive policies at a local level in his time in office, which began in 1901. A friend and follower of Henry George, his first act as mayor was to ensure that city land was not given to a railroad corporation. He expanded his city's infrastructure to make it more competitive, but also built amenities such as playgrounds to enhance the quality of life of its inhabitants. When the local electricity company charged prices that were too high for many Clevelanders, Johnson ensured that a new company was able to offer competition and drive prices down. When he died in 1911 he was buried next to Henry George. Johnson was one of the first of the powerful progressive mayors. His actions represented a deliberate repudiation of the unrestrained capitalism that had seen his predecessor wish to give land away to a railroad corporation, and he exemplifies the way in which the progressive impulse would come to prominence in the United States.

At state level, the actions of Robert M. La Follette (Senior) of Wisconsin and Hiram Johnson of California, both governors, are instructive. La Follette became Governor of Wisconsin (1901–06) and leader of the progressive Republicans, setting himself up in deliberate opposition to 'Stalwart' Republicans, which at this stage meant traditional non-progressives in the tradition of Benjamin Harrison. La Follette used taxation to regulate the railroads. He introduced open primary elections to reduce the power of the parties and promoted workers' and women's rights – classic progressive policies that he set against the capitalist impulse that had gone before. Johnson also campaigned for the direct election of US senators by the people – before nominating himself to the US Senate.

The first state to outlaw the direct nomination of US senators by the state governors and legislatures was California: by 1913 this had become enshrined for all the states in the US Constitution, as the 17th Amendment. A direct cause of this was a feeling that state governors and legislatures, and therefore US senators, were in the pocket of the powerful corporations: direct election would reduce their influence. Governor Hiram Johnson of California (1911–17), who promoted this law, also regulated the railroads through commissions, and made state governments more accountable by introducing recall (allowing Californian voters to remove politicians between scheduled elections) and initiatives and referendums (allowing voters to have a specific say on laws, including laws that they, rather than members of the legislature, proposed).

The traditional view of the Gilded Age and its aftermath is that the reaction came in terms of increasing class consciousness. Some of the most interesting work on the history of class formation has recently come from authors studying elites, James Livingston[1] and Sven Beckert.[2] For them, the most important social development of the post-Civil War decades was the formation of a self-conscious ruling elite. This largely fits with an older literature on the triumph of corporations. Here the standard work is Alfred Chandler's *The Visible Hand*[3], which focused on the rise of managerial hierarchies that allowed capital-intensive industries such as railroads to use dramatic new technological developments to monopolise markets.

There is also some interesting work by Robert D. Johnston[4] that challenges the view that this was a period of corporate dominance and deteriorating class relations. Johnston stresses the continued survival of proprietary enterprises in a wide variety of industries – 'mom and pop' stores, factories, and farms. In fact, small business owners controlled large swathes of the economy despite the rise of big business. Johnston even questions whether we should call these small business owners capitalists since they were advocates, he claims, of a 'moral economy'. These people were still advocating a republican political economy of small producers and often forged alliances at local level with workers, artisans, and so on. This, claims Johnston, was the underpinning of the anti-trust movement and also of the flowering of populist-style direct democracy.

And this is how history often works. At first it appeared that the reaction against big business was the growth of two different classes in America, with separate class identities. Then historians began to question whether, in fact, this picture really worked, moving their focus and suggesting that, perhaps, big business was not quite as dominant as it appeared. Alternatively, we might argue that the actions and motivations of small producers formed part of the reaction to the advent of unbridled capitalism.

Thematic link: economy and society

Governments, big business, and organised labour
American labour organisations made little progress during this period. One reason for this was that there were always plenty of people willing to work, most

of whom had come to the USA specifically for that purpose. New immigrants to the East could easily be used as strikebreakers, undermining attempts to organise labour against big business. There were few successes for labour unions except where the federal government came in, occasionally, on the side of the workforce. The exception was Samuel Gompers's American Federation of Labor, which was deliberately moderate and more successful. More often, local and national governments were firmly on the side of big business.

This was typical. Carnegie and Frick provoked a strike at the Homestead Steelworks, Pittsburgh, Pennsylvania, in 1892. They wanted to destroy the union, the Amalgamated Association of Iron and Steelworkers. They used the Pinkerton Detective Agency – a firm that provided agents to infiltrate workers and break up strikes – to do so. Although they nearly lost control – Frick was stabbed – the Pinkertons were successful. So much so that in 1893 Congress banned the federal government from employing Pinkerton agents; in practice this meant that the states employed them instead.

Robin Archer[5] presents some amazing statistics on the number of people killed in industrial disputes in the United States. Between 1877 and 1900, American presidents sent the US army into 11 strikes, governors mobilised the National Guard in somewhere between 118 and 160 labour disputes, and mayors called out the police on numerous occasions to maintain 'public order'.

At least 198 people were killed and 1966 were injured between 1902 and 1904 in labour disputes alone. In the 1890s in Australia, where there were also serious industrial disputes, only one worker was killed. In Western Europe, the figures are almost as low. The US therefore saw astronomically higher levels of violence than any other industrialised nation – indicating far, far greater levels of repression.

There were other developments:

- In 1894, the American Railway Union under Eugene V. Debs called a strike against the Pullman Palace Car Company of Chicago after a 25% reduction in wages. This was part of a wave of strikes. President Cleveland's **attorney general** issued a 'labor injunction' – a new device declaring the strike illegal on the grounds that it threatened the national interest. Cleveland sent in federal troops to break the strike, and the leaders of the American Railway Union spent six months in jail. This happened in the aftermath of the Panic of 1893.
- In 1902 President Roosevelt defeated the anthracite coal strikes of Pennsylvania, led by the United Mine Workers of America, by brokering a negotiation between the two sides. He threatened to send the army in to get the coal, and the mine owners conceded the workers' demands for more pay and fewer hours, but the union did not gain recognition for its efforts. This was a pragmatic solution, which set no precedents and prioritised the national interest over any other considerations.
- Also in 1902 the American Anti-boycott Association and the National Union of Manufacturers were set up to encourage 'open' rather than 'closed' shop labour forces, undermining the attempts of socialist leaders to organise and unite the working classes in opposition to capitalism.
- In 1905 during a miners' strike Frank Steuenberg, Governor of Idaho, was murdered in a bombing. Martial law was declared. The three miners thought

responsible for organising this went to trial and were acquitted. After his acquittal, their leader, 'Big Bill' Haywood, set up the Industrial Workers of the World (nicknamed the Wobblies) as an explicitly socialist organisation.

- In 1905 the Supreme Court found in the case of *Lochner v New York* that it was unconstitutional to limit the working time of bakers on the grounds that this was a violation of bakers' rights to work as many hours a week as they wished.

In 1912 'Big Bill' Haywood led a textile workers' strike in Lawrence, Massachusetts, to protest against a cut in wages that accompanied a reduction in the working week from 54 to 52 hours (see Figure 2.1). For the first time, there had been successful organisation of immigrant, unskilled, workers and women. By 1920 Haywood had been forced into exile in Russia and the Wobblies were no more; the dominant voice in the labour market was that of Samuel Gompers, the leader of the American Federation of Labor, who organised skilled workers to curb the excesses of big business but did not rock the boat overall. His Federation provided a form of social security for its members, but on a voluntary basis. Gompers believed that the role of 'organized labor' was to curb the excesses of big business, but not to challenge the system overall. His members had come to work, not to disrupt the system. Half of the country's wealth was owned by 1% of the population: for the most part, the other 99% were unconcerned.

Figure 2.1: Standoff between workers and militiamen at Lawrence, MA, 1912.

 Thematic link: ideas and ideology

ACTIVITY 2.1

What, if anything, was the policy of the American political class towards organised labour from 1890 to 1920? Is it possible to produce a coherent answer to this, or did it depend upon the precise circumstances?

The ideas and influence of Bryan, Roosevelt and Taft

The period from 1890 to 1920 was an era of big political ideas, all of which evolved over time. **Populism** grew up in the South and West, beginning as an expression of sectional dissatisfaction with the dominance of eastern commercial interests and southern Redeemer governments within the United States. Its major champion, William Jennings Bryan, was repeatedly defeated in his quest to become president, but his expression of the tension between the interests of East and West has survived in the politics of today and his agenda has largely been fulfilled. The People's Party failed to elect a president of its own, but had a profound effect on the Democratic Party.

Progressivism is most closely associated with the presidency of Theodore Roosevelt, although the word was not used during his time in office and his political achievements in the domestic sphere are less impressive than they appear. The progressive agenda, as originally conceived, was wildly successful – so much so that progressives ceased to exist as a distinct grouping by the end of the First World War, if they had ever existed as such. Roosevelt's protégé and then great rival Taft, often seen as among the least energetic presidents, had an agenda that was more practical than ideological, and he often had to settle for doing what he could, rather than what he wanted.

Wilson's New Freedom was certainly ideological, but it was also an electoral device designed to differentiate him from Roosevelt, who campaigned in 1912 on a platform of New Nationalism. As his presidency went on, he also adopted parts of Roosevelt's platform. His presidency was increasingly dominated by the First World War, and America's place in the world following it.

As you read through this section, it is very important to bear two things in mind:

- Ideological labels such as populism and progressivism can be deceptive, suggesting a body of opinion that does not really change, about which its adherents agreed. In fact many of the measures and politicians identified as, for example, 'progressive' were not seen as such at the time, and 'progressives' may not have realised that they would later be grouped together in history textbooks.
- Politicians and thinkers identified as leaders of ideological movements are not necessarily the originators of those movements, nor are they necessarily the most representative in terms of their beliefs. There are often other reasons why they assume an iconic role.

Hidden voices

The Triangle Shirtwaist Factory fire

One story from this period is particularly revealing about the way in which change occurred in the lives of American workers. In 1911 in New York City there was a horrific fire at the Triangle Shirtwaist Factory.

Nearly 150 workers perished, unable to use fire exits that had been locked to prevent their taking unauthorised breaks. The result was not immediate legislative reform. Nor was it union action. Instead, it was to inspire the progressive middle classes to campaign for better working conditions for those less fortunate than themselves.

Populism

Populism emerged in the 1890s as a response to the failure of the farmers' parties to make headway in the general election of 1888. The reasons why people in the West and in the South were discontented with the existing political parties in the USA were, in the short term, economic.

Poor harvests in the West began in 1886 and continued for roughly a decade. For the first time, the West was filling up – there was less opportunity for western pioneers to move to new, better, territory or expand. Some farmers could not be as productive as they needed to be, especially given that mortgage rates in the West were very high because of the scarcity of credit. This was set in the context of a long-term agricultural depression. Prices fell: wheat, which had cost $1.45 a bushel at the end of the Civil War, cost less than 50¢. Corn and cotton prices had gone the same way. One of the reasons for this was globalisation. US farmers had previously disposed of their surplus on the international market, but across the world there had been agricultural development – in Russia, Canada and Australia for example – which meant that there were fewer eager buyers for American surpluses. Steamships, telegraphs and extensive railroad networks meant that there was now a global market. Even those American farmers who had plenty of crops no longer had eager overseas markets to buy up their surplus, and they no longer had a guarantee that other Americans would buy from them.

Faced with these difficulties, western and southern farmers wanted their supposed commercial partners in the East to help. They did not. Banks tightened, rather than loosened, their credit: small-scale farmers were less able to cope with the bad times. Not for them the big business practice of absorbing a loss in the short term. Railroads remained very expensive, sometimes taking half the value of goods as payment for transporting them. By 1893 there was an industrial depression as well, and unemployment in industrialised areas rose to 20–25%. In Chicago in 1893 an estimated 100 000 men were looking for work. Hundreds of banks failed, and a quarter of the nation's railroad companies went bust (this does not mean that railroad trains stopped moving, though). If in the years leading up to 1893 the East had seemed unwilling to help the West and South, by 1893 it was not able to.

One possible solution to the problem was the 'money question'. Everyone agreed that, in a rapidly expanding economy such as that of the USA, the amount of money available had to increase rapidly enough to meet the economy's needs, or growth would be stifled. Those in debt, and primary producers whose commodities were selling at low prices (that is, western farmers) wanted a large money supply. The larger the money supply, the lower the value of money – and therefore the larger the value of inflation, which reduces the value of debts and increases the value of crops. Those who favoured 'sound money' – creditors, individuals on fixed incomes, those in the slower-growing sectors of the economy – wanted the opposite. One way to create more money, and the way on which national politics became fixated, was to allow coinage to be based on silver as well as gold. Those who supported an increased money supply, and inflation, were bimetallists. Their opponents, sound money men, were the goldbugs who supported a return to the gold standard. These differences transcended party lines

ACTIVITY 2.2

Make a list of as many reasons as you can why western and southern farmers were distressed in the late 1880s and 1890s.

Divide into groups representing:

- Eastern financiers.
- Eastern industrialists.
- The federal government.

Each group should produce a plan to address the farmers' complaints as fully as possible.

Now explain why these plans were not carried out: what stopped them?

and threatened party unity. Congressmen from Kansas, whether Republican or Democrat, tended to agree on an inflationary money policy, whereas congressmen from Massachusetts, from both parties, tended to support the gold standard. As far as possible, national parties, fearful of disintegration, tried not to talk about it.

The rise of the People's Party

Western farmers tired of watching eastern congressmen and businessmen squabble over expensive railroads. Their best chance of winning power was to win in elections, hoping perhaps that a re-elected President Cleveland would recognise a mandate for reform. They could, perhaps, use the Solid South to elect a president to suit their interests. Supported by their western allies, southern farmers sought to gain control of local Democratic parties, overthrowing the Redeemer governments in southern states. The new governor of South Carolina, Ben Tillman, would serve as governor and US senator for 30 years, but the farmers did not have overall success. The message of the elections of 1888 was that trying to create change through the Democratic Party in the South and farmers' alliances in the West was not likely to work.

The People's Party, often called the populists, was created to contest the 1892 election. Its candidates, James Weaver and James Field, were both veterans of the Civil War – although in an attempt to show sectional unity, they had been selected for the ticket as they had fought on different sides. Weaver had been the Greenback candidate for president in 1880, and was clearly identified as the candidate of the bimetallists. The first Populist manifesto, known as the Omaha Platform after the party conference in Omaha, Nebraska (see Figure 2.2), was a broad reform platform, reflecting the fact that the Populists were a broad party, seeking to gain support from West and South, and also trying to appeal to workers in the East.

The Populist Manifesto 1892

- Opposition to corruption in politics
- Criticism of the media, which does not criticise the Government or big business when it should
- Support for the formation of labour unions in cities
- Opposition to poor immigrants, as their arrival drives down wages for existing workers
- Criticism of Big Business for failing to support western farmers
- Support for bimetallism to increase the money supply
- Support for a shorter working day
- Support for the direct election of US Senators, rather than their appointment by state legislatures
- Support for a 'subtreasury plan' whereby the Federal Government agreed to buy cash crops at 80% of their value if necessary, to support farmers unable to sell their crops
- Characterisation of America as a 'land of tramps and millionaires'

Figure 2.2: The Omaha Platform, known as the Populist Manifesto, of 1892.

ACTIVITY 2.3

Look at the provisions of the Omaha Platform of 1892. For each provision, identify which group of voters it might be expected to appeal to. Is the appeal sectional? Is it class-based?

Weaver and Field received a million votes and 22 electoral college votes. They won Nevada, Colorado and Kansas, but failed to make any headway in the South or in the Midwest, where many farmers were doing somewhat better as they had diversified away from cash crops into raising cattle and pigs. The Democrat Grover Cleveland was returned to the **White House**. In Kansas, Mary Ellen Lease, one of the first women to come to prominence in American politics, had encouraged farmers to 'raise less corn and more hell'. Her unsympathetic adversaries called her the Kansas Pythoness. She became alienated from the People's Party as other party members worked more closely with the Democrats on the grounds that if you couldn't beat them, you had to join them.

William Jennings Bryan and the election of 1896

There are times in history when one person appears to encapsulate an entire movement. William Jennings Bryan was that man for populism, although he was not a member of the People's Party. Instead, he was a populist Democrat – the leader of a grouping that grew up inside the Democratic Party in opposition to the Redeemers. He propelled himself into the limelight with a speech that is as important an expression of populist ideology as the Omaha Platform is of populist policy.

Bryan had been a US Representative from Nebraska from 1891 to 1895, and a failed candidate for the Senate in 1894, when the Republicans won in a landslide victory. President Cleveland had failed to stabilise the economy after the Panic of 1893. The Populists, whose 1892 campaign had promoted **bimetallism**, found their ideas stolen by Republicans and Democrats. Bryan was among them. He used his time out of office to campaign for 'free silver' and absorbed the Populist message and rhetorical technique. By 1896 agrarian Democrats from the West and South, supporters of free silver, had gained control of the Democratic Party; Bryan was their leader, and was nominated for the Presidency aged 36.

Bryan was not a member of the People's Party but he did steal all their best lines. Although they nominated a different vice presidential candidate, the People's Party had no choice: it nominated him too. Bryan spoke for the plain people of rural America. His great speech, known as the 'Cross of Gold' speech, seemed blasphemous, and to call the East the enemy used the language of sectional conflict, which many Americans regarded with horror. Bryan was too young to remember the Civil War. His opponent, the former Speaker William McKinley, nominated by the Republican Party that had been shorn of its bimetallists just as the Democrats had lost their goldbugs, had fought in the great conflict. Bryan won the South and West but lost the election, which was a conflict between urban industry and the agrarian world but also between North and South, and East and West. Bryan carried 22 states in the West and South. McKinley carried one more state, but won nearly 100 more electoral college votes. The Republicans would control the presidency, the Senate and the House for the next 14 years. The Populists, meanwhile, were finished as a political force. An attempt to nominate a ticket for the 1900 presidential race merely resulted in their nomination of the same 'Stevenson' ticket as the Democrats. Their agenda, though, lived on.

Progressivism

McKinley's time as president (1897–1901) was notable for a few reasons. His was the most expensive successful presidential campaign: his supporters spent $3 million having him elected in 1896. The economy was improving, and the Gold Standard Act of 1900 settled the issue of the currency. America acquired for the first time an overseas empire of a sort, with the question of imperialism becoming one of the most important issues of the day. McKinley himself was not particularly in control of events: he seemed, instead, to dither while other voices made themselves heard. One of those other voices was that of Theodore Roosevelt, who talked himself onto McKinley's ticket for re-election in 1900 as the vice presidential candidate. Then, in September 1901, McKinley was assassinated, either as part of a global anarchist plot to mark the millennium by assassinating world leaders (which also claimed the King of Italy) or as a copycat assassination. Although he did not himself accept the label until 1912, Roosevelt would become the great progressive president.

Theodore Roosevelt was the youngest man ever to become president of the United States. His professional political career (he was among the first to have one) had stalled until he was able to persuade McKinley to appoint him to the Navy Department as assistant secretary. An enthusiastic proponent of war with Spain, Roosevelt, who had briefly been a cowboy and still romanticised the West, volunteered to help to lead a band he called the 'Rough Riders' in an invasion of Cuba, making himself a hero at the Battle of San Juan Hill in 1898. He won election as governor of New York later that year, and then as vice president in 1900. When McKinley died, the Republican 'fixer', Roosevelt's rival Mark Hanna, who had been

Key term

bimetallism: the economic doctrine that currency should be based on silver as well as gold. The effect of this would be to increase the money supply, as silver is far more plentiful than gold. Opponents, who wanted to maintain the gold standard, were called goldbugs.

happy to help him to the vice presidency as a way of keeping him quiet, remarked, 'That damn cowboy is president.'

Roosevelt remained among the most popular men in America until his death in 1919. He had a number of nicknames – 'the Colonel' for his adventures at San Juan, 'TR' and of course the affectionate form of his first name, 'Teddy', after which the teddy bear is named. At the risk of upsetting readers familiar with the romantic story of how Teddy refused to shoot a bear during a hunt in 1902, two facts stand repeating. The first is that Roosevelt refused to shoot the bear not because he wanted to save it but because it had already been subdued and he thought that shooting it would be unsportsmanlike: he asked his companions to kill it instead. The second is that he utterly loathed being called Teddy.

Progressivism was a reforming movement that sought to address social problems in varied, contradictory ways. All progressives sought to humanise industrial capitalism, as Populists had. Progressivism has been variously presented by historians as:

- A class project by an anxious middle class seeking to improve conditions for the working classes, often rationalised as 'civic duty'.

Hidden voices

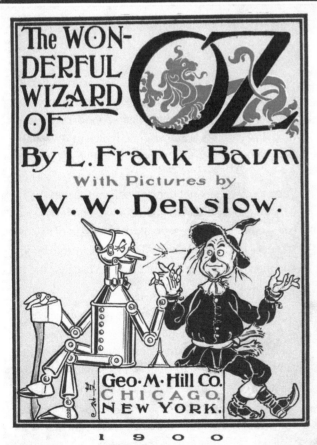

Figure 2.3: The cover of L. Frank Baum's *The Wonderful Wizard of Oz*.

In 1900 L. Frank Baum wrote *The Wonderful Wizard of Oz* (Figure 2.3). It tells the story of how Dorothy Gale is whisked away from her home in Kansas. She lands in Oz, a wonderful land controlled by an all-powerful wizard who turns out, in the end, to be a charlatan.

One reading of the novel is as an allegory of the populist message. An allegorical novel is one in which all the important details represent something in real life. In this reading of the work, Dorothy represents the plucky American smallholder, an independent hard worker from Kansas. The Wicked Witch of the East represents Eastern capital. The Yellow Brick Road, which the inhabitants of Oz insist everyone should follow, stands for the gold standard. The Emerald City is the colour of greenbacks – paper money – and Dorothy wears shoes made of silver, which gives her special protection. The scarecrow is an honest farmer, the tin man an industrial worker and the cowardly lion is William Jennings Bryan, the great charismatic failure of the populist movement.

ACTIVITY 2.4

Look at William Jennings Bryan's speech from 1896 in the Voices from the past box.

Identify the arguments that Bryan makes about what has gone wrong with America.

- A preoccupation with or search for order within America, imposing constraints upon a country that had recently gone through a period of radical growth.
- An attempt to impose government by experts – this was the first generation of university-trained professionals in the civil service and political classes, men like Roosevelt himself.

Progressive policies

There were many strands to progressive policy, and a key task for any historian of the period is to consider how to draw those strands together. Progressives certainly seemed to have taken on the populist preoccupation with corruption. A classic pattern for how corruption was exposed was this: a journalist would get a story and publish it in one of the many magazines that proliferated in the early 20th century (all in competition with one another, seeking the most sensational stories possible) (see Figure 2.4). Popular outcry among the magazine-reading classes would ensue and politicians would decide that something should be done. This could take the form of a reaction against the corrupt regimes of the Gilded Age, or of efforts to improve conditions in the slums, or of an assault on some social evil such as crime or drunkenness.

Voices from the past

William Jennings Bryan, 'Cross of Gold' speech at the Democratic-People's Party convention, Chicago, 9 July, 1896

'There are two ideas of government. There are those who believe that if you just legislate to make the well-to-do prosperous, that their prosperity will leak through on those below. The Democratic idea has been that if you legislate to make the masses prosperous their prosperity will find its way up and through every class that rests upon it.

'You come to us and tell us that the great cities are in favor of the gold standard. I tell you that the great cities rest upon these broad and fertile prairies. Burn down your cities and leave our farms, and your cities will spring up again as if by magic. But destroy our farms and the grass will grow in the streets of every city in the country.

'My friends, we shall declare that this nation is able to legislate for its own people on every question without waiting for the aid or consent of any other nation on earth, and upon that issue we expect to carry every single state in the Union …

'It is the issue of 1776 over again. Our ancestors, when but 3 million, had the courage to declare their political independence of every other nation upon earth. Shall we, their descendants, when we have grown to 70 million, declare that we are less independent than our forefathers? No, my friends, it will never be the judgment of this people. Therefore, we care not upon what lines the battle is fought. If they say bimetallism is good but we cannot have it till some nation helps us, we reply that, instead of having a gold standard because England has, we shall restore bimetallism, and then let England have bimetallism because the United States have.

'If [the great cities] dare to come out in the open field and defend the gold standard as a good thing, we shall fight them to the uttermost, having behind us the producing masses of the nation and the world. Having behind us the commercial interests and the laboring interests and all the toiling masses, we shall answer their demands for a gold standard by saying to them, you shall not press down upon the brow of labor this crown of thorns. You shall not crucify mankind upon a cross of gold.'

One of the most significant and successful victories of Progressivism was the anti-alcohol Temperance Movement. It was hardly new in American society to suggest that alcohol was a great and damaging evil: that kind of discourse had been around for half a century at least. When Prohibition (a ban on the sale or importation of alcohol) came as the 18th Amendment passed in 1919 to take effect in 1920, it represented the triumph of a long campaign. Temperance campaigners were often women, sometimes motivated by religion (men should be in church on Sunday morning, not in the saloon) and sometimes by a more middle-class puritanical analysis that the social problems of the working classes were caused by drinking. In the 1890s, when he was a member of the New York Police Board, Theodore Roosevelt had launched an ill-fated crusade against Sunday morning drinking, which had made him thoroughly unpopular with a number of people including his party bosses who saw that he might cost them future elections. After the First World War, helped by the association of beer as a German drink, Prohibition succeeded. This apparent progressive triumph was a false one – many historians think that the illegal bars (speakeasies) that sprang up in the 1920s made it *easier* to obtain alcohol, rather than harder.

Another victory of the Progressives was women's suffrage. This was granted nationally in 1920 in the 19th Amendment. That amendment was a direct response to campaigners, called suffragists, storming the White House in July 1917 – President Wilson pardoned them all and set the amendment in motion through Congress. Women had had the right to vote in Wyoming since 1869, and across the West, where women were perhaps more obviously equal partners in the settlement process, states were granting them the vote. By 1917 women occupied a fifth of manufacturing jobs; that number went up as American men prepared to fight in the war. Women's suffrage was certainly a progressive movement; it was led by the middle classes and aimed at widening democratic participation, which are two characteristics of Progressivism, but it would be wrong to say that the

 Hidden voices

Progressivism in a Transnational Context

Historians have only recently accepted that the progressive era was part of American attempts to strengthen the nation's social fabric in an international context. Especially through Daniel Rodgers's influential book *Atlantic Crossings,* historians have come to realise the importance of European stimuli for the development of American progressivism. The United States lagged behind some European countries in many types of social and economic reform, such as industrial injuries insurance, social insurance and pensions.

As Ian Tyrrell has shown,[6] the influence of Australia and New Zealand was also very strong. Reformers such as the irrigation promoter William E. Smythe in California proclaimed the need for 'New Zealandising' America. The 'Australian' ballot (i.e. secret ballot) was introduced in the late 19th century by 'progressives' wanting a more rational, deliberative democracy. You cannot really understand progressivism only by studying what's happening in America. International influences were key to American efforts to create a more organised, disciplined, efficient, economically productive, harmonious, *modern* nation-state at the same time as their competitors were doing likewise.

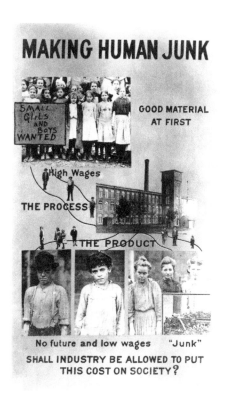

MAKING HUMAN JUNK

GOOD MATERIAL AT FIRST

High Wages

THE PROCESS

THE PRODUCT

No future and low wages   "Junk"

SHALL INDUSTRY BE ALLOWED TO PUT THIS COST ON SOCIETY?

Figure 2.4: This progressive era poster opposed child labour.

ACTIVITY 2.5

Make a note of progressive policies. Sort these policies into appropriate groups.

1. For each policy, identify whether it is the same as, or inspired by, a populist policy.
2. For each policy, identify whether there is a transnational context.
3. For each policy, identify whether it is likely to be a preoccupation of the middle classes seeking to help the working classes, or of those wishing to impose order, or of experts in government trying to professionalise American government.
4. Create a mind map to illustrate all of this information.

Progressives caused it. It had been coming in the United States since Roosevelt was a boy, and it was coming across the world in the early 20th century.

In general, progressive laws increased the regulatory powers of government over big business. This also tended to improve the lives of working people. Roosevelt's reaction to the anthracite coal strikes in 1902, when he improved conditions for the workers in order to prevent future strikes, is a case in point. In 1906 the Meat Inspection Act had the dual effect of improving conditions in meatpacking factories, especially in Chicago (where the press had exposed terrible conditions for the workers), and of reducing the chance of Americans being poisoned by unhealthy meat. This was not just about improving the lives of the working classes. Roosevelt and Taft broke up monopolies, reducing the power of big business against the 'little guy', but also regulated the market to prevent overheating. Progressivism both helped the working classes and allowed the government to regulate and in theory to calm the excesses of capitalism.

Progressives also secured a number of significant political changes, at least some of which had earlier been Populist goals. These measures all improved democracy – or, if you prefer, reduced the power of the political party hierarchies that distrusted progressives.

- In 1913 the 17th Amendment meant that every state had to allow for the direct election of senators, rather than their election by state legislatures.
- Direct primary elections meant that party candidates for other elections (including the general election for the presidency) could be chosen by popular vote.
- 'Recall' of unpopular politicians could now occur in some states – if a certain proportion of the electorate thought a politician should be removed between elections, he could be.
- Referendums and initiatives allowed ordinary people to put items onto the ballot paper to pass as state laws.

 Thematic link: ideas and ideology

The presidency of Theodore Roosevelt

The chief significance of Roosevelt's presidency was not that he was progressive. It was that he was energetic. This energy translated itself into an increasingly imperial USA, and into the beginnings of what would one day become an imperial presidency. Roosevelt viewed himself as the steward of the national interest, with a duty to make America as great as it could be. The death of McKinley had thrust him into centre stage earlier than he had planned: he would use his position to improve his country, adopting a 'bully pulpit' – a position of authority from which a speaker may express his views in the knowledge that others will listen – to do so. An academic called Woodrow Wilson wrote that Roosevelt assumed a position as the spokesman for the whole country, and moulded the views of the country to his own. He used the press for his own ends – he was perfectly upfront about his willingness to lie to them in the national interest, and also happy to join in on popular anti-corruption campaigns, although he condemned the authors of campaigns he disliked as 'muckrakers'. Roosevelt was the first reforming president to stand apart from the rest of the federal government and criticise it for not doing enough.

  Thematic link: government and politics

He was also (mostly) a perfectly sensible politician who knew how to pick his battles. During the anthracite coal strike he was carefully diplomatic until he obtained the result he wanted – at which point he declared victory over big business. He enjoyed a honeymoon period at the beginning of his presidency until, in 1902, he challenged J.P. Morgan in the Northern Securities case, invoking the Sherman Act to break up Morgan's monopoly (he would later work with Morgan to support the economy in 1907). He kept on using the Sherman Act, with varying degrees of success (he was often opposed by the Supreme Court), intending to regulate the economy to prevent damaging financial panics while also appearing to champion the little guy. The general progressive theme was also exemplified by the Hepburn Act of 1906, which set up the Interstate Commerce Commission to regulate the railroads; the federal government was now in charge of at least some infrastructure. Congress had done it, but Roosevelt claimed the credit.

Frustrated by his inability to act without constraint or congressional help in domestic affairs, Roosevelt became a foreign-policy imperial president. This was also a function of his rash decision in 1905 to announce that he would not seek election in 1908; he lost influence in Washington as Republicans began to consider the succession. Roosevelt deliberately focused on foreign affairs as an area where he, as president, had great influence. He viewed himself as like a king – an elected one, certainly, but nevertheless with a great deal of personal power. He set himself up as a major world statesman, winning a Nobel Peace Prize for his brokering of peace between Japan and Russia and making efforts to avert a potential European conflict. He was remarkably far-sighted about America's need to prepare for such a conflict, and for conflict with Japan.

If Roosevelt sought to raise the international profile of the USA, he also sought to define what it was to be American. He was obsessed by conservation, a legacy perhaps of his time in the West, and he had a nationalistic pride in a specifically American landscape. In his time many national parks were created as a bulwark against the rampant destruction of American's natural forests, which had been going on for two centuries as farmland was created. True, this was set like so much of Progressivism in an international context – conservationism was a popular European theme as well. And Roosevelt did not invent nationalism – another European import that had preceded his presidency. He did, however, become synonymous with a certain type of Americanism – pioneering, educated, energetic, confident and international.

Taft, Insurgent Progressivism and the Bull Moose

Roosevelt's successor, his secretary of war William Howard Taft (Figure 2.5), was a nationally respected man with a real sense of political ambition that was eventually fulfilled not in 1909 when he became president, but in 1921 when he became chief justice. This is not to say that Taft did not want the presidency – he

Figure 2.5: William Howard Taft, President 1909–13, who finally became Chief Justice, the job he had always wanted, in 1921.

repeatedly turned down Roosevelt's attempts to appoint him to the Supreme Court, having apparently made the absolutely accurate political assessments that he, rather than his Cabinet colleague Elihu Root, was the only real successor to Roosevelt as Republican nominee for the presidency, and that the Democrats could not win the presidency against the Republicans. Even so, he had to be persuaded to accept the nomination, which he did out of a sense of duty.

Taft was a Progressive, but he lacked both Roosevelt's drive and his political awareness. He took progressive actions, using the Sherman Act more often in four years than Roosevelt had in seven, continuing Roosevelt's programme of conservation and breaking up the Standard Oil monopoly. He could not, however, lead his party. His first political initiative in 1909 was to attempt tariff reform, a key progressive goal. He failed either to realise or to care that this would split his own Republican Party, which is why Roosevelt had entirely avoided the issue. The old Populists, not all of whom had been Democrats, wanted the tariff abolished entirely to lower the cost of living, perhaps to be replaced by a 'single tax' on land. The compromise that came up in Congress was to raise the tariff on manufactured goods, helping industry in the East, and to lower it on raw materials, penalising the West. The progressive president had awakened old populist sectional divisions, which now began to split the Republican Party. The pro-farming Midwest was outraged by the new tariff; Taft made things worse by claiming inaccurately that the compromise was all his idea, and publicly praising the bill. In his presidential memoir Taft later explained that, unlike Roosevelt, he simply thought that presidents should not take the initiative with Congress, and certainly should not veto such an important bill.

All this was of some alarm to Roosevelt, who was on safari in Africa. Worse was to come in 1910 when an internal row in the Department of the Interior, responsible for national parks and conservation, resulted in Taft dismissing Gifford Pinchot, a trusted Roosevelt confidant, from his position as chief of the United States Forest Service. Roosevelt took this well, but the progressive press took offence on his behalf. Taft had alienated the old guard of his party, irritated the new, and shown himself unwilling and possibly unable to pursue a presidency as vigorous as that of his predecessor.

Roosevelt launched a tour in 1910 that was supposed to heal the breach in the Republican Party, which was spreading to Congress where Speaker Joe Cannon's control was threatened by his own party. Roosevelt promoted the 'New Nationalism', a platform aimed at meeting what he viewed as a growing socialist threat, and arguing for:

- Social welfare reform.
- Regulation of business.
- Bigger government.
- Social justice as more important than property or capital.

In theory the Republican Progressive League (RPL), which did very well in the 1910 **midterm elections**, was led by Robert La Follette, the senator from Wisconsin. In 1912 the RPL tried and failed to deselect Taft as the Republican Party nominee. They used the primary elections to push their cause; Taft used patronage and threats to maintain his position, and he won the nomination. He presumably thought he could beat La Follette and whoever the Democrats might nominate. Over the spring and summer of 1912, Roosevelt allowed himself to be 'reluctantly' manoeuvred into accepting the nomination of the new Progressive Party, running on the platform of New Nationalism, and running on his own popularity and reputation. He characterised his campaign as that of the 'Bull Moose' candidate. This was in an attempt to differentiate himself from the Democratic donkey and the Republican elephant – and also a reference to his own uncompromising approach to argument, as well as to his love of hunting.

The presidential election was a landslide for the Democrats. The Democrats won 42% of the popular vote, Roosevelt 27% and Taft 23%. Debs, for the Socialist Party, came a very distant fourth on 6%, still their best result in an American general election. The victory of the Democratic candidate Woodrow Wilson had been achieved with fewer votes and a lower share of the vote than William Jennings Bryan, so often defeated for the presidency, had managed. Wilson won because of Roosevelt's progressive candidacy. It was Roosevelt, not the progressives, who did well in this election: in the Congressional election held on the same day, which the Democrats also won in a landslide, the Progressives won only 10 seats and were four million votes behind the Republicans.

 Thematic link: ideas and ideology

Wilson's New Freedom

The lucky Democratic beneficiary of the Republican insurgency was Woodrow Wilson, the academic who was governor of New Jersey. He had won the nomination of his party with support from Bryan. Wilson's platform therefore owed something to Bryan's populism, and was framed in opposition to Roosevelt's progressivism. Wilson himself, however, had become popular with progressives in New Jersey when he had shown independence from the party bosses there following his election as governor. In reality his policy platform stole many of Roosevelt's ideas, and over time his presidency became more and more progressive in character.

The key ideas of the New Freedom were:

- Opposition to monopolies.
- Support for 'free enterprise' (by which he meant small and medium-sized businesses rather than big business).
- Opposition to finance capitalism.
- Support for states' rights.
- A laissez-faire approach to government.

There is an inherent contradiction in that platform, in that Wilson's laissez-faire approach should in theory have prevented him from opposing monopolies or finance capitalism, each of which had naturally emerged during previous laissez-faire administrations.

ACTIVITY 2.7

How significant was the leadership of Roosevelt in the progressive movement?

When you are writing about Roosevelt's leadership, it is important to think about his presidency and also about his leadership of the progressive insurgents in 1912.

A key question to consider is this: how much of the progressive platform would have been expressed without Roosevelt? You might also consider that a lot of the progressive platform was, ultimately, enacted. How much of that relied on Roosevelt?

ACTIVITY 2.8

1. How much of the legislation of the New Freedom in 1913–14 was progressive?

2. How much of it was populist?

3. Is the distinction between 'progressive' and 'populist' sustainable in practice?

 Thematic link: ideas and ideology

There was a certain weight of expectation on Wilson's shoulders when he became president. He had a huge majority of Democrats in the House, and a large majority in the Senate. His own election had clearly been a product of the Republican insurgency, and it was only the South that was solidly behind him and could be relied upon to vote for him again. He was, himself, a southerner, although now a resident of a northern state, and he knew that he might be able to muster some cross-sectional appeal, but he also knew that he would have to act carefully in order to secure his own re-election in 1916. He imitated the style if not necessarily the policies of the man whose presidency he had analysed less than ten years previously – Theodore Roosevelt. Like Roosevelt, he argued that the president had a duty to use his powers, and he rediscovered for the first time in 100 years a presidential responsibility that is there in the Constitution. 'He shall from time to time', it reads, 'give to the Congress information of the state of the Union.' The State of the Union address that Wilson revived still takes place every year, and gives US presidents at least the illusion that they are directing the work of Congress, rather than merely implementing it. The growth of presidential power had reached another important milestone.

In Wilson's first two years Congress enacted various parts of the New Freedom platform:

- The passing of the 16th Amendment in the last month of Taft's presidency allowed the federal government to levy income tax. This allowed Wilson's government to reduce tariffs without losing income in the Underwood-Simmons Tariff Act of 1913.
- The Federal Reserve Act of 1913 established the US Federal Reserve, which guaranteed that national banks could not fail and took some of the risk out of capitalism. The same security did not necessarily apply to state banks.
- In 1914, the Federal Trade Commission Act established the Federal Trade Commission, which had regulatory powers intended to stop interstate corporations from using unfair anti-competitive practices.
- The Clayton Act in 1914 prohibited price discrimination (which was often an anti-competitive move allowing the promotion of monopolies) and also emphasised the legality of peaceful strike action.

The Progressive Party disappeared as a separate force in the midterm elections of 1914, making it clear that there would be a single Republican candidate, and a potentially difficult challenge, waiting for Wilson in the presidential election of 1916. Wilson responded by taking on some of their New Nationalist ideas, including regulation of child labour and attempts to professionalise the work of the federal government. He supported federal land banks to provide long-term cheap credit to rural communities, and introduced the Adamson Act, imposing an eight-hour day on railroad workers. This in particular signalled his abandonment of the rights policies of laissez-faire states. Meanwhile in January 1916 he put his advisor Louis Brandeis onto the Supreme Court. Brandeis had made his name prosecuting big business and regulating corporations.

The election of 1916 was very close. Wilson held steady in the South but predictably lost ground in the other sections. His campaign slogan was 'He kept us out of war', and this was probably crucial in determining his victories in the southwestern states, which feared a Mexican invasion backed by Germany. Having won re-election, Wilson took the United States into the First World War, which became the sole major focus of American politics. He would ultimately lose control of his own government while attempting to win the peace, and watching his own party fracture under pressure from Bryan, who had resigned as his secretary of state to campaign for peace. He also had to deal with his old antagonist Theodore Roosevelt, now in his late fifties, and whom he had been forced explicitly to ban from going to Europe to fight, and who was enthusiastically leading the calls for Germany to surrender unconditionally, while Wilson was trying to negotiate a settlement.

Economic change and developments

In 1890 the USA was a capitalist society in which the voice of socialism had hardly been heard. Big business ruled the roost, and all (rail)roads led to the big finance houses in New York City. Labour disputes occurred and were sometimes violent. If the federal government intervened, it was almost always on the side of the industrialists whose interests they equated with the country's. The two financial panics of the period had not caused permanent damage. In 1893, unemployment in industrialised areas rose from 20% to 25%. In Chicago an estimated 100 000 men were looking for work. Hundreds of banks failed, and a quarter of the nation's railroad companies went bust. In response, the laws allowing silver currency were repealed, and by working with the banker J.P. Morgan on four **bond issues** from 1894–96 Cleveland was able to stabilise the economy by preventing the federal government from defaulting on its loans. The recession that followed the Panic was ultimately ended in 1897, when a series of poor harvests in Europe gave American farmers a greater market share. The next Panic came in 1907; Roosevelt took action but pushed for more. The recovery was rapid but partial, and it was only really the stimulus of the First World War that fixed the American economy.

At its most basic level, an expanding economy has ready supplies of raw materials, labour and markets, which means there are plenty of people willing and able to buy the goods produced. It also has a favourable position relative to external competitors, which means there is not an international competitor willing to sell the same goods more cheaply. It also has a plentiful supply of currency to enable transactions to be made. If anything changes about this model, then the economy might contract.

Governments have various things that they can do to try to ensure that the economy continues to expand. These are often referred to as 'levers' (see Table 2.2). The difficulty of this, for a government, is fourfold:

- If there are economic difficulties, a government needs to decide which lever or levers to pull, by working out accurately what the problem is.
- A government has to resist the temptation to pull the wrong levers simply in order to be seen to be doing something.

Key term

bond issues: a bond issue occurs when a government attempts to raise money in the short term by borrowing, either on the international market or from its own citizens over the longer term.

Lever	Problem	Intended effect of pulling lever
Regulation of working conditions	Workers have poor conditions.	Regulate or allow unions to improve workers' conditions while sacrificing some productivity.
	Workers have good conditions but these are expensive for businesses.	Deregulation or banning unions to improve business productivity.
Tariff reform	Foreign goods are cheaper than domestic goods, and are putting American manufacturers or producers out of business.	Increase tariffs on imported goods to raise their price artificially, so American consumers will buy American goods instead.
	Foreign raw materials are too expensive, and American manufacturers cannot access them.	Lower tariffs on imported raw materials to lower their price.
Money supply	There is too much money, reducing its value and causing price inflation. This means that people who work in factories for fixed wages have less spending power.	Reduce the money supply to bring inflation down.
	There is too little money, increasing its value and causing prices to drop. This means that people who produce cash crops get less money for them.	Increase the money supply to encourage price inflation of cash crops.
Immigration reform	There are not enough workers to do all the available jobs. Corporations cannot grow quickly enough to meet the demand for their goods.	Relax immigration rules to encourage more immigrants to come to America.
	There are so many workers that the infrastructure of the cities cannot cope and slums appear.	Toughen immigration rules to ensure that overcrowding stops.
Territorial expansion	Industry and agriculture want more room to expand, and more markets into which to sell their goods.	Acquire new territory, either as part of the United States or as part of its trading empire.

Table 2.2: The levers governments might pull to affect the economy. Some levers can be 'pulled' both ways. Note that in the Gilded Age there was no central bank available to regulate interest rates.

- It may be that the problem is that the economy has grown to unrealistic levels, and that a period of contraction is needed to stabilise it: trying to put this contraction off might only make it worse.
- The consequences of taking action might turn out to be worse than the problem.

Governments, then, have a difficult time – even assuming that the capitalist model is broadly correct, as most Americans did, and assuming that those trying to manage the economy were men of good character trying to do their best for the country as a whole.

The first financial panic of the period in 1893 led to attempts by President Cleveland to reduce the tariff (the Supreme Court stopped him) and maintain the gold standard, restricting the currency. This led to political tension over bimetallism. Cleveland, who as president had to take a lead, declared himself a goldbug, but the issue split both main parties from 1894–96.

The Morganisation (organisation carried out by J.P. Morgan) of the railroads following the panic of 1893 had removed the threat that the whole system might go under. Finance capitalism had (for a price, and a seat on the board – naturally) streamlined and rationalised the major industries. The Interstate Commerce Commission had taken responsibility for the railroads and other vital infrastructure links, essentially doing what Morgan had done in the 1890s. The Federal Reserve had guaranteed that the major finance houses, and therefore the vital industries that they supported, would not go under – or at least, that if they did go under it would signal a crisis of the entire state. The major monopolies had been broken up – beef and banking in 1907, and Standard Oil in 1911 (which in any case did not control very much of the oil found in vast quantities in Texas and first extracted in 1900) – and much of the heat had been taken out of capitalism.

The next financial crisis came in 1907, with a new panic – more of a hiccup, in fact. Again, the economy faltered. The reasons were familiar – overexpansion had led to an overheated economy in which supply, demand, labour and the money supply could not keep up with one another. Speculators had involved themselves, some of them dishonestly, and enough companies failed to cause the market to correct itself. The recession lasted until 1909, after which recovery was patchy. There were two key differences this time. The first was that it was now a little clearer that something had to be done: the cycle of boom and bust (with panics in 1873, 1893 and 1907) was becoming more obvious. Laissez-faire capitalism did not involve smooth progress, implying that the government might be required to take some regulatory action. The second difference was that Theodore Roosevelt was a president who believed that he should be the one to lead action, and he and his successors did to a certain extent carry Congress along with them in an effort to get the federal government to act.

This recession led to a patchy recovery; the Great War that followed it helped the economy immensely as the USA lent money to other countries to buy American goods. By 1920 America was able to embark upon an age of prosperity (although as we shall see in the next chapter, this was not an age of prosperity for everyone). The boom of the Roaring Twenties, though, would be followed by another bust, this one the biggest of them all. The presidents of the 1920s had not learnt the lessons of the progressive era.

In 1920 the USA was a capitalist society in which the voice of socialism had been heard, and accepted, by 5% of voters in a presidential election. Although big business still mattered, life was easier for small and medium-sized enterprises especially in the West, and New York City did not seem quite so much to be at the centre of American life. The monopolies had been broken up, although usually only into holding companies that were still owned by the same people, the successors of the original robber barons. There was greater regulation of the working lives of ordinary people, and conditions were certainly better, at least in

ACTIVITY 2.9

1. Write down all the economic reforms made from 1890 to 1920.

2. Who or what had the most effect on the economy during this period: the federal government, the global market, big business, or small American businessmen and farmers?

part because of a progressive recognition that businesses function better with greater stability. If poor labour conditions appeared immoral to some Americans – well, they were at least *less* immoral than they had been, and there were still plenty of immigrants willing to work. Meanwhile, the cycle of frantic boom and panicked bust appeared to have been contained. There were, however, still some clouds on the horizon (see Figure 2.6).

1. The stock of companies such as US Steel was 'watered down'. Companies had borrowed money on the expectation that they would gain value in the future. If they did not, they would fail.

2. Automobile sales were becoming very important. There would come a time when everyone had an automobile.

3. The Panics of 1893 and 1907 had been caused by contractions in credit. Americans had not recognised this. The Panics had been ultimately solved by changes in global conditions. Were American governments really in control of the economy?

Figure 2.6: Economic clouds on the horizon.

 Thematic link: economy and society

The rise of US dominance as an economic and industrial power and the consequences of this

By 1900 the United States was the world's leading producer of iron, coal, steel, cotton, gold, tobacco and wheat. It was very nearly the world leader in production of petroleum and silver, and had a very large commercial carrying capacity. Its agricultural depression was largely lifted in 1897 when a decade of poor harvests in America ended, and there were poor harvests in Europe instead. At the same time foreign investors were beginning to invest in the American market, bringing capital. Although the battle for a silver currency had been lost, there were increasing numbers of banknotes in the 1890s and this cheaper money had expanded the availability of farm credit and therefore the agricultural base of the United States.

America did very well in the 1910s, and one of the key indicators of that success was the Model T Ford. Ten thousand had been produced in 1910; a million were produced in 1920. Its maker, Henry Ford, had realised two key things. The first was that demand could be created by marketing a product as essential, which is what he did with cars. The second was that a **production line** where individual workers performed single boring and repetitive tasks very well was a more efficient proposition than individual workers building the whole of individual cars. With reduced overheads and effective marketing, the Ford motor company became very profitable indeed. America's love affair with the automobile was underway.

When the war came in 1914, American farmers supplied food to Europe, and American manufacturers supplied arms and ammunition. America became aware that it might have a place at the top table of international diplomacy; another consequence of American industrial and economic might was security. It was inconceivable that America would have to defend her own borders and her own home territory, because no other power in the world would have the ability to raise a big enough army and transport it to the western hemisphere. This suggested that Americans could, if they wished, meddle in other countries' affairs with relative impunity.

A further set of consequences for the United States was internal. Relations between labour and capital (see the section on Governments, big business and organised labour earlier in this chapter) had reached an uneasy equilibrium during the First World War, but there was a clear pattern of success for the moderate policies of the American Federation of Labor, suggesting that the balance of power in the USA would remain broadly with the business owners. Meanwhile a precedent had been established that effort – and some money – would be spent on progressive policies. Income tax, on a federal level, had been introduced by the 16th Amendment to the Constitution. In this new, richer America, the federal government had become relatively more rich than the states.

Social developments

By 1920 the majority of people in the USA lived in cities. In the Northeast there was a clear pattern of urbanisation and rural depopulation beginning in the 1890s; elsewhere the issue was not that people were moving from the countryside. It was, rather, that more people were moving to the cities. Immigration continued apace, and began to cause social problems of its own.

The progressive era was not just about increased regulation and social democracy. It was also driven by exclusion. One of the most tangible ways in which US federal power expanded was in the policing of borders. Congress passed and enforced racially exclusive immigration control, beginning with the Chinese Exclusion Acts of the late 19th century, which also banned criminals and the mentally ill from coming to the USA and culminating in the Immigration Restriction Acts of the 1920s. Some of this racial exclusivity, which was characteristic of many progressive reforms, was driven by fear of radicalism generated by an internationally mobile proletariat moving across borders. Anarchists, terrorists, communists – all these national security threats from without helped to define the nation within. It was the USA that drove the growing use of passports for foreign travel with its

---

ACTIVITY 2.10

Draw a mind map of the consequences of the rise of US industrial and economic dominance. You might wish to revisit this mind map in the light of your reading of Chapter 3: Crisis of identity, 1920–1945.

 Key term

production line: a production line, often associated with Henry Ford, is an early 20th-century manufacturing innovation. Instead of individual workers building whole products, each worker was able to perform one repetitive task. This improved productivity.

increasing concern about the nature of European immigration. Workers were welcome, so long as they had come to work in freedom (which meant as it had for bakers in 1905, the freedom to work as hard as they liked in conditions as dangerous as they could bear).

Mass immigration and urbanisation and their consequences

From 1880 onwards immigrants to the United States came more from southern and eastern Europe, and from Asia, than they did from northern and western Europe. With insufficient capital to bring with them to do anything else, they came to the cities. In any case, the west was filling up: by 1890 there were few opportunities for jumping on the railroad and seeing where it took you. By 1910, two-thirds of the urban population consisted of first- or second-generation immigrants, often poorer and less skilled certainly than the immigrants who had preceded them. In Boston in 1894 the Immigration Restriction League emerged as a White Anglo-Saxon Protestant (WASP) organisation opposed to any other type of immigrant. It campaigned for a literacy test (in English) to be administered for any immigrant entering the USA. Presidents Cleveland, Taft and Wilson all vetoed literacy test bills. In the South, literacy tests were also used as another way to prevent black people from voting.

The immigrants came from southern and eastern Europe in greater numbers than ever before, driven to come to the USA by stories of how good life could be there, attracted by freedom and hope. In 1892 at Ellis Island, which is in New York Harbor, the immigration station (now a museum) opened, at which European steerage (third-class) passengers arrived for processing. Not everyone made it through the medical screening, but very many did. About half of these passengers were met by the friends or relatives who had paid for their tickets and invited them to join them in America; others were met by representatives from their national communities who went to Battery Island, at the southern tip of Manhattan, to meet their countrymen 'fresh off the boat'. From 1892 to 1924 about 12 million immigrants were admitted through Ellis Island, the curator of whose museum boasts that half of modern Americans are descended from them.

These 12 million were only the poorest passengers from Europe. Those who could afford to pay to cross first or second class were deemed automatically welcome. There were immigrants from Canada and Mexico, and a steady stream of immigrants coming from China, Japan and the Philippines across the Pacific, landing in California. Although families and older people did immigrate, the typical immigrant was young and single, seeking an opportunity for self-advancement; perhaps fleeing the poverty of southern Italy (Italians often entered the construction industry, although some also imported a particular brand of organised crime); or the anti-Jewish pogroms of Russia and eastern Europe (Polish and Russian Jews often entered the textile industry); or perhaps just seeking adventure in the New World rather than the prospect of having exactly the same lives as their parents had had in the Old. Although from 1890 to 1920 fairly consistently only around 1% of Americans were foreign-born, their children (that is, second-generation immigrants) came to dominate large areas of certain cities.

Why was there such opposition to new immigration? Some of it, undoubtedly, was racist or sectarian – and the emergence of the new concept of Americanism can hardly have helped. Some of the opposition was caused by an unwillingness to allow new immigrants – keener, hungrier, willing to work in ever more appalling conditions – to break strikes or undermine hard-won labour rights. There was serious opposition to German immigration by 1917, although stories of German atrocities had been heard throughout the war. This culminated in the Espionage and Sedition Acts. Eugene V. Debs, that recent presidential candidate, was imprisoned by Wilson and not let out until the end of his term.

With the frontier closed, immigrants tended to work in the cities, often in the same trade and geographical area as whichever group of their countrymen had met them off the boat. Immigration therefore implied urbanisation. Immigrants needed wages, and lacked the capital to buy land (increasingly expensive with the frontier closed) and so they worked in secondary industry. Some of the opposition to immigration, perhaps, was a response to the grim conditions that prevailed in many of the major cities of America by 1920. By 1910 there were 50 cities with more than 100 000 inhabitants in the United States. In 1914 alone there were 1.2 million immigrants, who essentially ended up somewhere between the East Coast and Chicago (and the closer to New York City or the Jersey Shore, where Ellis Island is, or to a direct railroad route to New York's Grand Central Station, the more immigrants there were). The problem of the slums was well known – Jacob Riis's 1890 work *How the Other Half Lives* led slowly to some efforts to clear and improve the slums, but not enough had been done to avoid slums growing up in Hell's Kitchen (in Manhattan) and Pittsburgh. The problem was beyond the capacity of even a professionalised Progressive government to deal with. They tried; their priorities included providing schools and roads.

Some of the opposition to immigration came as a response to the increasingly foreign character of major American cities, especially New York City. At the turn of the century, in response to concerns about immigration, the discourse of Americanism first began to emerge (Roosevelt was '100% American'). This in itself drew on decades of anti-Catholic politics, which had peaked in the 1850s and then again in the 1880s. In the last 20 years historians have looked at the emergence of the concept of 'whiteness'. The classic book in the genre is Noel Ignatiev's *How the Irish Became White*,[7] the title of which tells its own story – Irish people were literally regarded as a distinct simian race when they arrived, but by the early 20th century had become assimilated into a 'white' mainstream. This concept of 'whiteness' – meaning 'one who is able to participate in American politics' was of course particularly unhelpful to Americans who were not white at all.

It was perhaps more helpful for the Irish families of Boston, Massachusetts, who came to be part of the American mainstream. Most notable among them was the Kennedy family; in 1919, John F. Kennedy was born a fourth-generation immigrant (that is, his great-grandparents had crossed the Atlantic). He went on to be president. In 1894, when President Kennedy's father was only six years old, the Immigration Restriction League was formed in Boston. It sought the imposition of a literacy test for new immigrants, to be applied at Ellis Island. The official policy of the Immigration Restriction League was that eastern and southern Europeans were racially inferior to existing Americans. Its public voice was Senator Henry

Cabot Lodge – the same man who in 1890 had come up with the Force Bill, and argued against the racial discrimination being shown in the South. Lodge would later become an important voice in the Dillingham Commission (1907–11), which studied immigration patterns and recommended that various groups, including alcoholics, anarchists, the feeble-minded and homosexuals, should be barred from entering the country, and that East Asians should not be allowed in at all. One consequence of immigration was, perhaps inevitably, hostility to immigrants.

The position of African Americans

In the 1890s 90% of African Americans still lived in the South. A few had moved to northern cities, or west – often as cowboys – but most remained where their families had been for generations. In the South the position of African Americans was deteriorating, and becoming legally entrenched under the banner of **States' Rights**. The key Supreme Court case came in 1896. In the case of *Plessy v Ferguson* they ruled that the state of Louisiana (and by implication all the states) had the right to segregate public facilities such as schools and railroads. The iconic phrase was 'separate but equal', meaning that there was no obligation on states to integrate their facilities as long as white and black people had facilities of a similar standard. That idea was widely and immediately ignored. In 1899 the Court ruled in the case of *Cumming v Richmond Board of Education* that states (in this case, Richmond County in Virginia) could establish schools for white people even if they were not establishing schools for black people – this seemed to get round the idea of 'separate but equal' entirely.

There were roughly three assaults on the rights of African Americans at this time. Their civil rights, always precarious, were undermined as voter registration tests were introduced in southern states. Sometimes the fiction that black voters had failed the test was not even maintained – they simply were not allowed to register. On other occasions, though, black voters would be given forms to fill in in foreign languages, or their registration forms would be mysteriously lost by the white voter registration officials. Second, emboldened by the result of *Plessy v Ferguson*, state legislatures established 'Jim Crow' laws (see Figure 2.7). These laws set out the precise ways in which 'separate but equal' would be implemented, giving a legal basis to segregation. Third, black people, now lacking the protection of a white master, were in danger of being lynched.

Why did the federal government not stop this? It saw no reason to – in fact it had no law that could. Murder was criminalised by the states, and it was for the states to deal with it. From 1891 to 1911 the federal government was entirely controlled by Republicans, who had no serious presence in the South; none of these Republicans was interested in taking on the South, again, over the rights of black people. President Roosevelt entertained the black leader Booker T. Washington at the White House, but made a point of not making a fuss about it. Woodrow Wilson, the only southerner and only Democrat to lead the country in this period, extended the racist Jim Crow laws into the federal government, and certainly did not do anything to ameliorate the position of black people in the South.

Key term

States' Rights: the political doctrine that states should set their own social legislation. In practice, the term is often used as a shorthand for legislation designed to promote white interests at the expense of black people.

Speak like a historian

'One of the great pleasures of the age was baseball: although regarded as America's "national game" since the 1880s, it really came of age in the 1900s. Attendance at major-league games doubled during the decade to seven million a year and the World Series was inaugurated between the winners of the two rival leagues, the National and the American. Minor-league baseball was yet more popular; even small cities had their own team. Baseball, it was claimed, built civic pride … Baseball was not, however, a force for racial integration. Black Americans had to play in their own separate and badly funded Negro leagues.

During this booming pre-war era, owners pulled down the wooden ballparks, seedy fire traps, and replaced them with fireproof structures … These imposing new stadiums helped reposition baseball as a family game for the respectable middle classes.'

Source: David Reynolds, *America – Empire of Liberty.*[8]

ACTIVITY 2.11

What point or points is historian David Reynolds making?

 ## Thematic link: individuals and groups

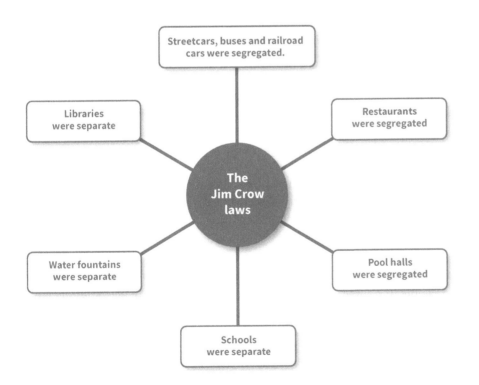

Figure 2.7: Jim Crow laws in the South.

The economic status of African Americans was not good, but nor was it entirely grim. The combined effects of laissez-faire capitalism and white racism had meant that there were large numbers of poor black people in the South, and those African Americans who had begun to move into northern cities in the 20th century found themselves on the whole on an equal footing with all the other poor migrants there. But the poorest African Americans in the South were becoming less poor: income was rising and life expectancy was increasing. An African American professional middle class was arising – often offering services that white companies in the South refused to provide to black people. There were shops run by black people for black people, for example, across the South. Black businesses often failed, but in roughly the same proportions as white businesses. Black businessmen offering services to black people were not on the whole as well off as white businessmen (they had a poorer client base, for a start) but things were looking up. The progress that was made was not perhaps as much progress as white people were making, but it was progress.

Black responses to white racism

With no help coming from the federal government, black people essentially had to help themselves. Booker T. Washington, the head of the Tuskegee Institute in Alabama, suggested reconciliation and accommodation with white people rather than opposition to segregation. In return for peaceful black acquiescence to the situation in the South, Washington sought white help in obtaining black schools and other institutions, and sought to enable black people to work in the North as well. This was the so-called Atlanta Compromise of 1895. From around 1897 there was indeed a substantial black migration to northern cities, for similar reasons as European and Asian workers were moving to the North – there was opportunity there. Twenty years later the First World War would see half a million black people moving North. Even Henry Ford, well known to be a racist, hired black workers. In 1917 nearly 400 000 entered the military. Meanwhile in the South there was an inward-looking revival of black culture – not quite, perhaps, what Washington had been looking for when he issued his advice to 'cast down your bucket where you are'. A rich culture began to develop in African American churches, and the music of the slave spirituals from southern farms began to move into southern cities such as New Orleans, Louisiana, in preparation for its rebirth as jazz and the blues.

W.E.B. du Bois was Washington's main black antagonist. He was a northerner, born in Massachusetts, but worked as Professor of Sociology at Atlanta University. His experience of white racism – and especially his witnessing of **lynchings** in Atlanta – brought him to oppose Washington by calling for an end to racism and the beginning of genuine equality. Du Bois founded the Niagara Movement in 1905 to fight for this. In 1909 he founded the National Association for the Advancement of Colored People, the NAACP. Advancement was needed because Washington, and his policies, were leading to a static situation.

In 1915 D.W. Griffith released a film called *The Birth of a Nation*, which depicted black men as slow-witted criminals (specifically, as potential rapists of white women). It also glorified the actions of that old white reactionary force the Ku Klux Klan. The film electrified the South, and the Klan was reborn in 1915. In July 1917 there were race riots in East St Louis, Missouri. In September of that year in Houston, Texas, black soldiers were provoked and then killed 17 white people, provoking lynchings. In the summer of 1919 there were race riots in Chicago. The reconstituted Klan turned on socialists, Catholics and Jews. President Wilson condemned the lynchings, but to little effect – in the 10 years after his comments

Key term

lynching: extra-judicial killing by a mob. In the popular image, this usually meant the hanging of a young black man from a tree, although not all lynchings were hangings. The vast majority of victims were black; many who were not were Hispanic. More than 100 lynchings occurred every year in the South throughout the 1890s.

in 1918 there were 454 lynchings in the United States. Of the victims, 426 were black. Wilson was not entirely innocent in this. One of the reasons why *The Birth of a Nation* had taken the country by storm was that he had selected it as the first movie ever to be shown at the White House. In any consideration of the Progressive Era, the growing segregation and violence directed against black people should not be forgotten.

Foreign affairs

In 1889 the great industrialist and philanthropist Andrew Carnegie wrote an article entitled 'Wealth' in which he outlined his belief that philanthropy was the duty of the very rich. His humanitarian interests extended to international relations, too, and he was instrumental in setting up the library of the Permanent Court of Arbitration in 1913. American money bought an international institution that was intended to bring about peace.

America was very active in foreign affairs during this period. Its presidents found themselves with an empire – reluctantly at first. American power was used by one American president to broker peace on another continent, and by another to attempt the same, but ultimately to put an end to a war; in both cases there was a tension in American motives between a desire to do 'the right thing', a desire to act as a dominant world power and a need to protect American strategic interests. The American army and navy began their journey to their ultimate rank as the best in the world, even though America itself suffered very, very few incursions into its own territory and faced absolutely no threats to its own existence.

Voices from the past

Booker T. Washington's speech in Atlanta, 1895

'A ship lost at sea for many days suddenly sighted a friendly vessel. From the mast of the unfortunate vessel was seen a signal, "Water, water; we die of thirst!" The answer from the friendly vessel at once came back, "Cast down your bucket where you are." … To those of the white race who look to the incoming of those of foreign birth and strange tongue and habits for the prosperity of the South, were I permitted I would repeat what I say to my own race, "**Cast down your bucket where you are**." …

'Cast it down among the eight millions of Negroes whose habits you know … Cast down your bucket among these people who have, without strikes and labor wars, tilled your fields, cleared your forests, builded your railroads and cities, and brought forth treasures from the bowels of the earth …

'Casting down your bucket among my people, helping and encouraging them as you are doing on these grounds, and to education of head, hand, and heart, you will find that they will buy your surplus land, make blossom the waste places in your fields, and run your factories … you can be sure in the future, as in the past, that you and your families will be surrounded by the most patient, faithful, law-abiding, and unresentful people that the world has seen … in our humble way, we shall stand by you with a devotion that no foreigner can approach … interlacing our industrial, commercial, civil, and religious life with yours in a way that shall make the interests of both races one. **In all things that are purely social, we can be as separate as the fingers, yet one as the hand in all things essential to mutual progress**.'

Source: http://historymatters.gmu.edu/d/39/

ACTIVITY 2.12

Read the Voices from the past box containing extracts from the speech made by Booker T. Washington.

What was Washington's message in this speech? The most famous metaphors he used are highlighted in bold.

ACTIVITY 2.13

Do you think that it is fair to criticise progressive era politicians for allowing the social injustice of the treatment of African Americans to continue?

Yet, the experiences of gaining an empire, and engagement in international affairs, came at a cost. America's foreign adventures laid the country open to domestic disputes and showed that its new immigrant populations, notably German and Japanese Americans, were not as thoroughly integrated into American life as they might have been. Wilson took America into a war after being re-elected largely because he had resisted the pressure to join in; America and its allies won that war, and America benefited from it, but the effort destroyed Wilson's presidency and his health, and quenched America's thirst for involvement in world affairs for 20 years afterwards.

 Thematic link: world affairs

Imperialism

Imperialism was a familiar enough term to anyone who knew about the politics of the 19th century: the European powers had gone to great lengths to acquire empires across the continents. America itself had begun as an unhappy part of the British Empire. European imperial nations had sought prestige, raw materials, and (preferential) access to new markets through their adventures. They had also often sought to convert native populations to Christianity. The British boasted of bringing Christianity, civilisation and cricket to their territories.

Not all Americans wanted imperialism. Figure 2.8 shows those who did. The Anti-Imperialist League brought together some unlikely bedfellows when it was founded in 1898 – Carnegie, Samuel Gompers and Mark Twain. President McKinley was himself reluctant – any empire would have to be administered by the federal government, implying a growth in federal power. His successor Theodore Roosevelt was of course less reticent about that. The major reason for Americans to support imperialism was that it offered a route for continued expansion. This does suggest that the American drive to expand was in some way analogous to America's expansion in the West in earlier years. Or was this driven by American industrial capitalism – a search for markets? Or by a cultural, nation-building project, perhaps to provide a 'safety valve' given the so-called 'closing' of the frontier at home? Or did different people have different ideas about what they were doing and why?

 Key term

imperialism: the drive for a nation to acquire an empire – a collection of separate territories that are not part of the homeland, but are administered by it and for its benefit.

1. Populists:

Wanted cheap transport and an effective merchant marine and navy to aid exports.
Wanted to reduce tariffs and support an increase in foreign trade.
The silver issue had a foreign policy dimension – a silver standard would ease sales to nations on a silver standard in Asia and Latin America.

2. Imperialists:

Imperialists on the British model, such as Roosevelt, exemplified a new breed of upper-class patricians, mainly educated at Harvard.
Saw America as successor to British Empire.
Josiah Strong, Protestant minister, founder of the Social Gospel movement, published *Our Country: Its Possible Future and its Present Crisis,* 1885.

3. 'New Empire' advocates:

Included Roosevelt when he became president, and Taft and Wilson.
Did not want US to have European-style colonies nor to be militaristic.
America could compete with other Great Powers in trade and commerce so long as there was a 'fair field and no favor' (John Hay, Secretary of State).
Hay advanced the 'Open Door' with China, demanding equal trading rights in even the British, Japanese, Russian and French spheres of influence.
Also involved impressing American models of democracy on the rest of the world.
Harvard Business School and Wharton founded around this time, which showed confidence in US business acumen.

Figure 2.8: Who favoured imperial expansion?

Engagement in international affairs

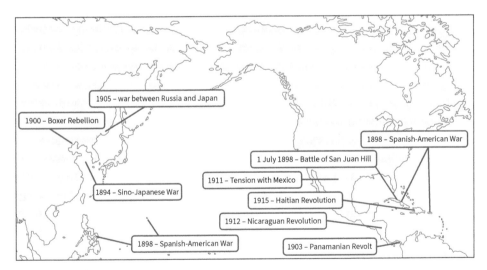

Figure 2.9: American engagement in international affairs, 1890–1915.

International affairs in the 1880s meant the scramble for Africa. This refers to the process by which the European great powers – and some minor powers – focused on carving up as much of Africa as they could. Africa brought with it new markets, natives to civilise and Christianise and, most importantly of all, precious metals and gems. The United States was in no position to involve itself in the scramble for Africa for a number of reasons, as detailed above, but by the 1890s the USA had the naval power, the political will and the economic imperative to seek colonies overseas. In the 1890s that meant Asia, where there were essentially two issues: would Spain be able to keep its possessions in the South Pacific, and which of the powers of East Asia – China, Russia or Japan – would prevail in their three-way struggle for supremacy? For the Americans, the Monroe Doctrine also meant keeping a close eye on the Caribbean. Figure 2.9 summarises American engagement in international affairs in this period.

East Asia

Japan had been a society closed to westerners until Americans had visited in 1852. Since then, there had been some Japanese immigration into California and some trade links had begun. China in the 1890s was a free-for-all for European powers, and Americans, keen to trade with the ancient empire. It was a prolific source of immigration into the United States. The Chinese defeat in their 1894 war with Japan over control of Korea had weakened the ruling Qing dynasty, and western powers were alarmed when the so-called Boxers – Chinese rebels – rebelled in 1898, leading to an all-out civil war by 1900. The United States contributed to the eight-nation alliance sent to help the Qings. The most significant part of this action is that President McKinley sent 5000 troops to fight without consulting Congress, and without a declaration of war, relying merely on his own powers as commander-in-chief and setting out the modern presidential doctrine of 'war powers'.

Roosevelt would go one better in his dealings with the Far East. Russia and Japan came into conflict over control of Port Arthur at the top of the Yellow Sea. Roosevelt intervened in this conflict in 1905, emerging with the Nobel Peace Prize. His personal interest was certainly satisfied by this; he had also fulfilled an American commercial interest by preventing Russia or Japan from taking control of Chinese trade, and had enhanced America's international prestige as an honest broker. The Japanese government blamed Roosevelt for robbing them of their coming victory – the Russians, beset by revolutionary worries of their own, were in no position to fight so far from their capital out in the west. In the meantime the 'yellow peril' in San Francisco – fear that Japanese Americans would not be loyal – had led to southern-style segregation there. Roosevelt managed to persuade the city of San Francisco to abandon segregation only by asking the Japanese government to refuse a passport to anyone seeking to emigrate to the USA. Roosevelt, meanwhile, privately feared that the Japanese Government's increased militarism might lead to later disputes over supremacy in the Pacific. More than 30 years later, he was proved right.

Spain and the Philippines

This is the story of the United States' accidental empire, but it is also the story of some very deliberate action. In 1897 there was a rebellion in Cuba against Spanish rule. The Cubans' major trading partner and investor was the USA rather than their imperial overlords in Europe; after all, Cuba is only 90 miles from the Florida coast. This was big news! And it was even bigger news when William Randolph Hearst, the proprietor of the *New York Morning Journal*, and Joseph Pulitzer, of the *New York World*, sent journalists there to cover events. These journalists were encouraged to hype up the events as much as they could – after all, there were newspapers to be sold. US commercial interests became alarmed, and there was substantial pressure on McKinley to do something. He sent the battleship USS *Maine* to Cuba in January 1898; by February 1898 it had sunk following an on-board explosion. The reasons for the explosion were, and remain, a mystery: the Americans claimed it was an external attack that had caused the explosion, and the Spanish claimed that it must have been an internal fault. The clamour for war in the USA became too much for McKinley to avoid – Assistant Secretary of the Navy Roosevelt even wanted to fight in it. The Spanish ambassador in Washington had criticised McKinley in a letter that was leaked to the press, and it seemed that war would be needed to avenge the dead of the *Maine* and to satisfy the president's honour. The war, in the summer of 1898, was swift and decisive. It also happened in two theatres, the Americans relieving Spain of its possessions in the Philippines, Guam and Puerto Rico, and finally formally annexing Hawaii, whose Pearl Harbor appeared to be an excellent location for a forward base for the Pacific fleet.

The question now was what to do with these new possessions. Cuba could not be absorbed into the United States following a Congressional decision (known as the Teller Amendment). Cuba, therefore, was helped towards independence – American business interests took tremendous care to ensure they were well represented there. In the Pacific the Philippines were something of an embarrassment. The Filipinos had assumed that the Americans were coming as liberators, intending to give them independence from the hated Spanish. They had not imagined that they were exchanging one overlord for another. Ultimately, the Americans appear to have thought that they needed to maintain a base in the Pacific to keep an eye on other nations such as Germany, which might wish to pick off Spain's colonies there. In the best imperial tradition, McKinley announced that the Filipinos were to be converted to Christianity. This came as something of a shock to them, since they were mostly practising Catholics anyway and had been for generations. The Philippine–American War that followed lasted from 1899 to 1902 and cost far more lives than the Spanish–American War before it; at its conclusion President Roosevelt sent his ally Taft to administer the new province. The Philippines were eventually promised that they would gain independence in 1944, and actually gained it in 1945 after the Second World War.

The American imperial experiment seemed more trouble than it was worth. Most Americans saw the action taken in Cuba to secure a trading zone as reasonably positive, and Puerto Rico is well placed to control access to the eastern Caribbean Sea. The Philippines and Guam gave America a welcome presence in the Pacific, but there seemed to be no need for any more.

The Panama Canal

There did seem to be a need, though, to complete a long-held plan by driving a canal through the narrow isthmus of Central America, creating a route between the Atlantic and Pacific. This would help American ships to trade in both oceans without moving all their cargo onto the transcontinental railroads; it would also allow the increasingly large American navy to move between its two potential theatres of war.

The French had tried to build a canal in the 1880s but failed as they were unable to control the outbreak of yellow fever among the canal builders in the jungle. Roosevelt was not deterred by this. Nor did he baulk at paying the French $40 million for building rights. It was more of a problem that the Colombian government, which at that point controlled Panama, was not willing to allow Roosevelt to buy the land required at a reasonable price. Roosevelt's solution in 1903 was simple enough: he encouraged the Panamanian people to revolt against Colombia, and bought the land from the new Panamanian regime that he had helped to establish. Roosevelt also paid a vast amount of money towards clearing the jungles in which yellow fever thrived, and the canal, begun in 1904, was completed in 1914. As the palindrome had it – a man, a plan, a canal: Panama.

Meanwhile Roosevelt added to the Monroe Doctrine. The Roosevelt Corollary to the Monroe Doctrine reserved the right for the United States to become an international police power in the western hemisphere if necessary. Along with his other actions the message was clear: the United States was opening up the Caribbean Sea to trade, and would not be stopped in doing so. In 1912 Taft sent marines into Nicaragua to stop a revolution that threatened America; in 1915 Wilson did the same in Haiti. Both of these presidents also had problems with Mexico, whose revolution in 1911 had led to incursions into the state of New Mexico in 1915. In 1916 Wilson had sent General Pershing into Veracruz on a punitive raid. The problem with Mexico was that Wilson was genuinely worried that the Mexicans might be tempted to invade in numbers – a fear that, perhaps, had momentous consequences.

The First World War – neutrality and entry

The First World War was both inevitable and a complete surprise. It was inevitable because to any neutral observer it was clear that irreconcilable tensions were building up in Europe. It was a surprise because the means by which it started following the assassination of the heir to the Austrian throne were unexpected. The most astute American student of foreign relations at the time was Roosevelt; he had not trusted the Kaiser (the leader of Germany) and had gently signalled to the British that, if necessary, the USA would observe benevolent neutrality towards them, meaning that they would continue to trade. In the event, there was little choice. The USA was, apart from Germany, the only nation producing industrial quantities of the dyes and drugs that Britain wanted. Meanwhile, the British had borrowed money on Wall Street to pay for American goods, and had blockaded German shipping, preventing neutral powers such as the USA from trading with Germany. What else was Wilson to do? It did not help that there was virulently anti-German propaganda doing the rounds in the USA (the general flavour of which was that the Germans were butchering babies), and it certainly did not help that Theodore Roosevelt's voice was raised against the Germans – and when he spoke, America still listened.

In 1915 the passenger liner RMS *Lusitania*, full of American passengers en route to Liverpool, was torpedoed by a German U-boat. True, it was carrying ammunition at the time – but the Americans had warned the Germans where it was. The American press was now even more violently anti-German. Wilson extracted a promise from the Germans that they would not use submarine warfare against

American targets, and kept on searching for peace. After all, while Americans could not trade with Germans, the war was bad for business. In 1916 Wilson was re-elected as 'He kept us out of war'.

To his dismay, the Germans resumed submarine warfare in January 1917, perhaps in desperation about the state of the war. The British then intercepted and published a copy of the so-called 'Zimmerman telegram' – a telegram from the German foreign minister to Mexico, inviting the Mexicans to invade the southern United States. Mexico, which enjoyed its continued independence from its mighty neighbour, had no intention of doing so, but the public pressure on Wilson was now such that he could hardly avoiding asking Congress for a declaration of war. In his speech to Congress he promised to bring democracy to the defeated nations. Over the next year the combined American army and navy went from a head count of 370 000 to nearly five million. The industrial potential of the United States was unleashed; by late 1917 the Atlantic had been cleared of U-boats, and by the end of 1918 the Germans had been forced to a negotiated ceasefire. The guns had fallen silent in Europe. Alone among the great powers, America was unscathed.

Wilson and the war

Wilson's background is important in understanding what he did during the war, and what he would then do during his efforts to win the peace (Figure 2.10). He was a southerner, a Calvinist, an academic and progressive. He alternated between humbling himself before God and being self-righteous because God had chosen him. His most famous book was *Congressional Government,* in which he advocated a parliamentary system with a strong central executive. He believed it was important to regulate society, and promulgate rules of behaviour. All this inclined him first to stay out of the war and then, once in, to run the show and try to use this God-given opportunity to create a new world.

Wilson came to believe (ironically like Lenin in Russia, whose solution was rather different) that imperialism was the fundamental cause of the war. He wanted to create a world of democracies based on free trade with a new League of Nations to help to keep things in order. He talked about a 'new world order', 'starting over again' and a 'war to end all wars'. There are three ways to understand this. It was a global version of the American 'open door' policy. It was an imposition of New Freedom – by this time, essentially Progressivism – on the whole world. Finally, in the League of Nations (see the section on Political reaction and renewed isolationism), he offered a view of global governance and regulation that was different from that of Lenin, who wanted to create world socialism starting in Russia. In these senses, Wilson's foreign policy in 1917–18 was the culmination of American foreign policy since 1890.

The USA by 1920

The America of 1920 was very different from that of 1890 and 1865. It looked different, filling a map with 48 fully formed states (the 'lower 48') rather than a group of states and territories. Its environment was less wild and more regulated and some of its forests were now conservation zones rather than natural woodland. It was united, viewing its period of division as a disastrous and yet heroic experiment. Some things, though, had not changed. It had two political

Figure 2.10: Woodrow Wilson, president 1913–21.

ACTIVITY 2.14

Create a timeline to illustrate American foreign policy from 1890 to 1920.

Can you see a progression in American diplomatic attitudes and thought?

With what did American presidents and diplomats mostly concern themselves at this time?

parties that won every election, with the Republicans dominating in the North and the Democrats in the South. It had a powerful president who viewed his time in office as an opportunity to rebuild, heal divisions and prevent future wars.

Economic power

The inflation that had arisen in the American economy during the war continued from 1918 to 1920, when American trade with Europe stopped. Instead, American banks began to call in the loans they had made during wartime. The American economy in 1920 was a powerful beast. The war had brought nearly full employment and streamlined industries. Europe needed rebuilding, providing American companies with the chance to do the work and knocking out a potential competitor for American market dominance worldwide. American labour relations were no longer utterly in favour of big business, but nor were they particularly burdensome. Capitalism was king, and it seemed that all Americans had to do was to carry on as they were, protected by the progressives' regulatory reforms from any further panics and crashes. The urban population of America was flexible, and there was room for further immigration: the future was bright.

Social and ethnic divisions

A play that opened in New York City in 1909 had been the first to refer to that city as a 'melting pot'. This meant that people of different races met in New York City and mixed together freely. Very little could have been further from the truth. Lower Manhattan was (and is) a patchwork quilt of ethnicities – Chinese here, Italians there and so forth. There was always the potential for conflict between nationalities in the great cities. In 1911 a report on immigration – the Dillingham Report – had stated explicitly that new non-white and Catholic immigrants were not suited to White Anglo-Saxon Protestant life in the North. Nativism like this was also promoted in Madison Grant's 1916 book *The Passing of the Great Race*. Inspired by *The Birth of a Nation* (1915) and by the beginnings of black southern migration to northern cities, race riots had begun in the North.

In the South, the ethnic divisions were even clearer. There, segregation was commonplace and legally protected, lynching went unpunished and the black community was itself divided over what to do about it. Those whose families had been slaves in the 1860s were free in 1920, but their freedom was circumscribed by violence, racism and an almost complete lack of civil rights.

Meanwhile another dominant social and ethnic theme of 20th-century American history was beginning to rear its head. At the end of the First World War, there was a false economic dawn in the USA. The mini-boom of 1919 was followed by an economic contraction and increased unemployment. Looking for someone to blame, Americans blamed not the system, nor the end of the war, but **communism**. The message of the Russian Revolution of 1917 appeared to be that a small group of extreme socialists could take over an entire country if allowed anywhere near the levers of power. Anarchists in America mailed bombs to capitalist leaders such as Rockefeller and they were blamed for every labour dispute (there had been 3500 in 1919). On 2 June 1919 they coordinated bomb attacks in eight cities. In January 1920 the General Intelligence Division of the Justice Department arrested more than 3000 people, mostly US citizens but some recent immigrants too – Ukranians, Jews, Russians and Poles, and held them for weeks in unpleasant conditions. Around 500 were ultimately deported to Russia. The leader of the General Intelligence Division was a young officer called J. Edgar Hoover; in 1920 the American Civil Liberties Union was founded to defend citizens against the countless violations of liberty that Hoover, and others, would commit.

This was the **Red Scare** – a concern that Reds (communists, whose flags and symbols were red for the blood shed during a revolution) might take over the country, and moreover that they were all around – 'the Red under the bed'. The immediate fear that there would be a revolution in 1919, with the president first absent and then ill, subsided.

Political reaction and renewed isolationism

Woodrow Wilson's plan for the peace after the First World War was idealistic and democratic. It was founded upon an imperial view of presidential power within America, and an imperial view of American power within the world. He made such a mess of his attempts to win victory and secure peace that his country retreated into an isolationism from which it would not be coaxed until its Pacific rival Japan forced its hand. Table 2.3 details his initial failures.

In Washington, Wilson worked so hard to secure the peace settlement that he ultimately lost control of his own government. He poured all his efforts into persuading the Senate to confirm his acceptance of the Treaty of Versailles. Unable to do so, he took to a speaking tour around the country to attempt to appeal directly to the people so that they might put pressure on Republican senators. For Republicans, the sticking point was Article 10 of the League of Nations Covenant, which would have to be accepted if the treaty were to be accepted. It allowed the League of Nations to declare war without reference to its member states, and

Key term

communism: also known as revolutionary socialism, is a political system based on the writings of Karl Marx, a 19th-century German economist and philosopher. Communists seek to have a society of equals, with no class structure and ultimately no leadership. They seek to overturn capitalism through a violent revolution, and to expand their socialist system throughout the world.

	Nature of failure	Reasons for failure
First failure	Failed to secure political consensus in 1918 – lost midterms heavily.	Wilson was concentrating on the war as a party political issue, which the electorate resented.
Second failure	Failed to secure the peace he wanted in Paris, as his Fourteen Points were not accepted.	The British resented the Fourteen Points as they weakened European countries and were clearly to America's advantage. The French resented the Fourteen Points as they were not harsh enough to Germany.
Third failure	Failed to persuade the Senate to accept the Treaty of Versailles.	Wilson did not take any Republicans to Paris; Republicans had had no input into the treaty, and they controlled the Senate, which it would have to pass. Wilson also failed to take account of the opposition of Irish Democrats who supported Germany as they opposed Britain, and German Americans in the Midwest.

Table 2.3: Wilson's failures in 1918–20.

would, if accepted, override the US Constitution's reservation to Congress of the right to declare war.

The League of Nations was the pinnacle of Wilson's creation, for which he won the 1919 Nobel Peace Prize. The concept was simple: nations would belong to an organisation that would mediate between them and prevent future wars in that way and through the threat of economic sanctions. Wilson had created a global peacekeeper to impose morality upon international affairs: Wilsonian democracy. Unfortunately for him, his own Congress was unprepared to give away its sovereign right to declare war.

Wilson had been unwell in the second half of the peace conference, and returned to the USA weakened. In September 1919 he suffered the first of a series of strokes. This left him incapacitated and unable to negotiate with the Republicans in the Senate, who had come close to agreeing a series of amendments that would have allowed the treaty to pass. Wilson, though, proved himself unwilling to compromise. The treaty was all or nothing – and he got nothing.

In America, meanwhile, there was horror at what Europe had done to itself. Men like Herbert Hoover, the food commissioner who had overseen the distribution of aid to Poland and then helped to reconstruct Belgium, found that the old world had failed to look after itself. Moreover, old world politicians were insufficiently grateful for the assistance of the USA in the form of loans and aid, and its offer to get them out of a mess of their own making. With their two great oceans and their mighty fleets to protect them, it seemed best to this next generation of American politicians that they should stay out of European affairs. Their president had bequeathed Europeans the League of Nations, and if the USA was not to be in it then this would be to the good of the USA. Meanwhile Wilson's presidency faded along with his health. His country was now beset by strikes and race riots, the effect of four million returning soldiers and the many immigrant refugees from Europe who would need jobs, and also had to deal with the deadly influenza that those soldiers had brought back with them – the final blow dealt by the war.

Look at the extracts from Woodrow Wilson's Fourteen Points. Draw a table like the one below, and use it to sort the Fourteen Points, explaining the reasons behind your selections. You might wish to place points in more than one column.

Points that seek America's advantage	Points that seek to promote international diplomacy	Points that are progressive (or part of New Freedom)

How realistic was it that Wilson's Fourteen Points would be adopted?

The year 1920 was the final sickly year of the presidency of Woodrow Wilson, who was not in full control. Access to him was managed by his aides and his wife, Edith, the first very powerful First Lady. This was hardly constitutional, but what was the alternative? By the end Wilson, a vigorous proponent of strong presidential government that sought to lead Congress rather than be led by it, was quite unable to lead Congress at all. His major preoccupation was with winning the peace rather than with winning the war; he realised that victory in war was meaningless if the peace was not satisfactory and lasting, and he had explicitly said back in 1917 that he wanted to avoid the advent of another war within a generation. The only Democratic president of his generation – the generation who had been children during the Civil War – left the Democratic Party out of popularity and out of power. It also left a challenge to the presidency. Theodore Roosevelt and Woodrow Wilson had been energetic presidents imposing progressive policies and intervening in foreign affairs. Their energy had been a reaction to the perceived weakness of the presidents who had gone before them. Even McKinley, who had helped to launch America's imperial ambitions, had been reluctant to do so. By 1920 America had found itself no longer the isolated power of 1890, but the victor of an international war – and threatened by its own president with having to guarantee the peace. Progressivism had, perhaps, run its course with its two great victories of women's suffrage and the prohibition of alcohol, which came at the end of this period. America's economy was booming. Perhaps it was time to take stock and return to conditions whereby America's economy could continue

 Voices from the past

Woodrow Wilson's Fourteen Points (extracts)

1. Open covenants of peace, openly arrived at, after which there shall be no private international understandings of any kind … Diplomacy shall proceed always frankly and in the public view.

2. Absolute freedom of navigation upon the seas, outside territorial waters, alike in peace and in war.

3. The removal of all economic barriers and the establishment of equality of trade conditions.

4. Adequate guarantees given and taken that national armaments will be reduced to the lowest point consistent with domestic safety.

5. Free, open-minded, and absolutely impartial adjustment of all colonial claims of sovereignty: the interests of the populations concerned must have equal weight with the claims of the government whose title is to be determined.

6. The evacuation of all Russian territory (occupied by foreign troops) and such a settlement of all questions affecting Russia as will secure the best and free-est cooperation of the other nations of the world …The treatment accorded Russia by her sister nations in the months to come will be the acid test of their good will, of their comprehension of her needs as distinguished from their own interests, and of their intelligent and unselfish sympathy…

12. The Turkish portion of the present Ottoman Empire should be assured a secure sovereignty, but the other nationalities which are now under Turkish rule should be assured an undoubted security of life and an absolutely unmolested opportunity of autonomous development.

14. A general association of nations must be formed under specific covenants for the purpose of affording mutual guarantees of political independence and territorial integrity to great and small states alike.

to grow unencumbered by progressive policies and international adventures. In the election of 1920, the Democratic ticket of James Cox, the governor of Ohio, and Franklin D. Roosevelt, the Assistant Secretary of the Navy and a rising star, was soundly defeated by Senator Warren Harding, also of Ohio. He was nominated after a disputed Republican nominating process as a compromise candidate, thought to be a safely isolationist and conservative pair of hands. He won the presidency easily.

Practice essay questions

1. How far do you agree that the greatest racial tension in America 1890–1920 was that in the South?
2. In what ways was the presidency of Theodore Roosevelt different from the presidencies of his immediate predecessors?
3. 'The most important cause of the USA's economic success from 1890 to 1920 was its liberal immigration policy.' Do you agree?
4. Assess the validity of the statement that America's foreign policy was unplanned and incoherent from 1865 to 1920.
5. 'Americans from 1890 to 1920 were more united than divided.' Explain why you agree or disagree with this view.
6. Using your understanding of the historical context, assess how convincing the arguments in the following three extracts are in relation to the ideas and influence of Populism.

Extract A

'Most populists sought economic and political reform, not the overthrow of existing systems. Culturally, too, the Populists, even those of an iconoclastic bent, tended to share common assumptions with many other Americans. The ethos of modernity and progress swept across the cultural landscape of late nineteenth-century America, driven by the winds of commercial capitalism. The Populists mainly shared this ethos. They mobilized to put their own stamp on commercial development. In doing so, the farmers and other reformers of the Populist movement were as committed to the notion of progress as any social group in post-Civil War America. A firm belief in progress gave them confidence to act. Because they believed in the transforming power of science and technology, they sought to attain expertise and knowledge for their own improvement. Because they believed in economies of scale, they strove to adapt the model of large-scale enterprise to their own needs of association and marketing. Because they believed in the logic of modernity, the Populists 'clodhoppers' attempted to fashion an alternative modernity suitable to their own interests.'

Source: From Charles Postel, *The Populist Vision*. [10]

Extract B

'The Progressive era was more than a response to the growth of industrialization and urbanization within the United States; it was also part of American attempts to strengthen the nation's social fabric in an international context. The United States lagged in many areas of social and economic reforms, such as in providing insurance against industrial injuries, even though the nation had an extremely high rate of accidents. Within the United States, progressivism reinforced the power of the Federal government in relation to the states. Social and moral reformers favoured national government intervention in the lives of the people to an unprecedented degree, and the American state structure would be morally intrusive as well as militarily competent. First introduced at the state level, laws against abortion, contraceptive devices and alcohol prohibition reinforced a strict middle-class, Protestant morality. But as in economic regulation, interstate influences corroded state efforts to protect communities and demonstrated the need for legislation at the federal level.'

Source: Adapted from Ian Tyrrell. *Transnational Nation: the United States in Global Perspective.* [11]

Extract C

'In the attempts of the Populists and Progressives to hold on to some of the values of agrarian life, to save personal entrepreneurship and individual opportunity and the character type they engendered, and to maintain a homogeneous* Yankee civilization, I have found much that was retrograde and delusive, a little that was vicious, and a good deal that was comic. To say this is not to say that these values were in themselves nonsensical or bad. The ideal of a life lived close to nature and the soil, the esteem for the primary contacts of country and village life, the cherished image of the independent and self-reliant man, even the desire (for all the snobberies and hatreds it inspired) to maintain an ethnically more homogeneous nation -- these were not negligible or contemptible ideals, and to those who felt most deeply about them their decline was a tragic experience that must be attended to with respect even by those who can share it only through some effort of the imagination.'

*homogeneous: all of the same kind, of one culture.

Source: Richard Hofstadter, *Age of Reform: Bryan to FDR.* [12]

 Taking it further

How far do you agree that the only really clear senses of American identity from 1890 to 1920 were negatively defined?

Chapter summary

After studying this period, you should understand:

- the ways in which populist and progressive policies and ideologies were adopted in America, even though populist politicians and the People's Party were themselves defeated
- the way in which presidential power and prestige grew
- the ideas of what it was to be American expressed by different individuals and groups within American society during this time – White Anglo-Saxon Protestants, Catholics, and African Americans had contrasting experiences
- the reasons why the USA came to be an industrial and commercial giant in this period, consolidating and developing its position as the most powerful economy in the world
- the changing American attitudes to foreign policy and international affairs
- the tensions within and between the different sections of the USA.

End notes

1 Livingston J. *Origins of the Federal Reserve System: Money, Class and Corporate Capitalism, 1890–1913.* New York: Cornell University Press; 1986.

2 Beckert S. *The Monied Metropolis: New York City and the Consolidation of the American Bourgeoisie, 1850–1896.* New York: Cambridge University Press, 2001.

3 Chandler AD. *The Visible Hand: The Managerial Revolution in American Business.* Cambridge: Harvard University Press; 1977.

4 Johnston RP. *The Radical Middle Class: Populist Democracy and the Question of Capitalism in Progressive Era Portland, Oregon.* New Jersey: Princeton University Press; 2003.

5 Archer R. *Why is There No Labor Party in the United States?* New Jersey: Princeton University Press; 2007.

6 Tyrrell I. *Transnational Nation: the United States in Global Perspective Since 1789.* Basingstoke: Palgrave Macmillan; 2007.

7 Ignatiev N. *How the Irish Became White.* New York: *Routledge; 2008.*

8 Reynolds D. *America – Empire of Liberty: a New History.* London: Allen Lane; 2009.

9 http://historymatters.gmu.edu/d/39/ [accessed 17 July 2015]

10 Postel C. *The Populist Vision.* New York: Oxford University Press; 2007.

11 Adapted from Tyrrell I. *Transnational Nation: the United States in Global Perspective Since 1789.* Basingstoke: Palgrave Macmillan; 2007.

12 Hofstadter R. *The Age of Reform: From Bryan to FDR.* New York: Knopf; 1955.

Part 2: Crises and the Rise to World Power, 1920–1975

Introduction

In 1920 the United States had assumed a position of tremendous global importance. As the only undamaged victor of the First World War, America had the greatest military power in the world, as well as the best economy. The next 25 years would be the story of the collapse of that economy, the rebuilding of American society in order to fix it, and the way in which America capitalised on the global cataclysm of the Second World War to become not just a power, but a Superpower. The 30 years after that would show how well America was able to capitalise on its new position, while assuming the responsibilities of world leadership that came with it. When President Kennedy was moved by the appearance of the Berlin Wall to claim that 'All free men … are citizens of Berlin', he might more accurately have said that, 'Culturally, geopolitically, and economically, all free men are becoming American'.

The role of the federal government and the powers of the president expanded, driven first by the need to repair the economy and then by the need to win the Cold War. Roosevelt's New Deal may or may not have worked in its long-term aim of improving the American economy (indeed, it may or may not have had a long-term aim) but it stabilised the economy for long enough to avert the complete disaster that seemed to be on the cards in the early 1930s. The next time the American economy appeared to be in serious trouble, in the 1970s, the effects on the American people were far less serious. Americans had on the whole become rich, and although there were still poor people, to be poor in America in 1975 was still to be comparatively rich.

In the 1920s, communism was identified as an existential threat, at least in the perception of those Americans for whom to be communist was to be by definition 'un-American'. This was stepped up to a new level during the Cold War; the anti-communist movement in the 1940s and 1950s has been likened to the witch-hunts of the late 17th century. As ever, the idea of being American (something to do with motherhood and apple pie, if many American movies are to be believed) changed according to time, place and circumstance. The idea of being African American, and how that fitted in, also changed. The racism experienced by black Americans would be addressed, if not the economic deprivation many of them suffered. The Civil Rights Movement of the second half of this period resulted in a renewed legal status for black Americans, and helped to create a tradition of left-wing American protest.

If we are not willing to accept that the rise of the USA was a function of its exceptional character or **manifest destiny**, how should we tell the story of how the Americans came to lead the free world? Just because we know what happened does not mean that we know why. I shall repeat the warning I gave at the end of the introduction to the first part of this book: as you consider the key questions about how America changed, which are outlined in the section on Themes in American history in the Introduction to this book, be careful not to assume that any of the changes we can trace (or indeed, any of the continuities) were inevitable.

3 Crisis of identity, 1920–1945

In this section, we will examine the way in which the self-confident, economically booming USA reacted to the economic disaster of the 1930s, and then transformed itself into a reluctant superpower. We will look into:

- Domestic politics: Harding, Coolidge and Republican conservatism; Hoover and the Depression.

- Franklin D. Roosevelt and the New Deals: conflict of ideas over the role of the federal government.

- The economy: boom to bust and recovery; structural weaknesses and the impact of the New Deals and the Second World War on economic recovery.

- Social and cultural developments: 'the Jazz Age' in the 1920s; new social values and the role of women; the failure of prohibition and its significance; the social impact of the Depression and the Second World War on economic recovery.

- Social, regional and ethnic divisions: countryside versus city; divisions between North, West and South; African Americans and the rise of the Ku Klux Klan.

- The USA and international relations: the extent of isolationism; FDR and the end of isolationism and the Second World War.

Americans in 1920 were a confident but exhausted people. There was a temporary economic slump, but the system seemed sound. They had had a series of vigorous – perhaps too vigorous – presidents, but that would soon stop. They had fought in the war to end all wars, and contrary to the warnings issued by President Wilson it was surely certain that no nation would actively seek war again. By 1945, the American presidency had been transformed and the basis of its economic success modified. The cycle of boom and bust had not quite been broken but certainly made less brutal. America was the dominant democratic nation in the world, with powerful agricultural and industrial sectors. Those dramatic changes were wrought on America both from within and from without.

America flowered socially and culturally, too, in this time. The 1920s brought jazz and movies and iconic American authors; the 1930s brought a cultural response to the economic depression, symbolised in a kind of pathetic fallacy by the dustbowl that parts of the West became. Americans experimented with banning alcohol (succeeding mostly in helping to build up organised crime). They continued to prevaricate over what rights to give African Americans in the South – with the result that African Americans living in the North found their lives much better than they would have been in the other section of the country.

The narrative of America 1920–45 has two remarkable features. The first is that it has a clear turning-point – the Wall Street Crash of 1929 (often used as a conceptual shorthand meaning, 'the Crash and the various failures that followed it') and the second is that it's dominated by one political figure. Only one man has been president for more than eight years; that man, Franklin D. Roosevelt, is one of the greatest and most controversial of American politicians.

Domestic politics

The fear of communism, which had begun in the Red Scare (see the section on Social and ethnic divisions in Chapter 2), continued. In 1927, after a seven-year trial, two Italian radicals, Bartolomeo Vanzetti and Nicola Sacco, were executed for murder. The trial, which seemed to have been part of a deeply flawed process, showed off a new American prejudice against immigrants, viewing them as anarchists – people who did not conform to the American mainstream. The Red Scare had claimed famous victims; some people in America and elsewhere believed that Sacco and Vanzetti were electrocuted not because they were murderers but because they were un-American. The historian Stanley Coben has likened the Red Scare to a revitalisation movement – an effort to purify the nation and call it back to its historic mission by ridding it of intruding ideologies and groups, such as Italian socialists.

Thematic link: ideas and ideology

The end of Wilson's presidency looked like the end of the Democratic Party as a party of government. It also looked like the end of the powerful presidencies of Democrats and progressive Republicans (Theodore Roosevelt) alike. See the section on Political reaction and renewed **isolationism** in Chapter 2 for a fuller explanation of the politics of 1920. The Republicans who followed Wilson – Harding, Coolidge and Hoover – would espouse a much lesser view of presidential power and authority. Harding was chosen by his party bosses in Congress because they hoped they might roll back the growth of presidential powers under Wilson. To a certain extent they did, but Harding ensured that Congress was not allowed to restrict his own constitutional powers over foreign policy. Coolidge was another accidental president, elevated to the presidency on his predecessor's death, and wildly popular for his habit of doing very little while saying even less, although what he did say often became a catchphrase. His successor Herbert Hoover had served all three of the other presidents of the 1920s in one way or another and was seen as a highly capable administrator. He was; but he was not equal to the task set before him of piloting America out of the economic collapse that came less than a year into his term. His belief in the restrictions that should be on federal and presidential power was at the heart of his inability to deal with the Depression; perhaps he also, like everyone else, was unable to see at its outset what its true scale would be. Hoover's was the final presidency that restricted itself for ideological reasons.

His successor, Franklin Delano Roosevelt (FDR), has been remembered as one of America's great presidents. Along with Washington, Jefferson and Lincoln he has a memorial along the West Potomac south of the White House; that is exalted company to keep. Elected in 1932 to lead an exhausted country, he was forced to watch for four months as the situation deteriorated before he was able to take office. Lacking the mobility to move around the country, he sent his formidable wife, Eleanor, to represent him. As a president he was innovative, resourceful and above all powerful, vastly expanding the role of the entire federal government and the power of the president at its heart. His New Deal created the conditions in which today's welfare state is possible. Without FDR, there could have been no **Medicare** and **Medicaid** under Lyndon Johnson, and certainly no Patient

Hidden voices

Not every American viewed communism in a negative way

'The Soviet Union, which would later become such an albatross around the necks of American leftists when the almost unfathomable depths of Stalinist cruelty became known, actually strengthened the appeal of left-wing reform in the early 1930s. Soviet communism seemed to be producing a dynamic egalitarian society that offered a viable alternative to the moribund capitalist economic order. Soviet leaders sparked the interest of American intellectuals in 1928 by announcing their first Five-Year Plan, which promised a rational, centralized economy that would create abundance by unleashing science and technology. Socialists and progressives had long favored intelligent planning over a seemingly anarchic system in which individual capitalists had made decisions

based on maximising profits. The concept of planning had inspired works as disparate as Edward Bellamy's 1888 socialist masterpiece *Looking Backward* and Walter Lippmann's 1914 *Drift or Mastery*, the bible of the Progressive movement …

'Many American intellectuals had also begun to see the Soviet Union as a place of intellectual, artistic and scientific vibrancy compared with the United States' stultifying bourgeois culture … Socialized medicine for all, remarkable scientific breakthroughs, dazzling economic growth – Soviet progress, many Americans believed, was vastly eclipsing that of its economically struggling capitalist competitors.'

Source: Stone O, Kuznick P. *The Untold History of the United States.*[1]

Protection and Affordable Care Act under Barack Obama. Roosevelt laid the foundations for an American economy that could and would boom, on and off, for the rest of the century. He also presided over the Second World War, which first stimulated that economy, and (accidentally) laid the groundwork for the **Cold War** that was to come. Roosevelt was the last president for nearly 60 years to have only domestic policy to concentrate on as his primary focus; his successors would all be war presidents too.

In 1921 the presidency of a Democratic president, a domestic reformer who had built on the achievements of his predecessors and taken a reluctant United States to victory in a global conflict, sacrificing his health in the process, came to an end. His immediate successors were internationally cautious and constitutionally timid in their dealing with Congress. In 1945 the next Democratic president died, broken by his efforts. He had reformed the roles of the federal government and of the presidency itself. His successors continued that reform; for the next 30 years every man elected president expected to preside over a powerful presidency as the leader not just of the USA but, like Wilson and Roosevelt, of the democratic world. Was the second President Roosevelt even greater than the first?

Harding, Coolidge and Republican conservatism

Sometimes the death of a president can enhance his reputation. Sometimes, the reverse applies. Nobody (including the man himself) had ever expected that Warren Harding (Figure 3.1) would be a great president. He was nominated by a Republican Party confident of victory in the presidential election as Wilson's popularity nosedived, taking the Democrats' chances with it. At his death, Harding was popular with the people entirely because he was affable and had done very little – much better than the moralising Wilson who had seemed intent on involving America in yet more international conflict. It was only after his death that the scandals began to emerge.

Harding was not himself implicated in any scandals; the problem was the people he surrounded himself with. Many of them were his cronies from his days back in Ohio. Harding was known to say that it was his friends, not his enemies, who kept him awake at night. The stories of the gambling and drinking that took place at the White House were, in this era of Prohibition, damaging. Rumours of Harding's extra-marital affair – conducted in the nooks and crannies of the White House for fear that Florence Harding might find out – were also unwelcome. But the real damage to Harding's reputation was caused by financial scandal. The head of the Veterans' Bureau Charles R. Forbes stole around $2 million dollars. Secretary of the Interior Albert B. Fall took kickbacks worth around $400 000 in leasing public oil reserves to private development companies in what became known as the Teapot Dome scandal.

These scandals affected Harding's reputation but hardly affected his presidency. He had campaigned on a return to 'normalcy' – a word he coined largely because it began with an 'n' and fitted well into an alliterative speech he was making. His view of presidential powers did seem to owe much to the era of weak presidents – not for him the activism of Roosevelt or Wilson. This is not a complete surprise; he had been picked as a candidate straight from the Senate (the first time a sitting

Figure 3.1: President Warren G. Harding (1921–23), referred to by his own party as 'the best of the second-raters'.

ACTIVITY 3.1

Warren Harding suggested that his presidency would represent a return to 'normalcy'. Write down what he did as president, or encouraged to happen during his time.

1. To what extent did Harding differ in his presidential actions and style from Roosevelt, Taft and Wilson?

2. What was Harding's view of 'normal' presidential government?

Figure 3.2: Calvin Coolidge (president 1923–29), a master of the political slogan.

US senator had become president) entirely in order to be a little more manageable for Congress. He let Congress get on with the job of running the country. Harding's main initiative was blaming strikes and the recession on the Democrats. He also freed the jailed socialist Eugene Debs. Otherwise his presidency consisted of right-wing economic measures that, with the benefit of hindsight, do not seem to have been wise. He pulled back from regulation, deliberately (perhaps) installing weak leadership in the Interstate Commerce Commission, allowing big business more leeway. Congress repealed some taxes and cut others, and in 1922 passed the Fordney-McCumber Act, which raised **tariffs** to a very high level, to the benefit of industry. These tariffs also had the effect of excluding Japanese manufacturers from access to American markets. By 1930 these policies had been partly responsible for an increasingly militaristic and desperate attitude on the part of the Japanese government, and an almighty boom in American industry that would be followed by an even more startling bust.

Harding's successor following his heart attack and death in 1923, Calvin Coolidge, was nicknamed 'Silent Cal' (Figure 3.2). He believed that the federal government should promote private enterprise and then get out of the way – and that was about it. His own simple charm, and the excellent economy, left him able to win a presidential term of his own with ease in the elections of 1924. Coolidge believed, in common with almost every political thinker of his era, that national debt was a bad thing – in fact, that it was *the* bad thing – and wanted to eliminate it. He did this by cutting government spending, and by using a combination of further tax cuts for the wealthy (in 1926) and keeping interest rates low (which, since the Federal Reserve had been set up, was an option available to American politicians) to stimulate business growth and reinvestment. In his time Congress also increased tariffs. During his presidency, the national debt was reduced by a quarter, which seemed a stunning success at the time.

Coolidge chose not to seek the presidency again in 1928, although he was perfectly at liberty to do so and would almost certainly have won the election comfortably. Why not? Perhaps it was because he had fulfilled the limited amount he wished to do, having proved that he could win a presidential term of his own. It was not because he had any great wish to give Herbert Hoover a chance to be president: the two men did not get on. Perhaps he had realised that the good times (which these undoubtedly were) could not last forever, and that the next president might preside over a time not of plenty but of despair.

What happened to progressivism?

There was pressure and even an expectation that the post-war order would see the culmination of many progressive demands, and, in some respects it did – women's suffrage and prohibition. But in most others it didn't. There was pressure for more reform from a few places. *New Republic* magazine approvingly published the British Labour Party's 1918 manifesto 'Labour and the New Social Order'. Progressivism, however, was a complex, heterogeneous and ambiguous force. Now, there were Progressives in Congress rather than in the White House, and they scored some victories:

*   Congress prevented Henry Ford from buying up Muscle Shoals Dam on the Tennessee River for very little money.

- The Treasury Secretary from 1921 to 1932, Andrew Mellon, did not get all the tax cuts he wanted.
- Farm credits were introduced to help western farmers.
- Robert La Follette of Wisconsin and Henrik Shipstead of Minnesota, representing the Farm-Labor Party, were progressive voices in Congress from 1922.
- Al Smith, the governor of New York, was a progressive Democrat.

When La Follette ran for president in 1924, he ran on a platform asserting that, 'the greatest issue before the American people today is the control of government and industry by private monopoly'. He harked back to a vision of 19th-century small-town America, but could not shake accusations of being a Red that were hardly helped by his endorsement by the Socialist Party.

Hoover and the Depression

Herbert Hoover (Figure 3.3) should have been a great president. He was an able administrator with real foreign policy experience. He had helped in the reconstruction of Europe after the First World War. So widely admired was he that his support was sought by both major parties in 1920; Franklin D. Roosevelt had thought that Hoover would one day make a great Democratic president. Hoover, though, was ideologically Republican. As Secretary of Commerce (1921–29) he promoted 'associated individualism', trade conferences to find a better way of doing things, and better statistics to aid government and business. Hoover's reputation was traduced following his presidency, not because he failed to prevent the Great Depression, but because he failed to deal with it. The precise economic effects of the Depression are dealt with in the section on The economy later in this chapter; any analysis of the political response Hoover attempted should bear in mind that historians today still argue about the causes of the collapse of the stock market that initiated the vicious circle of contraction that followed. How could Hoover be expected to have negated those causes? Figure 3.4 sets them out; the critical point is that the magnitude of the Great Depression that followed was increased by the government's responses to the crash.

At one level, what happened in October 1929 is simple to explain. Americans realised that the stock markets that regulated the money invested in big companies – the capital they needed in order to function – did not work. The practice of buying 'on the margin', which means investors buying shares with money that they did not yet have, but would have when, some days later, they sold the shares at a higher price had resulted in the overvaluation of almost every big company or corporation in America. Nobody knew what the real value of any company was any more; what began as a correction in the market ended as a crash. On 24 October, Black Thursday, 13 million shares changed hands as the market began to correct itself. High volumes of trade continued the next day, and on the following Monday, as nervous investors sought to 'cash out' by selling shares as early as possible. Shares were sold in such vast quantities that their prices began to tumble, and on Tuesday 29 October – Black Tuesday – the rush to sell became a stampede. American Steel collapsed first, then General Electric, then the Anaconda Copper Mining Company. By the end of the day the panic had spread across American stock exchanges. A staggering 14 billion dollars had been wiped off the value of American corporations, and the speculators who might have

Figure 3.3: Herbert Hoover, the president at the time of the Great Depression.

111

ACTIVITY 3.2

Historians are often said to possess '20/20 hindsight'. This means that historians tend to see the causes of a great event very clearly, and then to wonder why people at the time could not see it coming.

Look at Figure 3.4 and read through the section on Domestic politics. Identify:

1. Missed opportunities to avoid the Depression.
2. Political actions that might have made the Depression worse.

Now try to identify any area where US political leaders could reasonably have been expected to have avoided the Great Depression, without possessing hindsight.

invested in them had run out of money; the lucky ones had got their money out in time and were unwilling to expose it to the market again; some chose to take their own lives by jumping from the balcony at the Stock Exchange.

So why did nobody realise that the practice of trading on the margin was likely to result in catastrophe? The short answer is: they did. Early in Hoover's term the board of the Federal Reserve attempted to prevent banks from lending money to speculators who wanted to trade on the margin. This plan had been wrecked by the director of the New York Federal Reserve, himself a speculator, who had forced the board to apologise. Even recognising the dangers of trading on the margin, though, nobody had predicted the panic and crash that might ensue. In early October 1929 a leading economist described the stock market as reaching a permanently high plateau – meaning that it might not grow in value, but nor would it decline. Hoover thought that all was well. He had accepted the Republican nomination with the words, 'We in America today are nearer to the final triumph over poverty than ever before in the history of any land.' The prosperity on which that triumph would depend, however, itself depended on Americans being able to buy goods – especially automobiles – in increasing numbers. By 1929, though, most affluent Americans already had a car and only around 30% of Americans had become rich enough in the 1920s to afford one. The market was exhausted.

By the end of 1929 the question for Hoover was: what would he do? He did a lot, working 18-hour days to try to solve the problem. His responses were inadequate, for three main reasons:

- He did not know how bad the problem was. Nobody did: that only became clear over time. He believed that the capitalist system was fundamentally sound

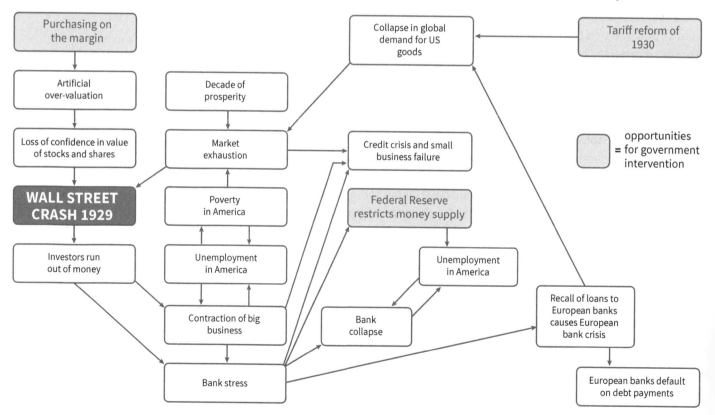

Figure 3.4: The causes of the Wall Street Crash, 1929, and the Great Depression that followed.

and that it would, given time, sort itself out. He repeatedly issued encouraging statements to this effect.

- Neither he nor anyone else in American politics believed that the federal government should involve itself openly with providing relief directly to impoverished people. That should be dealt via **voluntarism** and the role of business or charity, or if necessary of state and local government. There was no contradiction with his role 10 years earlier in reconstructing war-ravaged Europe: that had been an act of American charity.
- He did not believe that he, as president, could overstep his constitutional boundaries to solve the problem.

Key terms

voluntarism: in the American context means the belief that help should be given to the poor through charity, rather than as part of an organised programme of government.

What did his administration do? In 1930, against Hoover's wishes, Congress passed the Smoot-Hawley Tariff Act, which put a very high tariff onto imports and exports. By isolating America from world trade this destabilised other countries' economies and made the Depression worse across the world. Meanwhile, other countries retaliated with tariffs of their own and US imports and exports fell by 60%. Meanwhile Hoover tried to persuade employers to grin and bear it, by avoiding layoffs and pay cuts as far as possible. Set up in 1932, the Reconstruction Finance Corporation spent money on roads, bridges and buildings as a mild federal stimulus of $1.5 billion. He created the Federal Farm Board to help farmers – a progressive measure used to maintain America's ability to feed itself. It did not go far enough, and by 1932 farmers were blockading roads to try to persuade Congress to act further. He also encouraged rugged individualism – the idea of people helping themselves in a time of difficulty. Along with his emphasis on states and localities providing charity, this created mass migrations as people moved in search of jobs.

The defining moment of the last full year of Hoover's presidency, 1932, was the march on Washington by First World War veterans. They were asking to be allowed to access their war pensions, due in 1946, early. Because they were asking for money they became known as the 'Bonus Army'. Hoover ordered General Douglas MacArthur to deal with the situation. He dispersed them with tear gas, machine guns and tanks, and then burned down their shanty town on the outskirts of the city. Hoover's slim chances of re-election went up in smoke with it. He had eschewed the chance to be radical, perhaps because the thought of being more radical than he was had not even occurred to him. Everything he tried had been too little. His successor would not make the same mistake. He would, quite deliberately, do too much. Arguably, it still didn't work.

Hoover has been somewhat rehabilitated by historians in the last couple of decades. The popular myth – that he had fiddled while Rome burned (that is, that he had done nothing) – is clearly untrue. Ultimately, though, whether by underestimating the magnitude of the problem or by overestimating the ability of voluntarism to deal with it, he failed. The methods of the secretary of commerce in the boom times did not work for the president in the bust. Some historians now characterise Hoover as the 'forgotten progressive'. He recognised that government had an obligation to counter depression rather than allow 'natural' course correction as in the past. He inadvertently ran a large budget **deficit** of 4% GDP in 1932; this saved the economy from an even deeper slump. Herbert Stein argues that Hoover's fiscal policy was the prelude to the Keynesian fiscal revolution.

It's arguable that Hoover's one really significant failing was his total lack of publicly expressed empathy with the many victims of the slump. This could be why the response to the Bonus Army march was so important – precisely because it seemed to encapsulate his attitude. Hoover did not understand that part of the role of the presidency was to offer reassurance in times of crisis.

Divide into two groups in the class. One group should argue in favour of this point of view and the other group against it, using evidence gathered from the section on Hoover and the Depression and from your own research.

Hoover then made things worse by seeking to balance the 1933 budget. The Revenue Act of 1932 was the largest tax increase to date in US history, and it sucked spending power out of the economy at a critical time when the Federal Reserve was also restricting the money supply. Spending less had not worked in pulling America out of the Depression. The next president would have to try something different.

Franklin D. Roosevelt and the New Deals

Franklin Delano Roosevelt became president in 1933, and did not relinquish the office until his death. He brought industry, organisation and an understanding of how to get the best from talented subordinates to the problems he faced. As president during an economic crisis, he transformed the power of the American state; as the leader of the anti-Fascist alliance he helped to win the Second World War; as the leader of the Democratic Party he built an electoral coalition that restricted the Republicans' access to the presidency and made the Democrats the natural leaders of Congress for 60 years. He increased the power of the presidency and transformed the economic relationship between the federal government, individuals and the states. His assumption of the leadership of the western, democratic world was more effective than President Wilson's, 20 years earlier – so effective, in fact, that American presidents have never relinquished the role. FDR overcame a bout of polio, which left him unable to stand without crutches and in great pain; on the whole, the public was unaware of his difficulties.

As president he appointed the first female Cabinet minister, Frances Perkins (Figure 3.5) – but he appointed her on merit, not because she was a woman. His own wife, his distant cousin Eleanor (she came from the branch of the family that had spawned the first President Roosevelt) was a formidable female politician in her own right, both because she travelled around the country to promote his agenda and through her 'Eleanor Clubs', which encouraged other women to enter politics. They did not particularly have a love match, but their marriage was a formidable political partnership.

Roosevelt came to the presidency because he had been able to acquire the Democratic nomination: by 1932, Hoover and his Republicans were clearly discredited. Roosevelt was the governor of New York. He was not a pioneer of many New Deal style policies, but one of his policies was key. The very worst effects of the Depression were mitigated in New York State because he funded unemployment relief on a temporary basis, and because he gathered around him an exceptional group of people. He became president having heeded Hoover's call for the states to deal with the unemployed, and having begun to deal with the problems that New York and America as a whole faced and, perhaps most importantly, having watched Hoover fail in his efforts by, Roosevelt concluded, being too cautious.

Historians can without too much difficulty break the programme known as the **New Deal** – Roosevelt's own words, taken from his acceptance speech at the Democratic nominating convention – into three distinct phases, 1933–35, 1935–37 and 1938–40. The First New Deal focused on restoring the wellbeing of industry, agriculture and finance, to restore the confidence of producers and investors,

Figure 3.5: Frances Perkins, Secretary of Labor under Roosevelt.

using budget deficits to finance a federal and state stimulus package (one quarter of the total was paid for by the federal government). This was top-down reform. The Second New Deal focused on bottom-up reform – social security, labour rights and the redistribution of wealth. The Third New Deal made fiscal policy an instrument of economic recovery, building in deficit spending as a structural feature of the economy to stimulate it.

It's doubtful whether Roosevelt himself saw it like that: there are as many continuities as differences, and any assessment of whether this is a sensible division must focus on whether the aims of the New Dealers changed. As for Roosevelt himself – for he led the New Deal but was not its only architect – there are four main views. Was he:

- A pragmatic experimenter but only within limits of his ideology? (See William Leuchtenburg *Franklin D. Roosevelt and the New Deal, 1932–1940.*[2])
- The promoter of modern liberal public policy who lacked a coherent vision of **liberalism**? (See Alan Brinkley *The End of Reform: New Deal Liberalism in Recession and War.*[3])
- The saviour of capitalism? (See Barton Bernstein *The New Deal: The Conservative Achievements of Liberal Reform.*[4])
- The creator of big-government excess that Ronald Reagan would eventually tame in the 1980s? (See Steven Hayward *The Age of Reagan: The Fall of the Old Liberal Order 1964–1980.*[5])

The first hundred days

Franklin D. Roosevelt was not the most innovative economist of his day, nor did he have a particular ideological axe to grind. He had three great qualities. First, he appointed excellent people to positions of power and influence. He had the Brains Trust – Raymond Moley, Rexford Tugwell and Adolf Berle – economists from Columbia University who assembled to advise him. He had excellent and capable administrators from his New York days in Harry Hopkins, who took a variety of roles in the administration, and Frances Perkins, the Secretary of Labor. Second, he had tremendous energy: his philosophy was to try as many things as possible and see what worked. Third, he had the support of the country and knew how to leverage that to win people's trust.

In the period before coming to power – the four-month transition between election and inauguration – the state of the economy had deteriorated. Roosevelt refused to appear with Hoover to lend support, and drew criticism from Republicans; he did not want to be tainted by Hoover's failure to do what he should. Roosevelt survived an assassination attempt by the anti-capitalist Giuseppe Zangara. The mayor of Chicago, Anton Zermak, who had been with Roosevelt, was hit by a bullet; he later died of his wounds, but not before telling FDR, 'I'm glad it was me instead of you.' This only added to the weight of expectation surrounding Roosevelt. What would his New Deal involve?

The answer came on 4 March 1933 in Roosevelt's **inaugural address**. The only thing to fear, he declared, was fear itself. He would place before Congress a plan for 100 days of action, and if that failed he would seek broad executive power to declare war on the emergency. His words resonated with the American people, and so did his actions: he declared an immediate bank holiday (therefore preventing banks from opening and losing their capital in a run: in 38 states this had happened anyway) and ensured the heavily Democratic Congress passed a bank supervision law – the Emergency Banking Act. He cut civil service pay and government pensions to demonstrate his willingness that the government embrace the mood of austerity. He then addressed the nation by radio on 12 March in what would later be termed a 'fireside chat' – the idea being that the kindly president sat you down by the fire (where the radio was central to a living room) to offer reassurance that all would be well. The next day, the banks opened and there was no run. In fact, people began to return their money to the banks, building up investable capital. Roosevelt had clearly asserted his authority. When he asked people to be hopeful not fearful, they listened. There were two more legacies of this period. The first was that the Constitution was amended – for the 20th time – to reduce the time between election and inauguration by six weeks. The second is that, still, American politicians invoke the idea of an active 'first hundred days'.

One hundred days into his presidency, in June 1933, the economy was more stable. Deposits had picked up, and spending was increasing as confidence returned. Roosevelt created a number of government agencies, known by their acronyms as '**alphabet agencies**'. This became an iconic feature of the New Deal, and represented a major growth in power for the federal government. Essentially, any government agency fulfils an executive function that might otherwise be carried out by the states: the creation of a government agency makes the federal government more powerful. As these agencies function as branches of the executive, they also increase the president's power. Roosevelt had such popular support that he was not very vigorously opposed either by the desperate states or by Congress. Roosevelt did not necessarily intend to become more powerful: he wanted to repair the country. He passed the Securities Exchange Act to regulate the practice of buying shares on the margin, and set about repairing the damage that this practice had caused.

As the great administrator Harry Hopkins realised, long-term fixes could come later: 'People don't eat in the long run. They eat every day.' The first hundred days were for emergency measures. Other legislation included:

- The Federal Emergency Relief Act, which set up federally funded unemployment relief on a similar model to that FDR had used in New York.
- The Agricultural Adjustment Act, which provided immediate relief to farmers in danger of foreclosure. The Farm Credit Act, passed on the 100th day, consolidated it.
- A Homeowners Loans Act did something similar for homeowners.
- The National Industrial Recovery Act, which set up the National Recovery Administration (the NRA).

The NRA was run by Hiram Johnson, the progressive former Republican governor of California, and was designed to save the capitalist system by improving industrial relations. It also involved a three billion dollar public works stimulus programme, which Roosevelt quickly spun off into a separate agency, the Public Works Administration (PWA). This left Johnson to negotiate with corporate bosses big and small. He realised quickly and accurately that his actual powers as head of the commission were unconstitutional, so relied instead on persuasion – for example, he was able to persuade Henry Ford to raise wages and lower prices. The NRA and PWA were examples of the 'alphabet agencies' for which the New Deal is famous – see Figure 3.6.

The Public Works Administration created two million jobs building public infrastructure. The Civilian Conservation Corps and the Civic Works Administration (later in the First New Deal) did the same thing. This kind of injection of cash into the economy worked by giving people jobs, which meant that they did not need unemployment relief, and that they regained their self-respect. The message was: it's not your fault. Hoover had preached rugged individualism without realising that the government would have to provide a reward for hard work. So the stimulus programmes drew criticism over pointless jobs – 'boondoggling' – such as leaf-raking. A brief example of the effectiveness of this: when veterans turned up in Washington to see Roosevelt, as they had a year earlier to meet Hoover, Eleanor Roosevelt gave them a coffee and enlisted them into the Conservation Corps. The second major importance of the stimulus measures in the First New Deal is best illustrated by the most famous of Roosevelt's alphabet agencies, the Tennessee Valley Authority. This took a massive area along the Tennessee River, encompassing seven midwestern and southern states, and provided hydroelectric power. The plan was that once the initial work had been completed (providing jobs), there would be better infrastructure for new businesses to grow up and the region would be regenerated.

> ### Agricultural Adjustment Administration (AAA)
> Set quotes to reduce agricultural overproduction, and helped farmers to pay their mortgages.

> ### Civilian Conservation Corps (CCC)
> Created conservation jobs around the country improving National Parks.

> ### National Recovery Administration (NVA)
> Agency intended to coordinate the reform of all aspects of industrial capitalism.

> ### Public Works Administration (PWA)
> Provided jobs building public infrastructure and buildings.

> ### Tennessee Valley Authority (TCA)
> Built dams along the Tennessee Valley in seven states, providing electric power. Building the dams provided jobs; the presence of hydroelectric power would later provide a stimulus for new business to grow up in the region.

Figure 3.6: FDR's alphabet agencies established in the first hundred days.

The conflict of ideas over the role of the federal government

It was once fashionable among historians on the political left to accuse the New Dealers of conservatism. This radically underestimates the limits on what was possible, even in the crisis atmosphere of the early FDR years. The structure of the federal government in the 1930s was inappropriate to centrally directed radical reform. It had a small civil service and a lack of informed research, and there was a deeply entrenched hostility to 'big' government. The business interests affected by the New Deal, whose expertise was needed to implement the stimulus programmes, had an effective veto – when the Tennessee Valley Authority was set up, it was private companies working on the government's behalf who built the dams, not federal employees, and that gave them a lot of power. State governors could be obstructive, too – men such as Joseph Ely, of Massachusetts. They might divert federal money to balance state budgets, while increasing local taxation. Sometimes, they just became carried away. Eurith D. Rivers was elected governor of Georgia on a New Deal manifesto of pensions and welfare programmes, only to confess to his aides the next day that he had no idea how to proceed. The First New Deal was radical – and it ran into serious opposition that exposed fundamental issues about what the federal government should, and should not, be doing. Roosevelt expanded the federal government so much that in 1938 he requested an increase in the size of the bureaucracy. Perhaps fearing that presidential power might become permanent, Congress did not permit this, although a year later the Brownlow Committee set up to investigate the efficiency and effectiveness of the relationship between the White House and the federal bureaucracy would conclude that, 'the President needs help'.

The Supreme Court came into conflict with Roosevelt over his plans. This was inevitable: Congress was dominated by Roosevelt supporters, and the measures were hastily drafted and clearly not entirely constitutional. The NRA fell foul of the law in what has become known as the 'sick chicken' case as it tried to regulate the sale of kosher chicken in New York, and the Court found that Congress had not had the constitutional right to give the president that kind of authority over intrastate commerce. Roosevelt responded by redrafting the legislation more carefully. In 1936, the Court struck out the Agricultural Adjustment Act, which was immediately re-enacted as soil conservation legislation in response to the dustbowl affecting Oklahoma and Arkansas. Roosevelt overreached when, in 1936–37, he threatened to pick as many justices as he wanted (there is no law saying that there should be nine). He was upset that the nine justices were ideologically opposed to him; they had been there so long. Congress rejected the plan, but the Court got the message and became a lot more amenable, especially as he was able during his long presidency to replace seven of them with his own choices. Another side-effect of this was that the Chief Justice, Charles Evans Hughes, ensured that the Supreme Court's new building – the small courtroom in which there is very definitely only room for nine justices – was finished rapidly.

For some rich Republicans, who would not even name him, calling him, 'That man in the White House', Roosevelt was shockingly liberal. For others, on his own side, he was too conservative. Huey Long, the governor of Louisiana – and its senator – proposed a 'Share Our Wealth' programme to guarantee every family $2500 a year, twice the average wage. He intended to finance this by confiscating money from the rich. He was assassinated in 1935. Roosevelt's old friend Alfred Smith, his predecessor as presidential candidate and governor of New York, formed the American Liberty League in opposition to him. Charles E. Coughlin, a Catholic priest, launched blistering radio attacks on big business – and later on the Jews, and communists, and Roosevelt. Francis Townsend proposed that all elderly people should be given $200 a month by the federal government, on condition that they spend it – that was one way to stimulate spending.

The Second and Third New Deals

Roosevelt used the invalidation of the NRA as an excuse to launch 'a second hundred days of vital legislation'. One response was the so-called Wagner Act, named after the progressive senator who sponsored it. The National Labor Relations Act, as it was officially called, codified the labour relations provisions that had been invalidated. The Second New Deal was about bringing permanence to the best aspects of the first. The Social Security Act 1935 brought even more permanence – it would provide old age pensions, starting in 1942. This was aimed squarely at the Townsend Movement. A tax on wealth in 1935 alienated the rich even further, scooped up Long's supporters, and confirmed the view of the rich that FDR was a traitor to his class. The Works Project Administration (1935) was controversial as it used federal funding to create works of art and put on plays, as well as clearing slums, but those aspects seemed vital to Roosevelt's aim of restoring normal life to America.

In 1936 the Democrats and Roosevelt were heartily re-elected. At this point the New Deal seemed to have stalled. In 1937 Roosevelt tried to return to fiscal orthodoxy by working towards the elimination of deficit spending, and the result was another recession. Roosevelt, in common with almost all the other politicians of his time, believed that national debt should be avoided, and was at best a temporary measure – and while the country ran at a deficit the debt could only increase. His attempt to recover from this by bedding in a structural deficit to stimulate an economic recovery, following the economist John Maynard Keynes, was defeated by a coalition of both parties in Congress. Roosevelt's response was to try, and fail, to have those members of his own party who had defied him deselected in their primaries. The Third New Deal did produce some positive legislation – almost all of it progressive in character. The Wagner-Steagall Act of 1937 provided for slum clearance; the Farm Security Administration Act helped small farmers; the Agricultural Adjustment Act of 1938 extended credit to farmers even further, and the Fair Labor Standards Act of 1938 set a minimum wage and maximum hours. The Third New Deal was the most left-wing of them all (Table 3.1).

Further reading

The big historical questions about the New Deal are:

1.   What were its aims?
2.   What did it achieve?

In fact these are not just questions for historians but are still contemporary political questions, since the New Deal created a 'political order' – a set of assumptions about how politics works, what the key concepts at play are, how to win elections, what people can or should expect from government and how the economy works. The New Deal Order gave US politics a basic consensus about benefit of government programmes, about the federal government's role in regulating the economy to stimulate demand and borrow for investment and about the distribution of resources. That structure held firm until, arguably, the end of the century, and it's still challenged today. It was once fashionable on the left to accuse New Dealers of conservatism; now, however, the New Deal comes up in American politics as a bogeyman of the right.

Early scholars working on the New Deal debated whether it was the 'third' American revolution (see Louis Hacker *Short History of the New Deal*[6]). From their perspective it appeared that the New Deal might be as transformational and revolutionary as the American Revolutionary War (War of Independence) and the Civil War. From the 1960s onwards the New Deal was seen increasingly as a 'transitional reconstruction' of the American economy and society – Roosevelt's response to a new situation (see Carl Degler *The New Deal*[7] and Alonzo L. Hamby *The New Deal: Analysis and Interpretation*[8]). William Leuchtenburg, in *Franklin D. Roosevelt and the New Deal, 1932–1940,*[9] focused on the way in which the federal government promoted economic security and social justice.

In the 1980s Anthony J. Badger, in *The New Deal: The Depression Years 1933–1940*[10] emphasised urbanisation, managerialism and interest groups (rather than parties) in the origins of New Deal. For him, many of the trends attributable to the New

	Labour and social welfare	Relief	Business and industry	Agriculture, conservation and the environment
1933	Section 7 (a) of National Industrial Recovery Act	Federal Emergency Relief Administration (FERA) Civil Works Administration (CWA) Public Works Administration (PWA)	Emergency Banking Act National Industrial Recovery Act	Agricultural Adjustment Act (AAA) Tennessee Valley Authority (TVA) Civilian Conservation Corps (CCC)
1934			Securities and Exchange Commission (SEC) Public Utilities Holding Company Act	
1935	Wagner Act	Works Progress Administration (WPA) National Youth Administration (NYA)	Banking Act of 1935 Revenue Act (Wealth Tax)	Resettlement Administration (RA) Rural Electrification Administration (REA)
1936	National Labor Relations Board (NLRB) Social Security Act			Soil Conservation and Domestic Allotment Act
1937	National Housing Act			Farm Security Administration (FSA)
1938	Fair Labor Standards Act (FLSA)			Second Agricultural Adjustment Act

Table 3.1: Major New Deal legislation in four different categories.

Deal were happening anyway and were happening in other countries at the same time.

The current focus is more on the meaning of New Deal liberalism and its link to the nature of post-war reform – 'social' or 'commercial' **Keynesianism**. Ira Katznelson, in *Fear Itself: The New Deal and the Origins of Our Time*[11] argues that the New Deal was brought low by the need to compromise with the southern conservative block in Congress.

The economy

American presidents and congressmen in 1920 had far more control over the economy than their predecessors had had in 1890. By 1945, the federal government would actually be a major part of the economy. The cycle of boom and bust had finally caused so much damage that it was clear that it could not be allowed to continue. The details of the causes and nature of this crisis, and the

ACTIVITY 3.4

Look at Table 3.1 and read the sections about the New Deal.

Which way of organising the New Deal do you find more compelling: thematically, as in this table, or chronologically?

Read through the brief descriptions in 'Further reading' of interpretations of the New Deal. Choose one. As you read through this chapter again, find the evidence that you might use to support your chosen interpretation.

political attempts that were made (and not made) in an attempt to solve it, are given in the section on Hoover and the Depression and the section on Franklin D. Roosevelt and the New Deals. The America of 1945 had far more regulation than before. It had social security. It also had far, far more money than it had before. In 1945 America was a Superpower, arguably the only properly solvent nation in the world, and American prosperity was able to grow.

Before this period, growth had generally meant immigration. More people would come to the country, more work would be done and more money would be made. Encouraged – and horrified – by the flood of refugees coming to the country in the years following the First World War, in 1921 the new Republican Congress produced the Emergency Quota Act, which limited annual immigration from any country to 3% of the number recorded in the US Census of 1910. The 1924 National Origins Act reduced this to 2% of those resident in 1890, with the total number of immigrants limited to 150 000 from 1927 and all Japanese immigration was banned. In 1929 this became 150 000 people per year. Americans were worried that there would no longer be jobs for all these immigrants. They were worried that the immigrants might be communists, come not to work but to stir up revolution. They were worried that there was not enough to go around; they were rewarded with prosperity like never before.

Boom to bust and recovery

Politically, if the boom in the American economy in the 1920s was based on a laissez-faire approach, then so perhaps was the bust of the 1930s. When was the recovery? There may not have been a genuine recovery in the 1930s, but there was certainly a stabilisation. The recovery, which came in the 1940s, was greatly helped not just by the fact that the USA participated in the Second World War from late 1941, but by its bankrolling of the allies throughout their longer conflict.

In the 1920s manufacturing output doubled while the population went up by only a sixth. There was more money to go around, and more people shared in the prosperity (although not everyone benefited – certainly not more than half of the American people). At the heart of all this was the automobile (see Figure 3.7). By 1929, 27 million people had cars in America – one-fifth of the population. Apart from making Henry Ford (and General Motors, and Chrysler) very rich, car production employed a lot of people, stimulated the oil, rubber, steel and glass sectors (required to produce and run them) and encouraged road building. Cars also opened up suburbs – it was now possible to live a little further away, rather than within walking distance of everything. This, in turn, stimulated house building – in the late 1920s a million new houses were built every year. Cars could also be used to facilitate connections across the country, as could aeroplanes, which took off in popularity after the magnificent voyage of Charles Lindbergh, whose *Spirit of St Louis* became in 1927 the first solo plane to cross the Atlantic (Figure 3.8). It took him 33 hours. By 1930 commercial air routes criss-crossed the country. Figure 3.9 shows the new technologies and inventions of the period. Businesses were helped to sell their new goods not just by increased prosperity but also by the increase in debt – buying on instalment plan was very common. They were encouraged to buy by the new billion-dollar advertising industry.

The 1920s, the age of the automobile

- By 1929 there were 27 million cars on the road

- Americans owned 80% of the world's autos – 1 in 5 families owned a car

- 3.7 million people worked in the auto industry by 1929, by which time Americans spent $2.6 billion on new and used cars

- The American Automobile Association had 45 million members by 1929 and 2/3 of recreation costs went on cars

Figure 3.7: The 1920s, the age of the automobile.

Figure 3.8: Flying the *Spirit of St Louis*, Charles Lindbergh became a celebrity after becoming the first man to fly solo non-stop across the Atlantic in 1927.

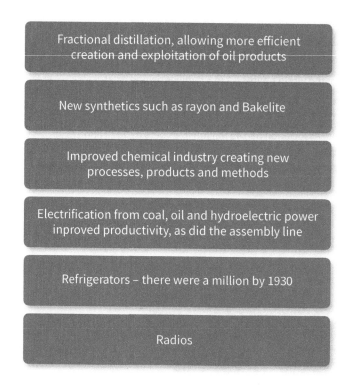

Figure 3.9: New technologies of the 1920s.

All was not necessarily well during the boom years. Even during Coolidge's presidency of unbridled plenty, 600 banks folded every year. In 1926 the Florida land boom in Miami had collapsed, after speculators were caught out selling undeveloped swampland, rather than houses, and buyers were further put off by the hurricanes to which southern Florida is so prone. This masked a deeper, structural problem. Just as those who could afford cars had largely bought one by 1929, so those who could afford a new home had largely got one by 1926. New buyers could not sustain the boom; by 1928 the stock market was the most reliable source of income.

The bust, when it came, seemed to American politicians to be heralded by a plateau. By the summer of 1929 all the major economic indices – such as inflation and unemployment – seemed to be getting worse. Taxes could hardly be reduced further to stimulate demand, and even had Hoover and Treasury Secretary Mellon thought of reducing the tariff, Congress would not have permitted it. Meanwhile the drive to invest spare capital continued. Americans had happily invested in Germany, and from 1927 they began to invest in American companies, and the American economy became an intricate web of indebtedness. The story of how plateau became contraction, contraction became panic, and panic became crash has already been told.

During the Depression that followed the Wall Street Crash, 5000 banks failed. Unemployment had reached 12 million (25%) by 1932, and many of those who were employed did not earn enough to live on. Investment – the amount of capital available for business growth – dropped by 90% from 1929 to 1933, industrial production by half and external trade by a third. The recovery, when it came, was at first partial. By 1936 unemployment had declined to 9 million, and earnings were up, although the supposed 'living wage' suggested by Huey Long, $2500, was in fact approximately the average wage. Roosevelt's Revenue Act of 1935 had made the rich a little less rich; in fact, the rich had not been too badly affected by the bust. They owned plenty of land and profitable infrastructure, and the very wealthiest in society had not, as had the aspiring middle classes, felt any incentive to invest almost all of their wealth in the stock market. For those middle classes sudden impoverishment was a shock, perhaps the more so as they had been used to the creature comforts of the 1920s.

For the very poorest, the bust was a disaster. Tenants found themselves evicted from their land as their landlords sought to farm it themselves; industrial workers were laid off. Official statistics show that fewer than 400 Americans actually died of starvation, but hunger was ever-present; even by 1940 around a million Americans failed the initial medical when they were conscripted for the army. Families forced to leave their homes by foreclosure or through lack of work became nomadic. Some lived in ramshackle shanty towns built to house migrant workers – these were nicknamed Hoovervilles – and lived off whatever state or charity handouts they could find.

In 1929, the richest 5% of American society had a third of the income, and the poorest 70% earned so little that they struggled to make ends meet; they certainly did not have a car, or visit the movies. Nor did they have electrical power. Most people in America spent the 1920s doing much the same work as had their parents' generation, for much the same reward. The boom of the 1920s had certainly been good for some sections of society, but its structural weaknesses were about to be exposed and nobody had thought, in the good times, to put some money aside for the bad.

Structural weaknesses and the impact of the New Deals and the Second World War on economic recovery

The weaknesses of the American economic system had been apparent even in the 1920s. The one area of consistent progressive legislation had been farming. There was a constant tension between the desire of rural farmers, now in the minority, for prices to be high, and that of industrial workers for prices to be low. There was a further tension because the increased efficiency in rural farms (especially for those with access to power) was greater than the increase in agricultural demand – the population rose comparatively slowly in the 1920s. The governments of the 1920s were moving towards dealing with this problem, which Coolidge recognised as beginning with the First World War. American farmers had been encouraged to become more efficient and overproduce; they found themselves with far too much to sell thereafter, a problem made worse by the European recovery of 1921, removing America's ability to sell its surplus across the Atlantic.

This strand of the New Deal represents the greatest continuity from what had gone before: the Agricultural Adjustment Act of 1933 paid farmers to produce less food in order to drive up prices. Six million pigs had to be slaughtered as part of this; sheep were slaughtered in their fields. In a land where there was hunger this

Write a list of who benefitted from the 1920s boom, and why and how they did so.

might seem perverse, but there was another problem. The demand for food was there, but those who needed the food could not afford to pay for it (because they had no money) at a price that covered the farmer's costs. In particular, the cost of transporting food was so high that many farmers found themselves in the position of taking a loss in order to get their produce to market. Roosevelt recognised that he needed to do three things to fix the problem. He had to get the farmers producing less (Agricultural Adjustment Act); provide more infrastructure to reduce the costs of transporting food to market (Public Works Administration); and ensure that those who wanted to buy the food had the money to buy it (alphabet agency job creation). The farms that emerged from the New Deal were bigger and more profitable; they had fewer tenant farmers and sharecroppers. Roosevelt also took America off the gold standard in April 1933, an inflationary measure designed to drive up prices.

Contemporary commentators, especially newspaper cartoonists, made great fun of Roosevelt, depicting him mixing together all the remedies he could to try to obtain a result. They might have had a point. Officially, though, his Brains Trust argued that there was a coherent plan, and that deep structural change was necessary. Conservative policies would not restore confidence in the system, but confidence was inappropriate. Bankers needed to be regulated, not told off; farmers needed to be supported but also reined in, and workers needed to be secure in their jobs, which would give them the confidence to spend money and stimulate demand. This was not the way to replace capitalism, but the way to save it. The experiment of unregulated capitalism was too brutal; although the cycle of boom and bust did move the economy forward in the long run, that was of no consolation to those who suffered in the bad years. The federal government would consolidate debts – the bigger the debt, the lower the available interest rate, borrowing on its own credit money, which it could repay when times were better.

It did not entirely work. In 1937, with unemployment falling, prices up and the stock market stable, and with new infrastructure in place, Roosevelt tried to move away from his emergency stimulus measures and just keep the longer-term changes. This caused another slump, and a change in thinking. National debt would have to be a near permanent feature of the USA. This was a step too far for some Democrats. By 1940 the national debt stood at $45 billion. Manufacturing had recovered to its 1929 level but further progress was slow. Unemployment was static at just over nine million. Farm income had doubled, but the drought and dustbowl (radical destruction of the farmlands of Oklahoma and Arkansas) had helped with that by reducing the number of farmers. By 1940 farmers were building up a worrying surplus for which, under the New Deal, the federal government would have to pay them. A still popular president (he was re-elected in 1940, albeit with a reduced share of the vote) had embraced a new system of economics, had restored confidence and had stabilised his declining country, but the system still tottered on the brink.

Then came the Second World War. A war fought at home is a destructive disaster, but a war fought abroad can be a useful stimulus. The mild rationing of meat, sugar and gas that was applied in the USA during the war actually helped to raise living standards; the 10 million Americans conscripted to the armed forces solved the unemployment problem; and the agricultural surplus could be sent to Britain, the USSR and France on a cash-and-carry basis. Inflation became a powerful force during the war, ultimately ironing out some American income inequalities by increasing the value of goods and labour over that of capital in the bank. By the end of the war steel production was up 20%, prices were up 28% and earnings were up 40%. The challenge for the USA in the aftermath would be to maintain this recovery.

Social and cultural developments

The 1920s was a decade of intense change in America – and Americans knew it. A key theme of the decade was the tension between progress and nostalgia. There was a celebration of modernity, combined with a longing for what had been lost. This was the period of **modernism** – authors Ernest Hemingway, F. Scott Fitzgerald and Ezra Pound wrote of a culture free from repression. There was a post-war cultural shift across the western world that saw the rise of the Austrian psychoanalyst Sigmund Freud, who undermined the Victorian belief that people could be complete masters of themselves. The cultural historian Warren Susman has written of the 1920s United States as the time when the idea of a 'personality' was 'invented' as a shift from the concept of 'character' that was the concern of the Victorians. New self-help manuals emphasised 'personality' as the 'quality of being somebody' in a crowd. This was the first age of fame (and infamy) and the 1920s saw the rise of cultural heroes such as Charles Lindbergh and the baseball player Babe Ruth.

So Americans in the 1920s appear to have believed both that the past was perfect and that progress was necessary. The historian Richard Hofstadter put it very well: 'The United States was the only country in the world that began with perfection and aspired to progress.' Americans believed both that America had a dramatic unfolding destiny, and that the nation was in a state of decline.

The car had a dramatic impact at a local level. By making people more mobile it fragmented communities. In Muncie, the Lynds found the town deserted on 4 July – people had gone back home in their cars (see Voices from the past box). Car adverts appealed to people to do just this: 'A man who works six days a week and spends the seventh on his own doorstep certainly will not pick up the extra

ACTIVITY 3.7

Historians sometimes argue that the Second World War was what really repaired the American economy. Make a case, arguing against them, that the New Deal was also crucial.

Voices from the past

Here are two examples of 1920s nostalgia for the past.

This is an extract from a pioneering sociological study *Middletown* by Robert and Helen Lynd – of Muncie, Indiana (1925). They recorded a Muncie woman saying:

'In the (18)90s we were all much more together. People brought chairs and cushions out of the house and sat on the lawn evenings. We rolled out a strip of carpet and put cushions on the porch steps to take care of the unlimited overflow of neighbours that dropped by. We'd sit out so all evening. The younger couples perhaps

would wander off for half an hour to get a soda but come back to join in the informal singing or listen while somebody strummed a mandolin or guitar.'

Similarly, the labour leader J.B.S. Hardman wrote, in 1924, of the demise of progressivism:

'The world has grown not only older but old … We seem to be growing away from the age of missions and large enterprise: only pilgrimage – to fleshpits – seems to be the order of the day.'

ACTIVITY 3.8

Produce a spider diagram to illustrate all the cultural advances of the 1920s.

dimes in the great thoroughfares of life.' In 1921 the first drive-through restaurant was opened, in Dallas, Texas, selling BBQ pork sandwiches. Life was sometimes so urgent that there was not even time to stop for lunch. The 1920s was the age of the car, of skyscrapers in New York City, of materialism – for all but the very poorest. Many Americans worked less hard and were more mobile, giving them greater access to cultural activities. The only problem was that the very poorest made up more than half of the population.

'The Jazz Age' in the 1920s

The 1920s was the age of play, and it witnessed a flowering of American culture. Jazz originated in 1917 in New Orleans and then spread to Chicago, Kansas City, New York and the West. It began as black culture and was adapted by white orchestras such as Paul Whiteman's. Jazz brought with it new dances including the intimate and risqué Charleston, creating a puritanical backlash. There were great black jazz musicians too – men such as the incomparable Louis Armstrong – and the movement spread across the Atlantic very quickly to take hold in Europe, where it was further transformed. Jazz is improvisational and informal, existing within a clear framework of musical rules. It symbolised the easy-going atmosphere of the 1920s. American classical music also came under the influence of jazz – George Gershwin's *Rhapsody in Blue* was written in 1924.

Jazz was the theme of the first 'talkie', Al Jolson's *The Jazz Singer*. Movies became increasingly popular in the 1920s, and, by the 1930s, making stars of Bette Davis and Greta Garbo as a movie industry built up in Hollywood, California. Use of radio also increased in the Jazz Age – there were 500 radio stations in 1924, covering sports and elections as much as news, and by 1929 there were 12 million sets.

There were great American writers too. Ernest Hemingway lived and worked in Paris on European themes, and the great poet T.S. Eliot was from Missouri but lived in London. F. Scott Fitzgerald wrote in *The Great Gatsby* in 1925 the key portrayal of the Jazz Age, or Roaring Twenties, as an age of decadence and social upheaval, of idealism and cynical excess. It was not popular until after Fitzgerald's death in 1940; now it's seen as 'the Great American novel'. In the South the Mississippi author William Faulkner wrote novels such as *The Sound and the Fury* (1929) and *As I Lay Dying* (1930), which took a nostalgic view of a fading southern society. Meanwhile, in Harlem, New York City, the Harlem Renaissance began with black writers such as Langston Hughes at its centre – he acquired a massive white following.

New social values and the role of women

In the words of the historian H.L. Mencken, 'It was Americans who invented the curious doctrine that there is a body of doctrine in every department of thought that every good citizen is duty-bound to cherish and accept; it was Americans who invented the right-thinker.' One example of this was the Scopes 'Monkey Trial' of 1925, which was also the final public contribution of the great populist William Jennings Bryan. The substance of the trial was whether it was legal for John Scopes, a teacher in Tennessee, to be allowed to teach the theory of evolution. Bryan argued that he should not be. Scopes was found guilty, but then let off his fine on a technicality. This mattered because the new **modernist** ideas had run into old-style American **fundamentalist** religious values. It matters still as the battle continues to be fought in America today.

During the Depression there was still a strong feeling that women should look after the home – mostly to free up the few available jobs for men. In the 1920s women made up only around a tenth of the workforce. The shock of the 1930s changed things: in practice, many women did whatever work they could in the Depression and they were sometimes their families' main breadwinners. By the time of the Second World War they made up a third of civilian workers, but their wages were lower than men's for equivalent work, and women certainly found it much harder (almost impossible) to make progress in professions like medicine. Women became more liberated and more able to ask for divorce. The availability of birth control did not quite lead to a sexual revolution but it made life easier for women – especially given that they no longer needed a chaperone when out in public, and might even use a car for an opportunity to 'go parking'. In the 1920s, though, for some young, middle-class women, there was another opportunity. They became 'Flappers'. Clara Bow, the star of the film *It* (1927), was a movie star and the original 'it' Girl – a role model for Flappers (see Figure 3.10). 'It' was a state of mind as much as a physical attribute; 'it' was confidence. If you had 'it,' everyone knew. Inspired by Bow, Flappers tried to have 'it'.

Flappers were all very well, but their cultural impact should not encourage us to overestimate the extent to which their lives reflected the actual reality for the majority of women in the USA. We know today that movie-star lifestyles are a cultural construct. The concept of 'it' sold movies, as did the presence of beautiful actresses (Figure 3.11). Some women smoked and drank, and attitudes towards sexuality were certainly becoming more liberal relative to the Victorian Puritanism that had gone before. At home, domestic appliances took some of the difficulty out of the lives of the vast majority of women of whom there was a cultural expectation that they would maintain the family home – but only in areas where the women had the money to buy domestic appliances, and where there was electricity to run them. Poor women were not Flappers; first- and second-generation immigrants, African American women in the North and the South, and those living out West on struggling farms with no mod-cons and no movie theatres were not particularly better off and had no idea of whether they had 'it'. The coming of the Depression made it even clearer that all of these things were a luxury.

Some women throughout this period became politicians, but at a national level they were almost always widows serving out their deceased husbands' terms, for example Representative Mae Nolan of California. The first female senator, Rebecca Felton, was the 87-year-old widow of a prominent Georgia politician and a prominent progressive in her own right; she was appointed to the Senate to fill a vacancy for one day in 1922. Others formed pressure groups such as the League of Women Voters (as, following the introduction of women's suffrage, they now were): this group's first cause was disarmament. The Women's International League for Peace and Freedom, a group with a similar cause, was accused of communism in the Red Scare almost as soon as it was formed.

Figure 3.10: A publicity poster for Clara Bow in *It* (1927).

Figure 3.11: Another well-known female icon was Louise Brooks, whose career in silent movies was curtailed by the advent of sound, and her refusal to participate in 'talkies'. She helped to popularise the bobbed haircut.

The failure of Prohibition and its significance

One of the great progressive reforms of the 1920s had been the enforcement of Prohibition – a complete ban on the production or consumption of alcohol except for medicinal or religious reasons. It would be fair to say that it was an utter failure. The desire of American people to drink alcohol was greater than the ability of the 1500 federal enforcement agents to prevent it. The temperance movement came to be associated with **fundamentalism**, and with the opponents of modernity.

So how did a thirsty American obtain alcohol?

- Set up an illegal distillery.
- Use communion wine from churches.
- Convert medicinal alcohol.
- Obtain a doctor's prescription for the increasingly common 1920s disease 'thirstitis'.
- Go to speakeasies – (not very) secret drinking clubs. It was in speakeasies that women started to drink on equal (equally illegal) terms with men.

One of the major effects of Prohibition was to create organised crime between gangs of bootleggers. Scarface Al Capone's Italians murdered leading members of Bugs Moran's Irish gang in a battle for control of organised crime in Chicago on Valentine's Day 1929 – the St Valentine's Day Massacre has since acquired iconic status. When repeal came in 1933 there were a number of reasons for it – Democrats argued that if production of legal alcohol could begin again it would cut organised crime, help farmers and bring in tax dollars from the sale of liquor. The real reason why it was repealed, though, was its failure.

Social impact of the Depression and the Second World War

The Depression had an immediate impact upon all but the very rich. At no point did the sale of Cadillacs drop off. The rich (men like Treasury Secretary Mellon) still became philanthropists, and still had money. The poor entered bread lines for free food and lived in Hoovervilles after being forced out of their homes. People moved West from the states hit most badly by the Oklahoma dustbowl and ended up in poorly paid jobs in California (some, but not all, of them as fruit-pickers). Some became nomads, hitching rides on freight trains from soup kitchen to soup kitchen. Americans found themselves thoroughly disconnected from the land on which they lived, as smallholding declined. It was no longer profitable to run a small farm. Meanwhile 20 million Americans were not getting enough to eat. Crime went up during the Depression, and the prison population in 1933 had increased by nearly 14% since 1929 – but violent crime had gone down. Crimes were committed out of economic necessity. The middle classes were also hit: their taste of the good life was stripped away, and their ability to run businesses was impaired. Professionals were not always paid – teachers in Chicago were not paid for years at a time. Some other human indicators of the Depression are shown in Figure 3.12.

The marriage rate fell from 10.14 per thousand persons in 1929 to 7.87 in 1932; the divorce rate fell too.
The birth rate decreased 13% from 1929–33 and only regained its 1929 level in 1940. Female employment increased a little; the number of married women emplyed outside the home rose by 50%; women mainly found work in clerical jobs, sales and services.
High youth unemployment meant that young people stayed longer in school (75% of youth attended High School in 1940, but only 48% in 1930).
Immigration in the 1930s was at 10% of 1920s levels.

Figure 3.12: Human indicators of the Depression.

When the war came, it solved the unemployment problem. Women entered the professions and made up a third of the total workforce. Roosevelt launched the Fair Employment Practices Committee by **Executive Order** in June 1941 to head off an African American march on Washington seeking equality in the workplace. With the exception of the Japanese-American community of California, which Roosevelt summarily and illegally interned, American society became more equal in the fight against fascism.

Social, regional and ethnic divisions

American society was divided at the start of the 1920s. The priorities of the wealthy, the very poor and the growing middle class were not the same. The progressive reforms of the earlier part of the century began to run out of steam, and they no longer had a presidential champion. In the South, life was poor for African Americans, who remained excluded from any real wealth; those who had moved to the North did not find any less racism there. The Depression, when it came, affected everyone in every region – not equally, for sure, but it affected them all. The restructured American economy was still unequal, and American society was too, but the rising tide of prosperity and sense of shared purpose brought on by the Second World War meant that America was stronger after the war than it had been before it.

The history of labour relations over this period is interesting: the power of the workers as opposed to business owners certainly grew. In the early 1920s not much changed. In 1921 Harding sent troops to break a miners' strike in West Virginia; in 1922, after miners in Illinois had launched a violent protest, Harding commissioned a report, that laid bare the awful conditions in which the miners had been working. He then ignored it. In 1922 he prevented a railroad strike through a court injunction. By the late 1920s companies were realising that their workers expected some sort of forum, and the 'American Plan' was born – of company unions, without national organisation, where individual issues (site-specific safety concerns) could be discussed. To want any more than the American Plan, it was hinted, was un-American.

The results were predictable – minor improvements in safety, more substantial improvements in the happiness of some workers, but no relaxation of the control of big business over wages and hours. The Wagner Act (or National Labor Relations Act) of 1935 was a key piece of legislation that took such decisions away from individual corporations and companies. Meanwhile the unskilled workers, often excluded from the American Federation of Labor (AFL), began to organise themselves into the Congress of Industrial Organisations (CIO). The CIO admitted black people and women; by 1938 it had four million workers. These new laws, and this new attitude, encouraged companies to recognise their unions – the new policy of sit-down strikes, first tried against General Motors by the Union of Auto Workers in 1936, helped too. It was very hard to defend against a situation where all the workers simply sat down and stopped. Labour relations during the war were mostly reasonable, with growing prosperity and plenty of orders to fill, and the businesses that might have pushed their workers too hard were still restrained by New Deal legislation. Roosevelt also banned some strikes when he deemed that they had impeded the war effort.

Countryside versus city

By 1920 more than half the population of the USA lived in cities, and although in practice that meant anywhere with a population of above 2500, it's still notable that across that decade three million Americans moved to the cities as farm prices fell and the rural textile industry of New England collapsed. By 1938 only about 25% of Americans made their living from farming, but they were a powerful interest group: one of the lessons of the Depression and New Deal appeared to be that the farmers had to be protected to ensure that the country would not run out of food. Modernisations in agriculture had had a profound effect. The idea of the American countryside was not quite a product of the romantic notions that Theodore Roosevelt might have had: it was being organised. Smallholders had less access to credit, less resilience to economic change. The era of the consolidated farm – of what would become known as agribusiness – was beginning.

Meanwhile in the cities not everyone saw the countryside in a positive light. It remained just as hard for labourers in the cities to understand the importance of keeping farm prices up and providing federal support for farmers' mortgages as it ever had. Intellectuals such as Sinclair Lewis, in *Babbitt*, even began to suggest that the traditional anti-modernist reactions of parts of American society to progress – the Red Scare, the Klan, the Scopes trial – were evidence of the power of backward rural communities, stuck in the past, forever stuck in the ideas of Puritanism and the pioneer spirit. These forces of traditionalism seemed to dampen the artistic spirit and restrict freedom – and they were obsessed by money, too.

Divisions between North, West and South

At the beginning of the 1920s the North was a Republican stronghold, the South Democratic and the West mostly Republican but potentially up for grabs. The aftermath of the First World War – overproduction followed by the re-emergence of European farming production – had been desperately bad for farmers, and saw the emergence of an alliance in Congress between the West and the Midwest in a 'farming bloc', which saw the election of a progressive senator in Wisconsin

(Capper), a Farm Labor senator in Minnesota (Volstead). This bloc also lay behind the Capper–Volstead Act of 1922, which exempted farm cooperatives from anti-trust laws, and the Intermediate Credit Act of 1923. This bloc remained intact during the New Deal, as the effects of the dustbowl were felt, especially, across the southwestern states. It was these progressive westerners upon whose votes Roosevelt was able repeatedly to rely.

The story of the South is not quite the story of African Americans, although the forces prompting them to leave the South are interesting. The agricultural model of sharecropping did not survive the Depression and the New Deal. New industries did not particularly take hold throughout the South, and southerners did not, as a whole, see any need to vote for the Republican Party, which had brought them Abraham Lincoln and which now, when it took an interest in farming, took an interest in farming western style.

The Northeast remained solidly Republican until 1928 when governor of New York Al Smith ran for the presidency. He was a 'wet' – opposed to Prohibition. More importantly, he was Catholic. The opposition to him was predictable. Hoover's supporters (without his instigation or, as far as we can tell, explicit approval) warned that a vote for Smith would be a vote for the Pope. George Fort Milton, a southern Democrat, warned that the primary appeal of Smith would be to aliens, Catholics and Jews, 'who feel that the older America, the America of the Anglo-Saxon stock, is a hateful thing which must be overturned and humiliated', and called upon 'the old America, the America of Jackson and Lincoln and Wilson' to 'rise up in wrath' and defeat them. Smith, the Democratic candidate, managed to lose Texas to Hoover on the back of this sort of rhetoric. He did, though, win in Massachusetts and Rhode Island, the two states in the North that were both most urban and most Catholic. The next time a Catholic ran for the presidency it would be a senator from Massachusetts who did so, and he would feel forced to set out in detail before the election that he was independent of the control of the Pope. His name was John Fitzgerald Kennedy, and he would be able to carry the North without being a White Anglo-Saxon Protestant.

African Americans and the rise of the Ku Klux Klan

In 1920 there were 152 000 African Americans living in New York City. They tended to live in ghettoes, for which they had exchanged segregation. They faced discrimination from white people competing for the same jobs as the full employment of the First World War contracted. This situation was made more difficult by the unwillingness of returning African American soldiers to be treated as second-class citizens. Black people who had moved to the North had expected that they would be moving away from the racism they had experienced in the South. The reality of the situation did not match up with their expectations, and amidst all the other social upheaval of July 1919 there had been race riots across the North, with the most serious, in Chicago, lasting 13 days.

The Ku Klux Klan, an obscure racist group from the Reconstruction era, had been revived in Georgia in response to the film *The Birth of a Nation*, which had come out in 1915. It was also a response to southern insecurity about the position of African Americans. Klansmen were behind a further spate of lynchings, and the

Why did northern states and black people sometimes vote Democrat by the 1930s?

As you come back to this section for revision, consider whether this represented the beginning of a permanent structural change.

phenomenon moved North – famously, there was a lynching in Duluth, Minnesota, in 1920. The Klan was by this stage a phenomenon of the Midwest and the cities. They saw themselves as regulators, imposing a modern order that was white, Anglo-Saxon and Protestant. They hated private schools, preferring to educate children publicly to ensure that they learned decent morality. They disliked Jews and Catholics, jazz and drinking. They expanded in those towns to which African Americans and other migrants moved, associating these new peoples with a threat to the 'good old days'. By 1925 there were 4–5 million of them and between 40 and 60 thousand marched on Washington, DC; later that year they began to fizzle out after an exposé of embezzlement of funds by their leaders, and a sex scandal in Indiana, one of their power bases, where a young girl who had been abducted by a Klan leader killed herself.

To the tension between Booker T. Washington and W.E.B. Du Bois was added a third voice – that of Marcus Garvey. His Back to Africa movement was critical of Washington's accommodationism and the National Association for the Advancement of Colored People (NAACP)'s failure in its legal battles. His attempts to persuade black people to return to Africa were not popular – especially with the government of Liberia, which feared him as a potential revolutionary. He was imprisoned in 1925 and then effectively exiled, but his idea of racial pride lingered on.

When the Depression came, black people suffered. Partly this is because they were disproportionately poor, and the poor suffered; partly it was because they were black. In the South, blacks were laid off in favour of white workers for even menial jobs; New Deal legislation such as the AAA displaced sharecroppers and tenants first. In the Southwest, Mexicans, some of whom were forcibly deported, even if they were legal US citizens, suffered the same fate. In the North unemployment among black people was at twice the national rate. Roosevelt did not challenge this – he did not wish to risk the votes of southern Democrats, allowing the TVA to set up new towns to which only white people had access and refusing to support a bill to make lynching a federal crime. Black people did benefit from the relief of the New Deal, though – about 30% of black people received relief in 1935 compared with 10% of whites. By 1939 a million African-Americans had benefited from the housing and schools built by the WPA. In the years that followed, they benefited from full employment during the war.

The USA and international relations

In 1920 it seemed like a mistake for America to have gone to war. Not enough had been gained, and the Europeans whom America had saved did not seem grateful. During the 1920s this idea gained strength, as America's debtor nations tried to wriggle out of their payments. Coolidge was indignant: the Europeans had, he said, only 'hired' the goods that they had received during the war.

The extent of isolationism

Americans did not step out of international society. They refused to join the League of Nations, but were soon attending League meetings in Geneva and supporting the International Labour Organisation, and participating in the League's work against slavery and drug trafficking. They had also volunteered more money to Europe, giving $100 million to Mediterranean countries and renegotiating the terms of German reparations through the Dawes (1924) and Young (1929) plans. These plans consisted of American banks absorbing German debts, effectively managing them so that their reparations could continue to be paid to France and Belgium. This was no great act of altruism; it was in the American national interest that Germany remain stable and not be invaded by other European countries, as American businesses were investing heavily in Germany. It did not seem to occur to anyone in Germany that this complete reliance on American capital was a poor idea as it depended on the stability of the American stock market. the Wall Street Crash is seen as one of the major reasons why Hitler, exploiting the economic misery into which Germans were subsequently plunged, came to power.

America pushed naval disarmament in this period – again, not for entirely altruistic reasons. The Washington Naval Conference of 1922 called for nations to reduce their naval capacity. In particular, the USA and UK would have more battleships than Japan. This benefited American interests in three ways:

1. Americans did not want another war, and the fewer warships there were the less likely one was.
2. The UK was thus weakened to the extent that Americans would not be excluded from trade, as they had been excluded from trade with Germany from 1914–17.
3. Japan's obvious ambitions in the Far East, stirred up by their success in the First World War, would be hampered. This was in America's interests as America wished to maintain an 'open door' trade policy with China.

The net effect of this on Japanese relations with America was negative largely because the Japanese realised what was going on. In 1927 Coolidge tried to extend this further by applying the limitations to smaller ships, but this failed at the Geneva Conference. In 1930 the United Kingdom bowed to the inevitable in the London Naval Treaty and accepted parity with the United States. The other major 'achievement' of the 1920s for American foreign policy was the Kellogg–Briand Pact of 1928 in which a number of nations agreed that they would never go to war. Nobody took it seriously even then.

While Harding and Coolidge intervened in Latin America (in Cuba in 1922, and in Nicaragua in 1925) and argued with Mexico in 1926, Herbert Hoover promoted the 'Good Neighbor' policy also adopted by FDR. Hoover, in the Clark Memorandum of 1930, publicly repudiated the Roosevelt Corollary to the Monroe Doctrine, and refused to intervene in the Brazilian Revolution in 1930. FDR continued this, withdrawing from Haiti in 1934 and Nicaragua in 1933.

By 1933, political sensibilities and economic realities meant that American isolationism seemed quite deeply entrenched; this did not mean that the US was entirely absent from the world stage, but it did not seem to seek leadership any more. Nor did it feel entirely the master of its own hemisphere. In 1937 the Bolivian government nationalised all of Standard Oil's possessions in their country; there was no real reaction. Emboldened, the Mexicans nationalised half of American oil interests in 1938.

FDR and the end of isolationism and the Second World War

By 1937, even with Mussolini's Italy and Hitler's Germany showing clearly hostile intent towards Europe, and with the Spanish Civil War that so fired Hemingway's imagination under way, 97% of Americans surveyed agreed: the USA should stay isolated. FDR was not quite the strict isolationist he appeared to be – he had campaigned as an isolationist in 1932 because he had to, and had been horrified by the praise he received from the Nazis at the 1933 London Economic Conference (the American delegation had refused to revise tariffs in an attempt to stabilise world currencies; the Nazis had called him an economic nationalist). His country was against any intervention, though, as it did not seem so important to intervene elsewhere with so desperate a situation at home.

In 1937 the situation between Japan and China, which had been simmering since 1931, degenerated into outright war, and Roosevelt's only real reaction was to go along with the Brussels Conference, which issued a moral condemnation. The Japanese, still smarting from the cessation of Japanese immigration in 1924 and the humiliations of the naval disarmament plans, and under an aggressive military regime, 'accidentally' attacked and sank the American gunboat the USS *Panay* in the Yangtze River. There was not a lot Roosevelt could do about Japan. He had tried to befriend the USSR in 1934 (their eastern lands were near Japan) but Stalin, their leader, had broken every promise he made. The reaction of Congress to the sinking of the *Panay* was to attempt to pass a law saying that America could not go to war unless there was an actual invasion.

Roosevelt, meanwhile, was doing his diplomatic best to avert the coming catastrophe in Europe, but he found no useful allies as the British and French governments attempted to appease Hitler. He had also been hampered by the Neutrality Acts of 1935–37, which essentially banned him from sending goods to one side in the war, as Wilson had 20 years earlier. The Neutrality Acts had been prompted by the report of the Nye Commission set up in 1934 under Senator Gerald Nye of South Dakota. This report presented the American entry into the First World War as the result of lobbying by the trigger-happy munitions companies seeking to make money from the conflict. It was a response to the Italian invasion of Abyssinia (modern Ethiopia) that was to bring the Abyssinian Emperor Haile Selassie to the League of Nations, of which America was not a part. The League, influenced heavily by the Italians, did nothing. 'God and history', Selassie said, 'will remember your judgement.' The Nye Commission's judgement was that America should not get involved. The Americans kept trading

 Voices from the past

This Republican campaign advert for the 1920 election expresses American feelings of isolationism.

'Harding and Coolidge stand for these things:

'Absolute control of the US by the US. No foreign dictation. No foreign control expressed or implied.

Americans can govern their country without Europe's assistance.

'This country will remain American. Its next President will remain in our own country, American public affairs will be discussed by American public servants in the city of Washington, not in some foreign capital.'

with Italy: Roosevelt was unable to take action to take his nation to war. This was the intention of the isolationists in Congress. It also accurately represented the intention of the majority of Americans.

In 1939, when war broke out in Europe, Americans mostly wanted the British side to win. A new Neutrality Act of 1939 allowed Americans to supply the allies; Roosevelt came up with various semi-legal schemes such as 'cash-and-carry' (in which the cash was not necessarily delivered) and 'bases for battleships' in which Americans gained basing rights in Europe in return for battleships. The new British Prime Minister Winston Churchill requested anything that could be sent; by the end of 1940 this was to be paid for by '**lend-lease**' – in goodsbecause Britain had entirely run out of money. Meanwhile Roosevelt was campaigning for re-election on a platform of 'keeping our boys out of war' while also instituting a peacetime conscription draft and dramatically increasing the size of the navy. An opposition arose led by Charles Lindbergh – a Nazi sympathiser – and the former President Hoover, called America First.

FDR gave many gestures of support to Churchill. In August 1941 they issued the Atlantic Charter, which was a statement of general democratic principles. By autumn 1941, after a German U-boat had attacked the USS *Greer*, which had been shadowing it, there was an undeclared war between the USA and Germany. Meanwhile the USA was applying economic sanctions against Japan every time they took more of China, and when diplomatic efforts to maintain the open door policy failed, Roosevelt was accused of being hell-bent on war. He probably was, perhaps because he saw the opportunities, perhaps because he regretted the loss of trading partners or perhaps because he recognised that the German war aims were morally evil.

 Voices from the past

Extract from Charles Lindbergh's speech to the America First meeting:

'There is a policy open to this nation that will lead to success – a policy that leaves us free to follow our own way of life and to develop our own civilization. It is not a new and untried idea. It was advocated by Washington. It was incorporated in the Monroe Doctrine. Under its guidance the United States became the greatest nation in the world.

'It is based upon the belief that the security of a nation lies in the strength and character of its own people. It recommends the maintenance of armed forces sufficient to defend this hemisphere from attack by any combination of foreign powers. It demands faith in an independent American destiny. This is the policy of the America First Committee today. It is a policy not of isolation but of independence; not of defeat but of courage …

'War is not inevitable for this country. Such a claim is defeatism in the true sense. No one can make us fight abroad unless we ourselves are willing to do so. No one will attempt to fight us here if we arm ourselves as a great nation should be armed. Over 100 million people in this nation are opposed to entering the war. If the principles of democracy mean anything at all, that is reason enough for us to stay out. If we are forced into a war against the wishes of an overwhelming majority of our people, we will have proved democracy such a failure at home that there will be little use fighting for it abroad…

'The America First Committee has been formed to give voice to the people who have no newspaper or newsreel or radio station at their command.'

The America First movement collapsed on the morning of 7 December 1941 – a day, Roosevelt said, which would live in infamy. The Japanese bombed Pearl Harbor, the American naval base in Hawaii, killing 2400 sailors, destroying 180 planes and sinking eight battleships. They later attacked the Philippines. In fact they had not done nearly enough damage; their attack, along with Germany's formal declaration of war a week later, united America's entire industrial might behind the war effort. By 1944, Roosevelt's election slogan was that he was a good soldier. Like Wilson before him, Roosevelt spent the war planning the peace, deciding that the United Nations – like the League of Nations, only more powerful – would be the way to do it. At the Yalta Conference between him, Stalin and Churchill in February 1945, Roosevelt ensured that Latin American countries that had not participated in the war would be able to join the United Nations; he also made a series of agreements with Stalin concerning free elections in Eastern Europe. We will never know whether he, unlike his successor Harry Truman, would have been able to persuade Stalin to keep those promises; Roosevelt died a month before the end of the war in Europe. Shortly after his death, the USA was, briefly at first, the world's dominant nation. It would never isolate itself again: a Superpower had been born.

Practice essay questions

1. To what extent do you agree with the New Deals were ultimately unsuccessful in meeting the problems of the US economy from 1920 to 1941?
2. 'The most significant American social and cultural developments of the 1920s and 1930s were all to do with the automobile.' Assess the validity of this view.
3. To what extent do you agree that the 1920s were a time of prosperity for all, and the 1930s a time of prosperity for no one, in America?
4. Assess the validity of the view that American isolationism was very strong from 1920 to 1945.
5. Using your understanding of the historical context, assess how convincing the arguments in the following three extracts are in relation to the new social values during the 'Jazz Age' of the 1920s.

Extract A

'The growing assumption on the part of both experts and the general public that sex was a vital part of a good marriage signaled another source of changing expectations about marriage. Philiss Blanchard and Carolyn Manasses, in a 1930 sociological study appropriately titled *New Girls for Old,* summarized the new way of thinking: "After hundreds of years of mild complaisance to wifely duties, modern women have awakened to the knowledge that they are sexual beings. And with this new insight the sex side of marriage has assumed sudden importance." At the root of the new weight given to sexuality in marriage was a changing notion of female sexuality. The Victorian moral code did not permit respectable middle-class women to admit to sexual appetites. The emphasis on women's sexuality coincided with the trend of women seeking more freedom in their social life. At the forefront of this change were the working-class young women who sought out the new urban amusements — dance halls, amusement parks, theatres and cinemas. This unchaperoned, relatively anonymous environment inevitably led to more sexual experimentation.'

Source: From Lyn Dumenil, Modern Temper: American Culture and Society in the 1920s.[12]

Extract B

'Chicago's workers regularly patronized neighborhood movie theaters near their homes in the 1920s, not "The Chicago," "The Uptown," "The Granada" and the other monumental picture palaces built during the period, where many historians have assumed they flocked. … Only rarely did workers' pay at least twice as much admission, plus carfare, to see the picture palace show. Despite the fact that palaces often claimed to be "paradise for the common man," geographical plotting of Chicago's picture palaces reveals that most of them were nowhere near working-class neighborhoods: a few were downtown, the rest strategically placed in new shopping areas to attract the middle classes to the movies. Going to the pictures was something workers did more easily and cheaply close to home. So it would seem that despite the expectations of mass culture promoters, motion pictures did not absorb workers – white or black – into a middle-class American culture. People resisted aspects of mass culture. But even when they indulged in it, these experiences did not uproot them since they were encouraged under local, often ethnic sponsorship.'

Source: From Lizabeth Cohen, *Encountering Mass Culture at the Grassroots: The Experience of Chicago Workers in the 1920s.*[13]

Extract C

'Until the advent of Prohibition, drinking in Butte was governed by clearly defined and understood social rules. Saloons were male preserves and reflected the ethnic and occupational strata of the community. Any woman who drank in a saloon was assumed to be a prostitute at worst, "loose" at best. When reputable women drank, they did so at home. Prohibition rattled these traditional patterns. It curbed some drinking, but, more significantly, it changed the drinking habits of youth and women. Blatant flouting of the law during Prohibition created new social spaces for drinking, and women began stepping up to the bat along with men, albeit in speakeasies and nightclubs rather than in the old corner saloons.… New watering holes welcomed young couples and groups of women, as well as men.'

From Mary Murphy, *Bootlegging Mothers and Drinking Daughters: Gender and Prohibition in Butte, Montana.*[14]

 Taking it further

To what extent did the experience of African Americans differ from the experience of Americans as a whole between 1920 and 1945?

Chapter summary

By the end of this chapter you should understand:

- the development of the power of the presidency in response to the emergencies faced by FDR, who transformed his office in a permanent way
- the reasons for, and consequences of, the Wall Street Crash, and the unwillingness (or inability) of politicians to prevent it
- the reasons for the end of American isolationism, and its emergence to leadership of the 'free' world
- the development of a new consensus about the role of the state following the New Deal
- the shifting cultural and social circumstances of Americans, including developments in ideas about what it meant to be American – this was not a uniform shift: the lives of different Americans changed in different ways
- changes in the position of American farmers during this period.

End notes

1   Stone O, Kuznick P. *The Untold History of the United States.* London: Ebury Press; 2013. p. 56– 57.

2   Leuchtenburg, W. *Franklin D. Roosevelt and the New Deal, 1932–1940.* New York: Harper Collins; 1963.

3   Brinkley A. *The End of Reform: New Deal Liberalism in Recession and War.* New York: Vintage; 1995.

4   Bernstein B. *The New Deal: The Conservative Achievements of Liberal Reform.* London: Chatto & Windus; 1970.

5   Hayward S. *The Age of Reagan: The Fall of the Old Liberal Order 1964–1980. Roseville, CA*: Prima Publishing; 2001.

6   Hacker L. *Short History of the New Deal.* New York: Crofts and Co; 1934.

7   Degler C. *The New Deal. Chicago*: Quadrangle; 1970.

8   Hamby AL. *The New Deal: Analysis and Interpretation. New York*: Weybright and Talley; 1969.

9   Leuchtenburg, W. *Franklin D. Roosevelt and the New Deal, 1932–1940.* New York: Harper Collins; 1963.

10 Badger T. *The New Deal: The Depression Years 1933–1940.* Basingstoke: Palgrave Macmillan; 1989.

11 Katznelson I. *Fear Itself: The New Deal and the Origins of Our Time. New York*: WW Norton and Company 2014.

12 Dumenil L. *Modern Temper: American Culture and Society in the 1920s. New York*: Hill and Wang; 1995.

13 Cohen L. *Encountering Mass Culture at the Grassroots: The Experience of Chicago Workers in the 1920s. American Quarterly* March. 1989: 41(1).

14 Murphy M. *Bootlegging Mothers and Drinking Daughters: Gender and Prohibition in Butte, Montana. American Quarterly.* 1994; 46(2).

4 The Superpower, 1945–1975

In this section, we will examine the way in which Americans, particularly American presidents, assumed leadership of the free world. From its previous isolationism, the USA found itself one of two Superpowers. Domestically, the economy boomed so effectively that even in recession things were not as bad as they might have been. Socially, the idea of being American changed, especially for African Americans, who had a new civic recognition (although not, perhaps, an equal share in economic opportunity). The power of the presidency grew and grew – until a president tried to set himself above the law, and failed. We will look into:

- Domestic politics: Truman, Eisenhower and post-war reconstruction.
- Kennedy, Johnson and Nixon; New Frontier; the Great Society; Nixon and Republican revival.
- Economic change and developments: the rise of the consumer society and economic boom.
- Ideological, social, regional and ethnic divisions: McCarthyism; civil rights; youth culture; protest and the mass media.
- The USA and international relations: the Cold War and relations with the USSR and China; the Vietnam War.
- The USA by 1975: its place as a Superpower; the limits of social cohesion; new cultural developments, including the role of women and the position of African Americans.

The story of 1945–75 is the story of the United States of America as a Superpower abroad. At home, it is the story of the fall of the New Deal Order – or perhaps of its painful unravelling. The Democratic Party relied on its New Deal coalition of white southerners, organised labour and northern workers in every successful presidential election of the 20th century. The fragmentation of this coalition, which had begun in 1964, was very clear by 1980. The Democrats lost control of the Solid South. President Lyndon B. Johnson predicted in 1964 that this would be the consequence of the participation of the three Democratic presidents of this period, with varying degrees of enthusiasm, in working towards civil rights for African Americans. Johnson predicted that the Democrats would lose the South for 50 years; with the exception of the unusual election of 1976, he turned out to be right. The United States, it seemed, were not very united at all. Meanwhile, America utterly dominated world trade, technology and culture. This dominance was both a consequence of the economic boom and a deliberate strategy in the Cold War. America's identity as the beacon of democracy, the shining light upon the hill, was forged and tested in battle. America battled best when she did not battle at all. The major military confrontations of the time – in Korea and Vietnam – resulted in a stalemate and a defeat. When America did not fight – in Berlin, in Cuba, over games of ping- pong in China, by establishing the capacity to destroy the world and managing not to use it – it emerged victorious.

Domestic politics

Truman, for much of the war, had been the man responsible for ensuring that America's wartime production was well directed and free from waste. Now he found himself in the Oval Office – not entirely unexpectedly given Roosevelt's obvious ill health. The war he inherited was rapidly replaced by another, this one undeclared, and then ultimately by a real shooting war on the other side of the world. He found himself with real domestic problems to face – real reconstruction to be done – but also with wars to win, communists (both real and imagined) to deal with and with a hostile Congress all too aware that his presidency had been delivered by a Democratic back-room fix and the infirmity of a revolutionary president already counted among the honoured dead of a righteous war.

It is now fashionable to stress the importance of the anti-New Deal politics of the immediate post-war years, seeing the astonishing Republican gains in 1946 as evidence of this (the Republican slogan was 'Had Enough?'). While the Second World War had greatly aided the ability of the government to do things ('state capacity' in the jargon of political science) it also rehabilitated big business, which had been the 'arsenal of democracy' and gave it huge power to achieve goals such as an end to price controls and limits on labour power as soon as peace came. The 1946 Republican intake were in a powerful position. They were able to pass the Taft–Hartley Act that enabled states to pass 'right to work' laws. At the same time the liberal New Deal alliance was fracturing – with social democrats like Henry Wallace on one side and conservative southerners on the other.

Truman inherited Democratic majorities in both chambers of Congress, and a notion of presidential power greater than anything that had gone before. He was able to hold enough of Roosevelt's voters together that he was re-elected in 1948. Famously, the *Chicago Tribune* ran the headline 'Dewey Defeats Truman' after the election (Figure 4.1): in fact, Truman had won with room to spare. He had found himself assailed on the left of his party by Henry Wallace, his own former secretary of commerce, who had formed a Progressive Party, and on the right by Strom Thurmond. Truman won because he had been able to hold farmers' votes, and those of organised labour, and also because he was able to build on the successes of his predecessors as Democratic candidate – Roosevelt and, in 1928, Al Smith – to secure the Catholic vote. Truman's policies included these:

ACTIVITY 4.1

To whom do you think Truman's policies would have appealed, and why?

- Civil rights are very important – Truman abandoned the idea of states' rights to segregate.
- Workers' rights, delivered by the New Deal, must be preserved.
- Communism should not be allowed to spread abroad.
- Farmers should be supported to ensure their prices remain high.
- The expansion of healthcare as part of social security.
- The president and Congress should be active in government.

Henry Wallace, Truman's left-wing Democratic opponent who identified as a progressive, opposed him largely on the issue of foreign policy – which meant communism. He had announced his candidacy in 1947, not long after leaving the Cabinet. Wallace's candidacy rested on assumptions that gained more traction at the time than they have among historians. First, Truman was overreacting in his aid programme to the countries of Europe that had suffered in the Second World War, and wasting American money. Second, Stalin would not be all that bad an opponent if only handled properly, and Truman did not handle him as well as Roosevelt. Truman was therefore being too tough on international communism, to the detriment of the United States. Early polls suggested that Wallace might get over 5% of the Democratic vote. With the benefit of hindsight we can see that his candidacy helped Truman by allowing Truman to demonstrate, in the midst of the Red Scare, that he was tough on Reds.

Figure 4.1: The *Chicago Tribune*'s inaccurate headline, 3 November 1948.

Truman's other opponent, Strom Thurmond, identified himself as a **Dixiecrat** States' Rights Democrat, and opposed Truman because Truman had begun to advocate civil rights, and because he supported the state of Israel. Thus began the movement that would ultimately see the Solid South realign itself with the Republican Party, as African Americans voted Democratic instead. Moderate support for civil rights turned to radical support at his convention. This was a political decision: Democratic bosses knew that it would split their party, but calculated that gains among African American populations in the northern cities would more than make up for the loss of parts of the South.

Truman, who in 1948 had been desperate to secure his own term and therefore his own mandate, chose not to run in 1952. He was by that stage thoroughly damaged by the Korean War, and he had lost the trust of some in his party by proposing civil rights legislation and a Fair Deal to build on the New Deal. His successor was Dwight Eisenhower, the Second World War general and Republican nominee whose personal politics were so unformed and little known that he had been approached by both parties. He was the subject of attempts by both political parties to 'draft' him for the presidency; his name had been put on the Republican primary ballot in New Hampshire without his permission. Eisenhower seemed like a reassuring presence. In fact, after finding that voters wanted Eisenhower to run

Figure 4.2: Campaign badge, 1952.

Voices from the past

Strom Thurmond

Figure 4.3: Strom Thurmond, whose career as Democrat, Dixiecrat and Republican exemplifies the political changes of the period.

Strom Thurmond (Figure 4.3) began his long career in the South Carolina Senate in the 1930s, and finished it in the US Senate in 2003, a month after his 100th birthday. In 1948 he ran for president from his position as governor of South Carolina, running on a Dixiecrat (i.e. Southern Democrat) **States' Rights** ticket. He won four southern states. By 1954 he had become US senator for South Carolina as an independent candidate in a 'write-in' campaign – he had not been on the ballot, but still won. By 1956 he had again joined the Democratic Party.

In 1964 he changed parties in response to the Democrats' support for civil rights. His state, which had voted for Democrats in presidential elections for 100 years, voted Republican, and with the exception of 1976, has done so ever since. Thurmond became an important voice within the Republican Party.

but did not know what they wanted him to do, Republican strategists came up with the 'I like Ike' campaign (Figure 4.2). Ike was Eisenhower's nickname, and the campaign strategy was reflective of the fact that the American people wanted a man, not a policy platform, for the presidency.

Truman, Eisenhower and post-war reconstruction

Figure 4.4: Truman had this sign on his desk.

Harry S. Truman (Figure 4.4) knew that he, as president, would be held accountable for the security and development of the United States during his time in office. He also knew that he would have a 'honeymoon' period at the start of his presidency, caused by the death of FDR – but that this would not last. When he came to power, the Second World War was nearly over; he had to plan for the peace.

In 1945 there was immediate discontent among workers. Miners and railroad workers wanted higher wages as they had lost their wartime overtime, thereby reducing their take-home pay. Worse, inflation was running high, and government-imposed price controls on some food stuffs, intended to benefit consumers hit farmers, who refused to market their goods at artificially low prices. By 1946 there was a serious meat shortage. Truman and Congress were unable to manage the situation, and the cost of living went up by 30% in the second half of 1946. Meanwhile, Truman was threatening legislation to draft striking workers into the army so that he could order them to return to work. His overriding aims appear to have been to ensure domestic stability and to avoid the slump he feared would be coming; the Roaring Twenties had not roared loudly for farmers, and Truman feared that this might happen again, undoing a lot of the work of the New Deal. He also wanted to avoid rolling back the gains of the New Deal for labourers, ultimately unsuccessfully vetoing the Taft–Hartley Act of 1947 – this was a piece of legislation designed to dilute the power of the Wagner Act, which gave workers the right to collective bargaining and representation.

In the immediate aftermath of the war had come the problem of how to rebalance the economy. A $6 billion tax cut provided a stimulus for growth, but the availability of cash together with high demand for agricultural goods triggered inflation of around 20% in food prices. This was part of the cause of the labour unrest that marked Truman's first two years in office. The issue became worse when Truman's efforts to get Congress to agree to price controls did not work; Truman, the Missouri farmer, was looking after his own. He was ultimately forced to concede in the face of a serious meat shortage, and the cost of living rose another 30% in the second half of 1946. No wonder the Democrats were hammered in the mid-term elections of that year.

The new, hostile, Congress passed income tax cuts over Truman's objections, in an attempt to redress the balance of the New Deal by stimulating the economy not by federal spending but through allowing wealth to 'trickle down' from the most wealthy. This model – high tax and high spend versus low tax and low spend – is still a major part of American politics. Truman was reduced to trying to get whatever he could out of Congress, ending up by increasing the provision of low-cost housing and social security.

Truman governed in 1947 and 1948 as a president in opposition to the 'Do Nothing' Congress, run by Republicans for the first time in more than a decade. With the cooperation of some southern Democrats, Congress slashed taxes even further and cut government spending – they were trying to roll back the New Deal, and in particular move away from the idea that government spending should be used as a direct economic stimulus. Truman's response was to put forward the 'Fair Deal' – a social programme that was doomed to failure but enabled Truman to be seen to be promoting New Deal ideas such as a national health insurance bill, which was branded 'socialist'. He did achieve a little more in building social security and low-cost housing. Levitt Towns were named after the administrator William J. Levitt, who built houses at the rate of 1.5 million a year on the grounds that new houses were needed, especially in the growing suburbs; the policy was also popular among those who thought that nobody who owned his own house could possibly be a communist.

America from 1945–53 was adjusting itself. Since 1917 it had been in a state either of wartime emergency or of what would turn out to be dangerous complacency. Truman sought, successfully, to avoid both a slump like that of 1919 and blame for a depression like the one that had begun in 1929. He was able to maintain high levels of production and productivity while managing the demands of labourers who had, on the whole, behaved in the national interest during the Second World War and now sought to promote their own interests. He was able to manage the demobilisation of an army (and was helped in this by the need to remobilise in 1950 when the Korean War began). On those grounds, his post-war reconstruction actually went rather well.

Eisenhower had been 'drafted' for the presidency because of his immense popularity as a war hero; he seemed preferable to the unpopular incumbent president, who felt unable to run again, and to any other professional politician who could be found. Both parties wanted him to run on their ticket. He chose the Republicans, and ran ahead of the rest of his party in the election; he won in a landslide, while the Republicans only narrowly regained the House and the Senate. This gave Ike something of a mandate to impose himself upon Congress. By 1955 he faced divided government as the House and Senate were recaptured by the Democrats (the former for 26 years, the latter for 40). Anything Eisenhower wanted to do to reconstruct the country would have to be acceptable to the Democrats. His 'Dynamic Conservatism' fine-tuned the recovery.

'Dynamic Conservatism' essentially meant the government maintaining the New Deal legacy of looking after welfare, while providing whatever stimulus was necessary. This was what the New Deal looked like when times were good. Eisenhower was not a slave to the New Deal – he believed in reducing spending and lowering taxes, and trying to reduce the size of the deficit. His policies included:

- Tax reduction.
- Creation of the Executive Department of Health, Education and Welfare.
- Exploitation of oil in the Gulf of Mexico to raise the revenue base.
- Supporting farmers through the 'soil bank' designed to prevent over-production.
- Building interstate highways.
- Establishing the National Aeronautics and Space Administration (NASA).
- The Atomic Energy Act to encourage the peaceful use of nuclear power.
- Raising the minimum wage.

Historians' initial reaction to Eisenhower was unfavourable; the first histories of his time were written in the light of the reforming Democratic presidents who succeeded and seemed to surpass him. Fred Greenstein, in *Hidden-Hand Presidency* (1982), began his rehabilitation, arguing that Ike's leadership style was indirect but effective; the modern view is that he did too little in terms of civil rights, social policy, and economic management.

Government and politics

Kennedy, Johnson and Nixon

Kennedy was only four years younger than his opponent in the 1960 presidential election, Richard Nixon. Nevertheless, the election, which was very closely fought, felt like a generational struggle. Nixon had been around for ages – leading the **House Un-American Activities Committee**, as senator, and as vice president to Eisenhower. He represented **White Anglo-Saxon Protestant (WASP)** America, and Kennedy (who was very rich) seemed to represent immigrants, the poor, African Americans – the full New Deal Coalition. The American people, upbeat after a decade of prosperity, elected the man who seemed to represent a glorious future. Kennedy's policies were new and forward looking. As for his opponent, Nixon – his policies had been useful in the 1940s.

Kennedy pushed civil rights, a little. He attempted to reform society with his policy of the 'New Frontier'. He achieved little. His successor, Lyndon B. Johnson, who became president when Kennedy was assassinated, was able to use Kennedy's legacy and his own mastery of the Senate to push civil rights and establish the 'Great Society' – a reform programme every bit as radical as the New Deal. In doing this, he helped to reform both the main political parties. The Democrats finally shed their segregationist southern members – this had been coming since 1948. The Republicans, meanwhile, forced into a serious discussion about their own policy positions, nominated Senator Barry Goldwater of Arizona for the 1964 presidential election. He was soundly defeated by Johnson, but his legacy was important as he established a tradition within the Republican Party that endures to this day. His conservative coalition, based in the West and South, was explicitly opposed to the New Deal. It was for the little guy and opposed to big business. It was in favour of states' rights.

Goldwater's campaign launched the political career of the B-movie actor Ronald Reagan, who ran for the Republican nomination for the presidency in 1968. The nomination and the presidency were won by Richard Nixon, running as a westerner with strong anti-communist credentials but on an otherwise moderate platform, with a northern moderate as his running mate. Nixon won in a tumultuous year because of his foreign policy experience – the Vietnam War was now the major issue in US politics – and because he seemed able to calm the howling protests that had afflicted America. He united his party around him. The Democrats, meanwhile, were falling apart. Their 1968 Convention has become known as the Battle of Chicago; it was attended by riots, and the Secret Service refused to allow President Johnson anywhere near. The eventual Democratic nominee, Vice President Hubert Humphrey, had not been the first choice. That had been Bobby Kennedy, JFK's younger brother, who was assassinated at the moment of apparently securing the Democratic nomination.

ACTIVITY 4.2

List the measures taken by Truman, Eisenhower and the Congresses of their time, to reconstruct the country after the war. In what ways do they appear to have learnt the lessons of the 1920s?

 Key term

The House Un-American Activities Committee: or HUAC, as it was known, had been set up in the 1930s to guard against fascism; its Republican members enthusiastically investigated communist influences on the New Deal and in the labour movement. In the 1940s and 50s it sought to investigate worrying rumours of communist infiltration, while at the same time defining being a good American as not merely being a capitalist but being actively anti-communist.

 Key term

White Anglo-Saxon Protestant, or WASP: a shorthand term with obvious racial overtones to describe Americans who were from particular white communities, in particular the Scots-Irish communities of the working-class North and South.

The New Frontier

The circumstances of President Kennedy's death, slain by an assassin's bullet after a presidency lasting little more than 1000 days, have established him as the stuff of legend. The myth of Kennedy, and his death, tends to obscure attempts at objective assessment of the achievements of his life. He was assassinated by a lone assassin, Lee Harvey Oswald, on 22 November 1963. Oswald's motivation? Nobody knows for sure, but he was a communist sympathiser and Kennedy's actions and rhetoric had been overtly anti-communist.

Kennedy and his team lacked experience in any form of politics. Kennedy's time in the House and the Senate had mostly been a preparation for election to high office; the most experienced Congressional operator in the administration was Johnson, but as vice president he was excluded from decision-making and the day-to-day running of the administration. The result of all this was that even the Democratic Congresses with which Kennedy had to deal were unresponsive to his requests. The southern Democrats, in particular, often voted with Republicans. Unable to manage Congress, Kennedy struggled to pass domestic legislation. His greatest achievements, and indeed the subject of his entire, famous, inaugural message, were in the realms of foreign policy.

The New Frontier was his domestic programme. He coined the term himself in his speech accepting the nomination of the Democratic Party for president, in the following words: 'We stand today on the edge of a New Frontier – the frontier of the 1960s, the frontier of unknown opportunities and perils, the frontier of unfilled hopes and unfilled threats. … Beyond that frontier are uncharted areas of science and space, unsolved problems of peace and war, unconquered problems of ignorance and prejudice, unanswered questions of poverty and surplus.' Inspired by the Soviets' achievement in making Yuri Gagarin the first man in space in April 1961, two and a half months into his presidency, Kennedy challenged NASA to put a man on the moon by the end of the decade. In his foreign policy he aggressively challenged communism. He was a reluctant champion of the Civil Rights Movement. In his economic and social policy, he was a Democrat in the progressive, New Deal tradition.

Or at least, he tried to be. On the face of it his legislative record seems impressive; around 60 percent of his suggested legislation passed. It had often been watered down by Congress, reduced to its basics in order to secure votes: Kennedy's team lacked the experience to prevent this. Sometimes his policies were unsuccessful. He tried and failed to enact healthcare and to create a Department of Urban Affairs. Instead he managed to expand social security, pushing the pension age down to 62 and raising the level of unemployment benefits, and to address slum clearance and water pollution. He was also successful in passing an Omnibus Housing Act in 1961, a classically progressive piece of legislation and New Deal-style stimulus. Equally progressive was his support of farmers – his Farmers Home Administration (1961) dealt with the age-old problem of mortgage foreclosures and falling farm prices.

The New Frontier is summed up in Figure 4.5. A key question to consider when thinking about the New Frontier is what it was designed to do. Was it:

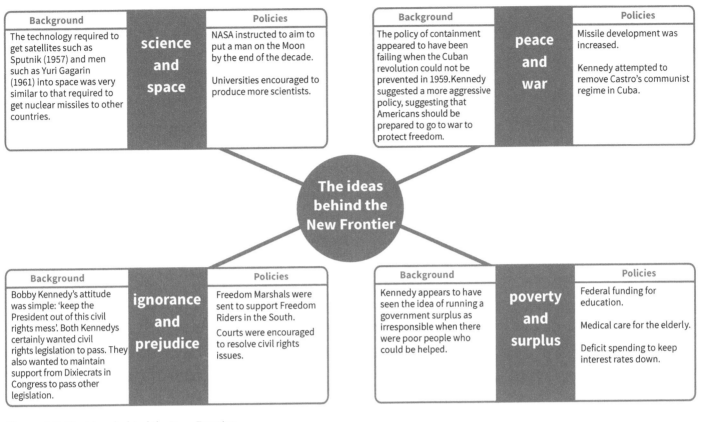

Figure 4.5: The ideas behind the New Frontier.

- Classic progressive legislation in the New Deal tradition (placing Kennedy in a line of Democratic presidents from Roosevelt to Johnson)?
- A series of attempts to restructure an economy in downturn, providing stability and trying to avert a repeat of the pattern of boom and bust that had followed the First World War?
- Aimed at improving America's image and standing abroad: America was a beacon of hope for the free world, after all?
- An attempt to preserve some form of Democratic coalition that could win elections, given the apparent loss of the Solid South because of the Democrats' support for civil rights?

The Great Society

When Kennedy died, the presidency was inherited by Lyndon Johnson. He had been the Democratic leader in the Senate through Eisenhower's time in office and was vastly experienced at pushing legislation through Congress. He was a committed liberal in the New Deal tradition, who sought to create a second set of New Deal legislation – this one to be carried through while the economy was excellent. He intended to reshape American society. He referred to his reform plans from May 1964 as 'the **Great Society**', which he often characterised as a woman to be cherished and protected.

After his first three years his reforms had been largely completed; besides, by that stage he had an all-consuming war to deal with in Vietnam. The five main strands of Great Society legislation were:

- Civil rights

ACTIVITY 4.3

List the elements of Kennedy's New Frontier.

For each element, explain whether it is (a) progressive, (b) in the New Deal tradition or (c) neither.

Key term

The **Great Society:** the label first applied in May 1964 to LBJ's radically liberal domestic policies.

Year	Legislation	What it provided
1964	24th Amendment	Banned poll tax in federal elections
	Civil Rights Act	Banned discrimination in public accommodations and employment
	Urban Mass Transportation Act	Provided financial aid for urban mass transit systems
	Economic Opportunity Act	Authorized the Job Corps and VISTA (domestic Peace Corps), established the Office for Economic Opportunity
	Wilderness Preservation Act	Barred commercial use of 9.1 million acres of national forest
1965	Elementary and Secondary School Act	Provided $1.3 billion in aid to schools
	Medicare	Provided medical care for the elderly
	Voting Rights Act	Forbade literacy tests and other voting restrictions, reinforcing the provisions of the 24th Amendment
	Omnibus Housing Act	Created Department of Housing and Urban Development; provided rent supplements to low income families
	National Endowment for the Arts	Provided federal assistance to the arts
	Water Quality Act and the Air Quality Act	Required states to establish and enforce water quality standards
	Immigration reform laws	Repealed 1920s immigration restriction, fundamentally altering the countries of origin of new immigrants in favour of Latin Americans
	Higher Education Act	Provided federal scholarships for university and college education
	Highway Beautification Act	Controlled billboards along Interstates, and encouraged scenic roadside development
1966	National Traffic and Motor Vehicle Safety Act and the Highway Safety Act	Sets federal safety standards
	Model Cities	Rehabilitated slums

Table 4.1: Legislation of the Great Society.

- Economic stimulus
- Conservationism
- Healthcare
- Education.

More details of the legislation are shown in Table 4.1.

Making America beautiful

Johnson enacted legislation to preserve the wilderness and beautify the highways, operating in a progressive tradition worthy of the first President Roosevelt, because he thought that Americans should be able to live in a country with beautiful surroundings, and because he thought that journeys on the interstate should be more than merely functional: they should be beautiful. He followed Franklin Roosevelt in producing legislation to allow federal patronage of the arts.

ACTIVITY 4.4

Examine Table 4.1. Create a mind-map to illustrate Johnson's Great Society legislation.

In a time of relative prosperity, Johnson wanted to invest in the unnecessary, luxurious things in life on behalf of his nation.

Kennedy's New Frontier looked similarly impressive, but was beset by failure and Congressional efforts to water down his policies. Johnson's key policy of Medicare was beefed up by Congress to include Medicaid. Johnson knew that the idea of providing healthcare on a social-security basis might be controversial, which is why he waited until 1965, after his re-election in 1964, to secure it. His initial priority had been civil rights legislation, in which he proved tenacious. He was able to pass Kennedy's Civil Rights Act, push for the Constitution to be amended to make it clear that the right to vote could not be denied for any reason (the 24th Amendment) and in 1965 pass the Voting Rights Act to enforce this.

Johnson also capitalised on the economic prosperity that, whether through luck or judgement, Kennedy had restored after the temporary downturn of the late 1950s. His Economic Opportunity Act was a billion-dollar stimulus passed in 1964, which also set up a Job Corps, a domestic equivalent to the Peace Corps, and the Office for Economic Opportunity. In August 1964 he declared war on poverty. He then won a sweeping victory in the presidential election against Barry Goldwater, the Republican candidate who instead proposed declaring nuclear war on North Vietnam. Meanwhile, Johnson reduced taxes, provided federal stimulus for building mass transit systems and produced progressive conservationist legislation to improve water and air quality, and the Wilderness Preservation Act to regulate further expansion. He also passed federal laws about education at every stage from kindergarten to college, ensuring minimum standards and access. The Supreme Court was also extremely liberal over issues such as contraception, censorship and obscenity.

It seemed clear to many that this was the time of a liberal consensus. Where had this idea come from? The Cold War had created a form of consensus in American society, which the Red Scare of the 1950s had tested. The historians of the time, men such as Louis Hartz, had begun to argue that America had been born liberal. In the early and mid-1950s there had been a decline in liberal activism, with no real attempts at identifying and addressing new social problems. To identify social problems (the most obvious being civil rights) might lead to conflict, perhaps to class conflict, and that might allow communism in. The liberal consensus was characterised by three assumptions:

- America was in a cycle of increasing prosperity.
- Americans had shared values and goals.
- American exceptionalism rested on pragmatic avoidance of class conflict, which would harm the image of America abroad.

If America could look like this, then Americans would have a legitimate claim to global leadership. In global terms, Johnson saw liberalism as a way to defeat communism, which shared these assumptions about what a perfect society might look like but had very different means of getting there. The Great Society was Johnson's way of achieving this goal.

The Great Society played a role in the changing perception of what 'liberal' meant. There are two issues here:

ACTIVITY 4.5

Prepare a short presentation arguing that Johnson's motivation for launching the Great Society programme was one of the following:

1. Creating the situation whereby the liberal consensus would be a permanent feature of American society.

2. Integrating the New Deal into American life so thoroughly that it could never be unpicked.

3. Achieving as many liberal goals as he could because he knew that a revival of Republican conservatism was inevitable.

4. Fulfilling the legacy and honouring the memory of John F. Kennedy.

1. **Welfare**: The title of Gareth Davies's book *From Opportunity to Entitlement*[1] captures one perspective on what happened in these years: 'big government' support for people ceased to be something that aided an entrepreneurial individualistic society and became one in which certain sectors of society (the shiftless, work-shy, etc.) developed a sense of entitlement. This is about a shift from a conception of government as a helping hand for everyone (though in fact social security was discriminatory in racial and gender terms) to one in which 'welfare' (which became a dirty word) went to 'special interests' and 'minorities'.

2. **Multiculturalism**: the Great Society also seemed to be divisive in a cultural sense, by promoting groups and interests that seemed to challenge the mainstream. For the majority of white, Protestant Americans, who had benefited from social security and labour rights in the New Deal, and had learnt from FDR that government was on their side, the Great Society seemed increasingly alien – its beneficiaries were not people like them but those hitherto marginal to US politics – black people and other racial minorities.

Both of these issues pushed the term 'liberalism' away from that associated with, for example, FDR. Rather than meaning an assertive, confident use of government power to benefit the majority, it now meant wasteful government spending for the benefit of so-called 'welfare queens'.

Nixon and the Republican revival

'As we look at America,' Nixon told the delegates at the Republican nominating convention of 1968, 'We see cities enveloped in smoke and flame. We hear sirens in the night. We see Americans hating each other; killing each other at home. And as we see and hear these things millions of Americans cry out in anger: Did we come all this way for this?' He promised that he would speak 'for another voice, … a quiet voice … It is the voice of the great majority of Americans, the forgotten Americans, the non-shouters, the non-demonstrators … those who do not break the law, people who pay their taxes and go to work, who send their children to school, who go to their churches … people who love this country [and] cry out … "That is enough, let's get some new leadership."' To Americans who feared the new permissive society's assault on traditional family values and notions of respectability and authority, Nixon offered himself as a man who had lived

Hidden voices

Daniel Bell, in *The End of Ideology: On the Exhaustion of Political Ideas in the Fifties,*[2] argued that social science yoked to modern technology would allow capitalism to realise a frontier of abundance.

'Ideology, which once was a road to action, has come to a dead end … Few seriously believe any longer that one can set down "blueprints" and through "social engineering" bring about a new utopia of social

harmony … In the western world, therefore, there is today a rough consensus among intellectuals on political issues: the acceptance of the Welfare State; the desirability of decentralised power; a system of mixed economy and of political pluralism …The ideological age has ended.'

And he thought that was a good thing because moral visions created conflict, which can only damage a society.

the American Dream by raising himself from poverty and as a firm defender of morality, true patriotism and social order.

Was there, yet, a Republican revival? Nixon's victory was entirely due to the split in old New Deal coalition, which had won so many elections for the Democrats – the showing of former Alabama governor George Wallace, who challenged the Democratic candidate, Hubert Humphrey, was the best since Robert La Follette's in 1924 – but even so, it was close. Nixon made carefully pitched appeals to swing the South behind him, with the former Democrat Strom Thurmond at his side. Nixon's appeal to 'the forgotten Americans' was bound to appeal to the insecurities of white southerners who had voted Democratic in the past only because their grandfathers fought for the Confederacy. In *The Real Majority* (1970) Ben J. Wattenberg and Richard Scammon characterised the typical American swing voter – the type of voter who might decide an election by changing their vote from Democratic to Republican – like this: 'She was a white 47-year-old machinist's wife from Dayton, Ohio, afraid to walk the streets alone at night, with a mixed view about blacks and civil rights because before moving to the suburbs she lived in a neighbourhood that became all black, with a brother-in-law who is a policeman, without the money to move if her new neighbourhood deteriorates, deeply distressed that her son is going to a community junior college where LSD was found on campus.'[3] Nixon won by appealing to a sense of colour-blind middle-class entitlement rooted in a culture of work and reward – playing to their identities as homeowners, taxpayers and parents. It was not just the careful application of the race card.

In 1972 Nixon would characterise his presidency as anti-drugs, anti-abortion, pro-army and pro-peace; in contrast, his opponent George McGovern was anti-'**middle America**'. This was true, but only because Nixon had effectively won the battle to define what 'middle America' meant. He was able to assert that the patriotic compliance of the 1950s, and the sense of duty (both personal and national) of the 1940s, were what 'normal' Americans felt, as opposed to the damaging liberalism that had enabled the protests and decline of the 1960s. Nixon's slogans were about self-help and local control. Accordingly he dismantled some of the more expensive federal guarantees in the Great Society, such as the Office of Economic Opportunity, and called a halt to any new spending on education, health and welfare. He announced a Family Assistance Plan to get people back to work – like FDR, he believed that there was a moral element to doing a hard day's work, which had to be encouraged. He tried to slow down the pace of desegregation; in the case of *Alexander v Holmes* in 1969, which related to Mississippi, the Supreme Court overruled him. He denounced public busing of black students to schools in white areas. The reason for this was that he was trying to appeal to Wallace supporters so that they would vote for the Republicans, not for the Democrats, in 1972. He wanted to keep the Democratic Party disunited.

Nixon believed in the imperial presidency – the presidency should be the most powerful of the three branches of government and the president could do what he wished, without fear of the law. His domestic reforms were only part of the story. He campaigned for his own leadership as a cultural phenomenon – he represented patriotism, morality and religion, and would work hard to help the **silent majority**. His policies did not help the rest of the Republican Party; the idea

 Hidden voices

In *Fear and Loathing on the Campaign Trail '72,*[4] Hunter S. Thompson attempted an analysis of the reasons why Nixon was so popular:

'He speaks to the werewolf in us, on nights when the moon comes too close.' [He represents] 'that dark, venal, and incurably violent side of the American character.'

ACTIVITY 4.6

ACTIVITY 4.6

Make a supported case for each of the following statements:

1. 'There was no general Republican revival under Nixon. What really happened was a Democratic collapse.'

2. 'Nixon's victory in 1972 demonstrated that the New Deal coalition was finished, and that American politics had swung back to the right.'

Which argument do you find the more convincing, and why?

of a Republican revival is misleading; Republicans did not win the Senate until 1980 (briefly) or the House until 1994. What Richard Nixon did, very well, was to win elections for himself.

The Watergate Scandal

During the election campaign of 1972 Nixon formed the Committee to Re-elect the President, which was nicknamed CREEP. Among many other activities, CREEP activists broke into the Democratic Party campaign headquarters of George McGovern, the presidential candidate, in the **Watergate** hotel, which overlooks the Potomac River in Washington, DC. The burglars were caught. This set off a series of events that led to Nixon's resignation, two years later, when it had become clear that he had lied about the extent of his involvement in the burglary itself and the subsequent cover-up.

 Taking it further

The new right

Conservatism, once an unfashionable subject, is now the most fertile area by far in post-war political history. The story was not just about Nixon and Reagan.

Lisa McGirr's study of political organising at the grassroots in Orange County, suburban Los Angeles, CA (*Suburban Warriors: The Origins of the American New Right*[5]) shows the importance of the 1964 Goldwater campaign.

In *The Origins of the Urban Crisis: Race and Inequality in Postwar Detroit*[6] Thomas J. Sugrue argues that at the local level (his is a study of Detroit), competition over resources like housing triggered an urban anti-liberalism from the 1940s on. Sugrue shows how white working-class Americans defined their security and their sense of entitlement in conservative and individualistic terms, specifically as the right to a private home (secured for many by the GI Bill) often in racially segregated neighbourhoods.

In *Up from Liberalism*[7] William F. Buckley Jr described Eisenhower as unprincipled because he tried to please everybody, and argued against the Civil Rights Movement thus:

'In the South, the white community is entitled to put forward a claim to prevail politically because, for the time being, anyway, the leaders of American civilisation are white – as one would certainly expect given their preternatural advantages of tradition, training and economic status.'

 Thematic link: ideas and ideologies

Economic change and developments

The gross domestic product (GDP) of the United States went up by a factor of 10 from 1945 to 1980, when it reached $2.7 trillion. Over the same period of time the demographics of the United States changed radically; by the mid-1970s over 70% of Americans lived in cities, of whom more than half lived in the suburbs. Labour relations changed in character; after Truman's time there would never again be waves of strikes running across industries. In part this is because the nature of American labour changed, with white-collar workers coming to outnumber blue-collar workers by the 1970s. In part it is because the AFL and CIO had merged in the 1950s, which put a lid on the CIO's greater radicalism. In part it is because some industries, such as the auto industry, proactively improved conditions for their workers (the United Auto Workers were at their strongest and most successful in the 1950s and early 1960s). In part it is because relations between the new corporations that grew up in the 1960s and their workforces were of a different character. The new corporations were global, and so were their workforces and manufacturing bases. They were often hi-tech, with more highly qualified employees who seemed less replaceable and were therefore treated better.

The economic boom of the United States was not a given in 1945. The first issue was what to do with returning servicemen. The GI Bill of Rights of 1944 had provided $13 billion dollars for returning soldiers to start businesses or go to college. Neither group added to unemployment, and both in different ways repaid the investment in them by bringing skills or productivity to the economy. Although he had his differences with Congress over the best way to manage post-war reconstruction, Truman was able to run for re-election on an economic platform, pointing to low unemployment. Then the first six years of Eisenhower's presidency saw a time of steady economic expansion fuelled by the consumer society – Americans had more money, and spent it on American goods. Expansion slowed in 1958–59, but although the economy was less buoyant the general standard of living of Americans was high enough that this did not plunge vast numbers of them into distress. When Kennedy came to power he acted to support farmers in the usual way, with price controls and help to prevent mortgage foreclosures. He also worked to keep inflation down and create a mild stimulus (mild because Congress watered his proposals down). Kennedy was content to create a budget deficit in order to stimulate recovery, and it worked: during his 1000 days GDP expanded by 5 percent a year on average, unemployment went down and production rose by 15 percent. Kennedy's economic policies were very successful. Kennedy's successor Lyndon Johnson chose to invest the new American prosperity in his Great Society programme of social reforms.

The end of American prosperity?

The economy Johnson inherited was excellent; the economy he bequeathed to Nixon was teetering on the brink of disaster. Part of the reason for this was structural, part was cyclical and part was Johnson's fault. One structural problem with the economy was American overreliance on oil. The military used oil; manufacturing industries used oil for power and raw materials; in this consumer society everyone used gasoline to move themselves and their goods around. Whole communities were growing up in the southern Sun Belt where

ACTIVITY 4.7

1. List the reasons why the American economy faltered in the late 1960s.

2. What, in your view, was the biggest single reason why the American economy faltered in the late 1960s? Justify your answer.

3. Compare your answers to question 2, which is a very tough question, with the answers of others in your class

air conditioning and cars were vital to maintaining the standard of living that Americans expected. The cyclical problem underlined a further structural problem. Since the 1940s, the American economy had benefited from exporting goods and raw materials that other countries either did not make or could not process efficiently enough. During the 1960s, countries in Europe, and Japan, recovered their pre-war positions. America entered the decade a net exporter of textiles, steel and household goods (such as washing machines). By 1969, America was a net importer of all these goods. Instead, America began to export construction machinery – the kind of machinery that refined steel and made washing machines.

The net effect of this change was that by 1969 the American balance of trade had reverted to a more normal position, but American economic planning (now, under the Great Society, quite obviously the domain of the federal government and therefore of Johnson) had at its heart the dangerous assumption that the good times would continue. To be fair to Johnson, one reading of the Great Society is that he was attempting to spend money while times were good in order to cushion the blow should times become worse. He spent on infrastructure and job creation, and educational spending is also about looking to the future. The cumulative effect of the rising prosperity enjoyed by Americans, and the federal support given through the New Deal and Great Society programmes, meant that even in a downturn there was no danger of the sort of collapse that had begun in 1929.

The economy had boomed during the 1960s, and now the boom was slowing down. Part of the problem was that Johnson was spending a lot of money. Johnson had invested in the Great Society; he also invested in a very expensive war in Vietnam. He knew that to do so was to endanger the Great Society by diverting vital funds; so it proved. Paying for social security and for the war put the country in serious economic danger. Rising fuel costs did not help; the American economy relied to a disproportionate extent on oil, both because fuel was needed to power manufacturing and move goods around, and because car manufacture was such an important part of the economy. The higher the price of gas, the less affordable were cars. Nixon's response to this was to restrict the money supply to control inflation, which was running out of control; this proved insufficient and in August 1971 he froze wages and prices for 90 days, followed Kennedy in abandoning the idea of a balanced budget, and attempted to stimulate the economy through a tax cut. This did not work; he would ultimately have to devalue the dollar after oil prices rose steeply in 1973 when the Organisation of Petroleum-Exporting Countries (OPEC), based in the Middle East, raised the price. Oil prices went up by a factor of four in 1974, leading to massive inflation. By 1975 Ford presided over an economy suffering from 'stagflation' – a baffling combination of a stagnant economy, rising unemployment and rising inflation. His economic advisers agreed that such a situation should not be able to exist – but it did, and the tax cuts of March 1975, intended as a stimulus, were only partially successful. The crisis was not fatal. The underlying economy remained solid, and even during this crisis average disposable income was rising.

The rise of the consumer society and economic boom

From 1930 to 1965 the average family income doubled. Fueled by wartime savings, the consumer boom that occurred after the war transformed the nature of

American life. At the heart of it all was the car. By 1960, 90% of suburban dwellers owned at least one, in which they used to travel to malls where they could buy other goods. They might travel on highways funded by federal governments. Even the existence of the suburbs in which they lived was conditional upon the car, which enabled suburban communities to be built up within commuting, rather than walking, range of jobs. Suburban dwellers moved into available housing. In 1960, 25% of the available housing had been built since 1945. Arthur Levitt, the building contractor from Long Island, New York, and Henry Kaiser, a shipbuilding magnate from California, built houses that could be bought with assistance from the Federal Housing Administration or Veterans Administration for ex-servicemen.

Suburban dwellers were encouraged by advertising to be aspirational, and often affluent suburban dwellers brought largely similar things. Consumers could get into their easily affordable car, drive on a well-maintained road – perhaps even using the federally-funded Interstate network – and go anywhere they wanted. They might stay in a motel – a hotel for the motorist. They might go shopping in a mall – there were only eight in 1945, but 4000 by 1960. They might buy white domestic goods, new furniture and books, bought from travelling salesman on hire purchase agreements, with their credit cards, or from malls. They might eat out, perhaps at a McDonalds, which was founded in 1948, but became big in the 1950s. They might read comics, collect baseball memorabilia, or enjoy the Superbowl (first played in 1967) on the television: by then there were 55 million TV sets and over 500 TV stations. The consumer boom was a suburban phenomenon, but it was not universal. By 1962 a quarter of Americans were still under the poverty line – but poverty now did not mean homelessness or hunger. Michael Harrington's book *The Other America: Poverty in the United States* (1962) brought this to the mainstream popular consciousness. So did popular musicals such as *West Side Story*. Americans could also be aspirational about their personal lives, and self-help plans and psychotherapy became increasingly popular. Table 4.2 shows the kind of people who lived in the suburbs.

Many middle-class people reacted to the consumer boom by wanting more possessions, which drove the growth of the economy. The less well-off reacted either by becoming aspirational or by becoming angry if that prosperity was denied them. This applied to black people in the segregated South, who lived among the new restaurants, movie theatres and rock and roll clubs to which they were not allowed to go.

✔	✘
• WASPs • Whites from a non-WASP background – Poles, Italians and Jews • Petro-chemical workers in Texas • Defense workers in California • Retirees– attracted to the 'Sun Belt' now that air-conditioning had been invented.	• Black people – Levitt refused to sell to black people. • Poor people – who moved to the cities, from which the suburbanites had come. • Asians (Korean, Japanese, Chinese) – many suburbs had 'restrictive covenants' which prevented sales to Asian people. These were illegal, but that did not stop them.

Table 4.2: Who lived in the suburbs?

Ideological, social, regional and ethnic divisions

From 1945–75 the concept of what it was to be American changed dramatically. By the 1960s there was a tension between a 'liberal consensus' and a conservative 'silent majority'. Should Americans support and promote freedom across the world, or should Americans live in freedom at home? Was it patriotic to exercise the right to freedom of speech even if that speech was used to criticise the government? Could Americans be properly American while criticising their country? America was the America of Superman, who fought for Truth, Justice and the American way, Batman the rich man helping the deserving poor, and Spiderman ('With great power comes great responsibility'). Interestingly none of the American superheroes about whom children read in their comics ever made the world better; they only stopped it from getting worse.

McCarthyism

McCarthyism is named after Senator Joseph McCarthy, Republican of Wisconsin, who made his name as an anti-communist campaigner. From the moment in February 1950 when McCarthy claimed that he had a list of 205 communists working in the State Department, the anti-communist movement was associated with him. Throughout his career, McCarthyism did not uncover a single actual spy.

Voices from the past

The wording of this General Electric advertisement from 1956 exemplifies the consumer boom in America.

People's Capitalism – What Makes it Work for You?

Around the world, the term 'capitalism' has been applied to economic systems which bear little resemblance to each other.

Our American brand of capitalism is distinctive and unusually successful because it is a 'people's capitalism'; *all* the people share in its responsibilities and benefits. As we see it, these are its distinguishing characteristics.

1. We in America believe in providing opportunities for each individual to develop himself to his maximum potential.

2. We in American believe in high volume, and prices within the economic reach of all – not low volume, and prices only a few can pay.

3. We in America believe in high wages, high productivity and high purchasing power. They must occur together. One without the others defeats its own ends, but together they spell dynamic growth and progress.

4. We in America believe in innovation and in scrapping the obsolete. By reinvesting earnings in research and in new production facilities, American business is creating more jobs, better products, and higher living standards for everyone.

5. We in America believe in consumer credit …

6. We in America believe in leisure for our people through a comparatively short and highly productive work week …

7. We in America believe in broad share ownership of American business …

8. And finally, we in America believe deeply in competition versus the cartel …

As we see it, the more the principles of America's distinctive brand of capitalism become known and understood, the more certain everyone can be of continued progress …

Progress Is Our Most Important Product
GENERAL ELECTRIC

There really was a Communist Party in the United States of America, and it really did take orders from the Soviet Union, in theory at least – historians know a lot of detail about its workings because it was so thoroughly infiltrated by the FBI. There really had been spies. In 1947, the newly Republican House of Representatives used the House Un-American Activities Committee to investigate. In 1948 HUAC claimed a major scalp when Alger Hiss, a State Department official under FDR, was convicted of perjury for denying an allegation that he had passed film to Soviet agents. HUAC, under the leadership of a young congressman named Richard Nixon, became very popular.

Under severe pressure from HUAC and accused of being soft on communists at home, Truman conducted a review of federal workers in the Loyalty-Security Program in 1947; 2000 resigned and 200 were fired for suspected communist sympathies. Nixon, meanwhile, continued to press. By 1949 HUAC had extended its reach to examine people working in the movie business (based close to Nixon's district in California) and those who refused to testify could be jailed or blacklisted, meaning that they could no longer work in the industry. There were several prominent Jews in Hollywood – often of eastern European origin – and HUAC's activities came to resemble a WASP crusade against them.

The anti-Semitic nature of the Red Scare was further boosted by the event that led to McCarthy's dramatic revelation – the arrest in February 1950 of Julius and Ethel Rosenberg. They were accused of stealing information from Ethel's brother, who worked on nuclear weapons. They were convicted and executed in 1953. Although it was not known at the time, the FBI had secured a Soviet codebook that demonstrated their guilt. McCarthy made a series of accusations of communism over the next four years, both general and specific, against people working at the State Department and in the army: they were working for the Soviets; they were homosexual and subject to blackmail; they were 'un-American'.

Joseph McCarthy had rarely focused on actual threats such as the USSR or China. Even the change of administration from the presidency of Truman, the Democrat, to that of Eisenhower, the Republican, had not deterred him from attacking the executive branch. In 1954, he referred not to 20 years of treason (the Roosevelt and Truman presidencies) but to 21 years. Eisenhower refused to give him the satisfaction of engaging with him. Meanwhile McCarthy's targets became wilder

 Hidden voices

Arthur Miller

Arthur Miller (1915–2005) was an American playwright whose life and work provide an interesting window into American life. Four of his plays neatly illustrate the different demands of the 1950s:

Death of A Salesman (1949) and *All My Sons* (1947) are criticisms of the American Dream, and of the way in which ordinary Americans have their values distorted by trying to live up to an impossible standard that fails to take account of individual weaknesses. *Death of a Salesman* is about the consumer society and *All My Sons* about a morally defective corporation.

The Crucible (1953) is an allegory about the Red Scare, and partly reflects Miller's own experiences after being called before HUAC in response to *All My Sons*.

A View from the Bridge (1956) is about corruption at the New York City docks.

and wilder. After some pressure he dismissed the staff officer J.B. Matthews, of the Senate Permanent Subcommittee on Investigations that he (McCarthy) chaired, for an attack on communism among the Protestant clergy – an attack that appeared to have originated with McCarthy himself.

In 1953–54 McCarthy held public hearings about communism in the army. They were televised, which was not to his advantage. He bullied and hectored and rambled. His victims began to fight back, challenging him to produce his lists of communists whom he claimed to be working for various divisions of the army. It became clear that his attacks were ill-founded and ill-mannered, and he was criticised in print as being a barrier to effective anti-communist measures. The journalist Edward R. Murrow created a series of documentaries, critical of McCarthy, for his *See It Now* series. Public opinion began to turn against McCarthy; by the end of 1954 he had been censured by the US Senate and his crusade was over.

McCarthy, once feared, was shunned. On one occasion in 1956 when he was almost photographed sitting next to that other anti-communist campaigner Vice President Nixon at a campaign event in Wisconsin, an aide asked McCarthy to leave; he did so without demur, but a journalist later spotted him weeping. He died from alcoholism later that year. Nixon, the other Congressional leader of the movement that had come to bear McCarthy's name, was yet to reach either his own highest office or his ultimate disgrace.

The Red Scare in general, and McCarthyism in particular, did have some notable effects:

- In September 1950, the McCarran Internal Security Act was passed over Truman's **veto**; a further version was passed in 1952. These acts outlawed doing anything that would promote a totalitarian dictatorship, and denied admission to the United States to foreigners who had ever been communists.
- J. Robert Oppenheimer, the creator of the atom bomb who, in 1949, opposed the development of the more powerful hydrogen bomb on moral grounds, was denied security clearance to work for the Atomic Energy Commission because of his 'communist sympathies'.

 Thematic link: ideas and ideology

Civil Rights

In 1945 African American communities across America hoped for advancement. Voting rights for black people were patchy in the North and non-existent in the South. Lynching was still commonplace. Black people were disproportionately poor. Over the next 30 years the Civil Rights Movement reached its famous heights; the legal barriers to black participation in society were removed and lynching stopped. The story of civil rights was the story of legal struggle, direct action, peaceful protest and violent revolution.

1947	CORE supporters illegally ride on public buses in the South; Jackie Robinson joins the Brooklyn Dodgers, becoming the first African-American to play major league baseball.
1948	Truman issues an order to desegregate the armed forces.
1954	In the case of *Brown v Board* the Supreme Court bans segregation.
1955	Beginning of the Montgomery Bus Boycott in Alabama.
1956	Creation of the Southern Manifesto by 101 members of Congress promising 'Massive Resistance' to integration
1957	Eisenhower sends federal troops to support the integration of a school in Little Rock, Arkansas; Congressional liberals pass a weak Civil Rights Act.
1960	Sit-ins begin in Greensboro, North Carolina
1961	**Freedom Rides** begin across the South; Kennedy calls for government contractors to take '**affirmative action**' in their recruitment procedures.
1962	James Meredith is personally turned away from the University of Mississippi by the state Governor.
1963	Protests in Birmingham, Alabama, make global news; March on Washington – Martin Luther King's 'I have a Dream' speech
1964	24th Amendment and Civil Rights Act; Freedom Summer in Mississippi
1965	Three marches from Selma to Montgomery; Assassination of Malcolm X; Race riots in Watts, Los Angeles; Voting Rights Act
1968	Assassination of Martin Luther King
1969	Richard Nixon stops public bussing of students in urban areas; Nixon begins to enforce affirmative action among federal contractors in the construction industry.

Table 4.3: Major civil rights events and developments.

The progress made by African Americans occurred in fits and starts and was incomplete. In 1945 the picture was not entirely bleak; in 1975 it was not entirely rosy. The New Deal had helped African Americans because it had helped poor Americans, and the Second World War had had three main effects. Northern African Americans, who had moved to the cities, were usually trained for the army in the South, where most training camps were; there, they witnessed for themselves the horrors of segregation. African Americans began to acquire a states-wide group consciousness. Second, African Americans who fought – and fought bravely – in the Second World War came back less willing to accept a second-class status. Third, the rising tide of prosperity that came after the war provided the economic backdrop that would be necessary for reform. The big developments in the way historians have viewed the Civil Rights Movement over the last 20 years have been to do with the 1940s, and the 'long' Civil Rights Movement, and with an emphasis on the grassroots activists of the movement, and not just with the leaders. Table 4.3 lists the major developments in civil rights in the 1940s and beyond.

It is possible to see the Civil Rights Movement in terms of 'stages' of progress, but this should not distract from the essential messiness of the process. It was not centrally planned, although various agencies and pressure groups did engage in planning. There were leaders, who emerged chaotically, and whose leadership was not always accepted. If there were stages, perhaps they were something like those that follow – but please do not accept such delineation uncritically.

1945–55: African Americans in the South bided their time in terms of direct action; any direct action that occurred was essentially an effort to be arrested (as in the Freedom Rides) so that a legal challenge could be launched on the grounds that segregation was unconstitutional. This was a time of legal challenges, the most famous of which was the case known as *Brown vs Board of Education of Topeka, Kansas.* The case itself was of great importance to the 10-year-old Linda Brown, who had not, three years earlier, been allowed to go to the school closest to her home; the segregated all-black school she was sent to was not as good and further away. This was standard practice across the former Confederate states and it was upheld in the courts on the grounds that segregated facilities were 'separate but equal' and therefore did not violate the 14th Amendment guaranteeing equal rights to all citizens. The District (lower) Court that had upheld the decision by Topeka to segregate had specifically cited the case of *Plessy v Ferguson*, an 1896 Supreme Court case permitting segregation in railroad cars. By 1954, the case was about the whole legal basis for segregation. Specifically: could a state decide to provide 'separate but equal' facilities without violating the equal rights clause of the 14th Amendment? The segregation of the South – in buses, restaurants and water fountains – depended on it. Chief Justice Warren, realising that the Court had a majority in favour of Linda Brown, ensured that the decision that came down was unanimous. He did this to emphasise the momentous nature of the decision: the entire legal basis for segregation was thrown out. In theory, that would be the end of segregation in the South.

1955–63: This was the period in which the famous protests that form the core of the Civil Rights Movement began. When, in December 1955, a civil rights activist working for the Southern Christian Leadership Conference named Rosa Parks (Figure 4.6) was arrested for refusing to give up her seat on the bus in Montgomery, Alabama, breaking the local segregation law, a local pastor named Martin Luther King Jr. was called upon to pass comment. Under his leadership, the boycott that grew up in Montgomery, as black people simply refused to use the buses, resulted in a local change in the law and plenty of national attention, not least for King himself.

Figure 4.6: Rosa Parks with Martin Luther King, the local pastor who spoke to the media on her behalf in December 1955 and became a globally famous leader of non-violent protest.

In 1957, President Eisenhower used federal troops to enforce the desegregation of a school in Arkansas. Elsewhere, however, segregation remained largely unchallenged. It was in response to this – which was effectively recognition of the failure of legal attempts to desegregate the South – which further direct action occurred. King was involved with this, often creating publicity rather than providing the initial impetus for action. So when he came to bring publicity to the Albany Movement, already under way, he found himself immediately caught up in a wave of arrests. As was his habit, he chose to go to jail to write letters to the press rather than pay his fine. The local chief of police, Laurie Pritchett, was so concerned at this that he paid King's fine for him and had him released.

For King, this was the era of seeking publicity to highlight the injustice and oppression of life in the South. He moved his operation away from Albany because Pritchett had refused to provide him with the publicity he wanted; instead he moved into Birmingham, Alabama, where he knew that the local police chief, Eugene 'Bull' Connor, would be more obliging. And so he was. King's campaign led to violence by the police; dogs were used against protestors and the pictures went around the world, where America's claim to democratic leadership began to seem hollow. Jailed again, King wrote a letter explaining why he was there – because injustice was there.

The culmination of this phase of the Civil Rights Movement was the March on Washington (for Jobs and Freedom) in August 1963. Although the different groups involved did not initially agree about what they wanted the march to achieve – whether it was a gesture of support for the Civil Rights Act the president had been promoting, or a more generalised protest against black economic exclusion – they did agree to march together. Bused in to the sound of protest songs such as '*We Shall Overcome*', which characterised the sit-ins and other peaceful protests,

250 000 people turned up in Washington to listen to a platform of singers and speakers including Bob Dylan, a young singer of protest songs, and King, who gave a speech in which he consistently repeated the refrain, '*I have a dream*', describing a future world in which segregation, especially in education, did not exist.

1964–65: The next phase of the Civil Rights Movement began in the aftermath of the assassination of President Kennedy. The new president seemed willing to pass legislation, but King had come to change his mind about his goals. During 1964 he clearly turned towards promoting not economic opportunity and general liberty, but voter registration. The greatest injustice, he decided, was that African American voters in so many of the southern states were unable to vote to overturn the mayors, governors and police chiefs who oppressed them. Once again, this was not his idea; voter registration drives had been going on for some time and King had been in Florida, not Mississippi, during the Freedom Summer, which was aimed at voter registration. In 1965, King sought a Voting Rights Act to go with the Civil Rights Act of 1964, which it was clear had changed little in Mississippi.

He chose to campaign with a four-day march from Selma to Montgomery, the capital of Alabama, in March 1965. It was the setting for the murder of two civil rights volunteers – as in Mississippi, the victims were both black and white. As the marchers reached Montgomery, the Confederate flag could be seen flying from the state capitol building. The local sheriff in Selma had used electric cattle prods on the protestors. The Voting Rights Act of 1965 was passed in response to the events in Montgomery.

There were three attempts to march. The first, on 7 March, became known as Bloody Sunday after Alabama's state troopers gassed and beat local protestors. The second, two days later, attracted national attention from the start, and was attended by many protestors from out of state; the state troopers stood aside but a wary King obeyed a court order not to march. That evening James Reeb, a white minister from Boston, was killed. In the face of national and international outrage, President Johnson went to Congress to push for the passage of the Voting Rights Act, declaring that Selma represented a pivotal point in history. On 21 March, the march to Montgomery finally went ahead, with federal troops protecting the marchers whom Governor George Wallace – like Johnson, a Democrat – refused to protect.

1965–75: The Voting Rights Act was, broadly, successful. African American enfranchisement resulted by the early 1970s in the creation of a 'New South' in which segregation melted away. The focus of the Civil Rights Movement shifted to the North, where it was unsuccessful because the problems it sought to address were not the same. In the last three years of his life King campaigned against poverty. He campaigned against the Vietnam War. He visited Chicago to campaign against the poor housing endured by poor (black) people there. The issues, there, were different. The problem was not of African American exclusion. It was of the exclusion of poor people who were very often black and living in the city centres vacated by white people moving to the new suburbs. On the night before he died, King spoke in Memphis, Tennessee, on behalf of striking sanitary workers (who happened to be black: that they felt underpaid and mistreated was a function not of their race but of their poverty).

Grassroots and presidential agency in the Civil Rights Movement

A common view of the Civil Rights Movement is of reluctant presidents pushing legislation upon even more reluctant members of Congress, under severe pressure from a mass movement of African Americans and white liberals led by inspirational figures and opposed by racist southern whites. The reality is far, far more nuanced. President Truman had a far greater impact on the Civil Rights Movement than he might have anticipated. It was not his idea to campaign for civil rights in 1948 in anything more than a moderate way, but he embraced the ideas of the mayor of Minneapolis, Hubert Humphrey, in calling for real civil rights in North and South. He began the transformation of the Democratic Party into one that would fight for civil rights, and deliver major changes two decades later under Johnson, and in memory of Kennedy. By embracing civil rights as a Democratic issue, Truman also made it into a northern as well as a southern issue. Conservative Republicans were sometimes enthusiastic about civil rights for political reasons. Senator Taft of Ohio had attempted to drum up support for civil rights in 1946 as part of an attempt to re-engage the Republican Party with the African American vote, which it had begun to lose as a result of the New Deal. In 1957, Nixon toyed with the idea of trying to push a Voting Rights Act through Congress in order to fragment the Democratic Party. He had already worked with Senate Majority Leader Lyndon Johnson in order to pass the Civil Rights Act, which supported the *Brown* decision. The leadership of both parties sought to use the Civil Rights Movement to their own political advantage.

Presidents and congressional leaders were not the major movers of the movement. The various groups that took part in the Civil Rights Movement as it progressed from legal challenges to direct action are summarised in Table 4.4. There were also key characters – Linda Brown, she of the legal case of 1954, was still fighting segregation in Topeka schools in the 1990s.

The real importance of the initial legal challenges to segregation, which saw segregation itself (and therefore every Jim Crow law) declared illegal, was that it meant that peaceful protestors could deliberately get themselves arrested, so that they could challenge the arrests and gain publicity for the cause. Martin Luther King Jr., aimed to use non-violence to provoke arrests and violence, and for gruesome pictures to be beamed around America and the world. It was legal action that gave Eisenhower the chance to demonstrate his support for the Supreme Court, if not for Civil Rights, by sending federal troops to enforce the Supreme Court's decision that schools in Little Rock, Arkansas, should be integrated in 1957.

There were all sorts of reasons for integrating schools: education was important, after all, and the protests against school integration were also great publicity. Being publicly arrested was the entire point of Freedom Rides, which were never an all-black affair, and it was part of the point of sit-ins and bus boycotts. This needed organisation, but the organisation often happened at a very low level – Freedom Rides came from university campuses, for example. Leaders might then emerge – King emerged out of the Montgomery bus boycotts. King's influence transcended that of his organisation, the Southern Christian Leadership Conference (SCLC), and his message of non-violent protest, inspired by Mohandas Gandhi in India, came to dominate the Civil Rights Movement in the South.

Sit-ins and boycotts spread around the country, with added publicity from the relatively new medium of television. They were at their most effective when they had a direct economic impact on businesses. When black people stopped riding the buses in Alabama, bus companies felt the pressure and many reversed their policies. This economic pressure led to retaliatory violence and the return of the Ku Klux Klan. Ultimately, the violence and the marches convinced Kennedy to act; his successor Lyndon Johnson pushed through much of the legislation in his name.

Johnson accepted that white southerners objected to civil rights but gambled that he would attract enough liberal votes to compensate, and he saw the need for liberal reforms. Although the legal reforms of 1964–65 ultimately sorted the South out, the North was still divided. The issue there was urban deprivation as much as it was the failure to provide separate schools; there were whole areas that had no formal segregation because they were entirely black. In the cities the Civil Rights Movement took a different tone. The Nation of Islam was violent and separatist, wanting not segregation but equality and respect. A famous member of the movement, Cassius Clay, changed his name to Muhammad Ali, rejecting his 'slave name'. He rejected his status as an American hero (a hero because he was the charismatic heavyweight champion of the world in boxing). He would later be jailed for refusing to fight in Vietnam. Here was a man whom Americans wanted to praise, but who refused to accept an American identity.

Reform never really happened in the North. The race riots that began in 1965 were also urban riots about poverty. The concept of 'Black Power' was about the power of poor blacks. It was possible to be black and do well – to become middle class – but being middle class was a white mode of existence. The Nation of Islam and the Black Panthers argued for separate black identity. In the South, reform did ultimately occur. Future president Jimmy Carter, when governor of Georgia in 1971, became part of the wave of '**New South**' Democratic governors who refused to allow segregation to occur: they had been able to come to power at least in part because of the enfranchisement of black voters in their states.

Martin Luther King Jr. and Malcolm X

The two most famous civil rights leaders of their day did not see eye to eye (Figure 4.7). They shared a mutual respect for their shared aim of achieving racial equality, but there were several differences between them. Martin Luther King Jr. was a Christian preacher who practised and preached non-violence and believed that a combination of economic action, voting reform and protest would produce integration. Malcolm X was a Muslim who believed that relations between white and black people had irretrievably broken down in America, and that only a violent black response could prevent further white violence. He advocated 'the ballot or the bullet'. X was, obviously, a pseudonym: the Nation of Islam's practice was for adherents to abandon their 'slave name' (his was Malcolm Little). X left the Nation of Islam for its refusal to cooperate with other civil rights groups: members of the NoI (Nation of Islam) assassinated him a year later.

Group	Leader(s)	Founded	Aims	Major events
Black Panthers	Huey Newton Bobby Seale	1966, Oakland, California	Protection from police brutality. Becomes a Marxist revolutionary group.	Considered by the FBI to be the biggest threat to national security
Congress of Racial Equality (CORE)	James Peck Bayard Rustin	1942, Chicago, Illinois	Non-violent resistance to segregation	Freedom Rides, March on Washington, Freedom Summer
National Association for the Advancement of Colored People (NAACP)	Thurgood Marshall Rosa Parks	1909, Baltimore, Maryland	Legal challenges to segregation	Brown v Board Montgomery Bus Boycott Little Rock March on Washington
Nation of Islam (NoI)	Elijah Muhammad Louis Farrakhan Malcolm X	1930, Detroit, Michigan	Black power Equal rights Violent response to white violence	Assassination of Malcolm X
Organization for Afro-American Unity	Malcolm X	1964, New York, New York	Heightening the political consciousness of black Americans Pan-Africanism	Freedom Summer
Southern National Leadership Conference (SCLC)	Martin Luther King, Jr Bayard Rustin Ella Baker	1957, Atlanta, Georgia	Non-violent direct action against segregation	Birmingham Campaign March on Washington March from Selma
Student Non-violent Coordinating Committee (SNCC)	Ella Baker Stokely Carmichael (1966)	1960, Raleigh, North Carolina	Direct-action protests, voter registration. Peaceful (before 1966) Black Power (after 1966)	Sit-ins Freedom Rides March on Washington Freedom Summer

Table 4.4: Major civil rights events and developments.

Figure 4.7: Malcolm X's only public meeting with Martin Luther King Jr. 26 March 1964.

ACTIVITY 4.8

Ella Baker, another civil rights activist, commented of Martin Luther King Jr that, 'Martin didn't make the Movement: the Movement made Martin.' Do you agree?

As well as what you have read in this section, you should consider the following:

- King was an excellent publicist who knew how to use his fame.
- While he was a leader of the SNLC, he was not its chief planner.
- King chose his campaigns for maximum impact.
- He had not set out to speak on behalf of Rosa Parks in December 1955, and had had very little notice of the opportunity to speak to the media on her behalf.

ACTIVITY 4.9

Record details of the Civil Rights Movement in the appropriate columns in the table. Which of those methods was the most effective in gaining civil rights?

Direct action peaceful protest	Violent protest	Legal action	Lobbying the government

 Thematic link: individuals and groups

Youth culture

The cliché is that teenagers were invented in the 1950s. What the cliché means is this: in the 1950s there were for the first time specific activities for young people to do, and sufficient leisure time in which to do them. The social movements of the 1920s (jazz and Flappers) had been curtailed by the Depression. The 1950s, though, were an age of plenty. The separate youth culture only applied to young people with money. Poor slum-dwellers or those still scraping a living on subsistence farms did not have their lives transformed.

Actually, some of them did, because Johnson's educational reforms established an absolute expectation that every child would go to school and the real possibility of even the poorest winning a merit scholarship to university. This might have had a transformational effect on some very poor communities were it not that those favoured enough to leave for university often did not come back. For others, especially by the later 1960s, university was more about having a convenient excuse to avoid the draft.

The activities, which are described below, are more of a menu than a prescription. Some young people enjoyed and followed them; others did not. Some of them were enjoyed while still at school. Others were the preserve of students at universities. Some of the elements of youth culture were:

- Rock and roll music – stars included Elvis Presley and Bill Haley and the Comets (as early as 1954). By the 1970s this might involve disco dancing to the Bee Gees.
- Crazes such as hula hoops (1958).
- Movies – especially drive-ins – that featured film stars such as Marilyn Monroe (d.1962) and James Dean (d.1955).
- Sexual freedoms brought about by a decline in traditional morality on the one hand and increased availability of means of contraception including (early 1960s) the birth control pill.

- Long hair, outrageous clothes and drug use – cannabis or LSD (although some young people were horrified by this and viewed all these things as unpatriotic).
- Increased political participation – from joining in with protest movements to voting at the age of 18 (1971).
- Fast-food restaurants such as McDonalds (which began to hit it big in the mid-1950s).

What underlay all this? Affluence and opportunity, certainly, but also practical things like the availability of televisions and music radio, which enabled the quicker spread of cultural ideas. As with everything else in American life the car was a vital tool for young Americans wanting to congregate away from their families, or to go to university across the country, or to have some privacy on a date.

ACTIVITY 4.10

The two photographs in Figure 4.8, the first from the Berkeley Free Speech Movement in late 1964, and the second from an anti-war march in Berkeley in 1967, illustrate the pace of change in youth culture. Make a list of what appears to have changed in three years in Berkeley. Account for the changes.

Figure 4.8: The Berkeley Free Speech Movement.

Protest and the mass media

Youth culture, the Civil Rights Movement and the Vietnam War led to the creation of a culture of protest in the 1960s. By the end of Johnson's time in office there was a deeply embedded conflict between what Richard Nixon called the 'silent majority' and vocal, sometimes violent protestors – in fact the conflict was so deeply embedded that it must have been there before. The later 1960s were a perfect time for protest for a number of reasons:

- The economy was sound, but turning down – this was enough to provoke protest without placing people under so much economic stress that they did not have time to protest.
- There was a large younger generation – the **Baby Boomers** – who were educated and available for protest.
- Communications technology meant that local protests could quickly become global through the medium of television.
- There were clear focuses for protest, including an unpopular war.

These factors created between them a situation whereby protest was almost inevitable. By 1968 youth culture in America was synonymous with opposition to the Vietnam War. The point was not lost on young people – the draft affected them. They were less ready than their parents' generation had been to embark upon a far-off war, especially when, as with Vietnam, the causes of the war seemed murky, the reward uncertain and the opportunities for glory and pride seemed far distant. The protest movements of the 1960s were virtually all youth movements at heart – if not in leadership, then in their activists. Young people had time, they had ideas and they had ideals. A 20-year-old could risk or even encourage arrest in the cause of civil rights far more easily than a 40-year-old with a family to support.

A Free Speech Movement began at the University of California, Berkeley, in 1964 (Figure 4.8) after the university attempted to restrict student political activity on campus. By 1968 student protest was so serious that President Johnson could barely leave the White House. Protest did not end with Johnson's presidency, but it did become less popular. In 1970, when student protestors were killed by the National Guard in two separate instances (four at Kent State University, Ohio, and two at Jackson State, Mississippi), President Nixon's opinion polling found that 90 percent of the country was on the side of the federal troops. The protests of the youth movement seemed to many Americans to be out of hand. There were cultural reasons for this:

- Many Americans felt the traditional unease that the older generation has when the younger generation rebels.
- Some Americans also felt that it was un-American to protest when the economy was failing and the country was at war.
- Others felt that any form of protest was contrary to the WASP work ethic, showing these students (with all this free time) to be overprivileged.

The Peace Movement, as the Free Speech Movement became, was characterised by draft-dodging (fleeing to Canada or burning your draft card, which could carry a six-month prison sentence) but also by protest songs, hippies, flower power and drugs. As befitted a peace movement with its organisational origins at least partly in the Civil Rights Movement, its methods were peaceful.

The calls for peace were made stronger by the media. The American army now deployed with journalists embedded with them; occasionally these journalists did not prove compliant when the army tried to censor their output. Word got out about American disasters, of the massacre of civilians, of indiscipline in the ranks and of the messiness of war. Journalists were forbidden from covering the repatriation of the bodies of dead American soldiers, lest the images fuel further unrest. When Walter Cronkite, a respected journalist, was openly critical of American strategy after the Tet Offensive in 1968, LBJ was heard to remark that if he had lost Cronkite he had lost America.

The Black Revolt

In the late 1960s, radicalised, violent African American leaders became more noticeable than peacemakers like King. The reasons for the Black Revolt, as this new protest became known, were clear enough. In the North, black unemployment was twice the national average and black poverty twice as bad. Schools were worse, housing was worse and there was little money in the affected communities to repair this. The radical Nation of Islam, under Elijah Muhammad, had splintered. Malcolm X had left to form the Organization of Afro-American Unity and brought even greater publicity to the idea that white and black people had fundamentally different needs and goals. In the wake of Malcolm X's death and the riots that began in 1965 other groups were formed, such as the Black Panthers in Oakland, California (1966). The idea of Black Power recalled Marcus Garvey's call in the 1920s for racial consciousness and pride. Black Power wanted black businesses, homes, schools, politics – and even guerrilla warfare. This was not peaceful protest at all.

Feminism

There were other protest movements in the 1960s. Feminism made great strides. Betty Friedan's *The Feminine Mystique* (1963) criticised the way in which women were referred to in relation to men – they were someone's wife or mother or daughter. Nixon had let slip in the 1959 Kitchen Debate his expectation that women should be grateful for all the new labour-saving devices in their homes. The family, with the mother playing a traditional role in child rearing, represented the new aspirational suburban lifestyle where a nuclear family would live in a family house with a family car, going on family vacations. Feminism grew up to argue that women should have equality as people. Pickets attacked the Miss America pageants to argue that women should not be objectified. For women, the legal battle was partly won by 1970. The Equal Rights Amendment that was pushed by the National Organization for Women failed in the 1980s, with southern states declining to ratify lest women who wished to be housewives should feel oppressed.

In the Kitchen Debate Nixon had measured the progress of a society by how much women were helped at home. Legally, this was not the position at all – women were fully autonomous – but in practice women's rights had a long way to go. As late as the 1970s, women often had difficulty obtaining credit without a man's signature. Female politicians were still the exception rather than the norm – there were two female senators in the 1960s, one of whom, Margaret Smith of Maine, made a spectacularly unsuccessful attempt to gain the Republican presidential nomination in 1964.

The National Organization for Women ('What do we want?' 'Equal rights!' 'When do we want them?' 'NOW!') was formed in 1966 by activists including Friedan. Feminism as a political movement had been a long time coming. Why did it come in the 1960s? Figure 4.9 gives some suggested reasons. By the end of the 1960s, feminism was a force both on the ground and in Congress, where the interracial nature of the movement became apparent when Shirley Chisholm, Democrat of New York, emerged as a leader of women's rights, saying that she felt she had faced far more discrimination over her gender than over her race. A remarkable woman, Chisholm would later gain greater fame when running for the presidential nomination in 1972. She visited George Wallace, the segregationist former governor of Alabama, who had been seriously wounded in an assassination attempt while he was also running for president, because it was in her view the right thing to do.

The position of women is also touched on in the section on new cultural developments, including the role of women and the position of African Americans.

The same pattern has applied to gay rights. Homosexuality became legal in the 1960s, although many states retained creative ways of punishing homosexual acts. The Gay Liberation Front was formed in 1969 in response to a police raid on the Stonewall Inn in Manhattan, New York.

The USA and international relations

From 1945 to 1990 international relations across the world were dominated by the Cold War. Superpower status seemed to bring a particular sense of responsibility with it. One area in which this was expressed was the Middle East. In 1948 the British had retreated from control there, unable to sustain their power because of their failing post-war economy. There were, in the aftermath of the Holocaust, persuasive calls for a Jewish homeland to be established in Israel. Truman backed these calls for domestic electoral reasons, as well as out of a sense of American guilt over turning Jewish refugees away in the late 1930s. The identification of America as Israel's greatest ally, and the importance of the Jewish vote in New York, New Jersey and ultimately Florida, have been compelling themes in American foreign policy ever since. When Israel went to war with its neighbours in the 1960s and 1970s, the Americans were dragged in. When the Organisation of Petroleum Exporting Countries (OPEC) – which included many Islamic and Middle Eastern countries – put punitive tariffs onto oil prices in 1973, America would suffer.

The Cold War and relations with the USSR and China

The Cold War was an ideological, economic and geopolitical conflict set against a background of nuclear weapons. The major players in the Cold War were always the USA and USSR, which were more-or-less identified as leaders of their sections of the world, but that clear picture of a **bipolar** world was disrupted in the 1960s

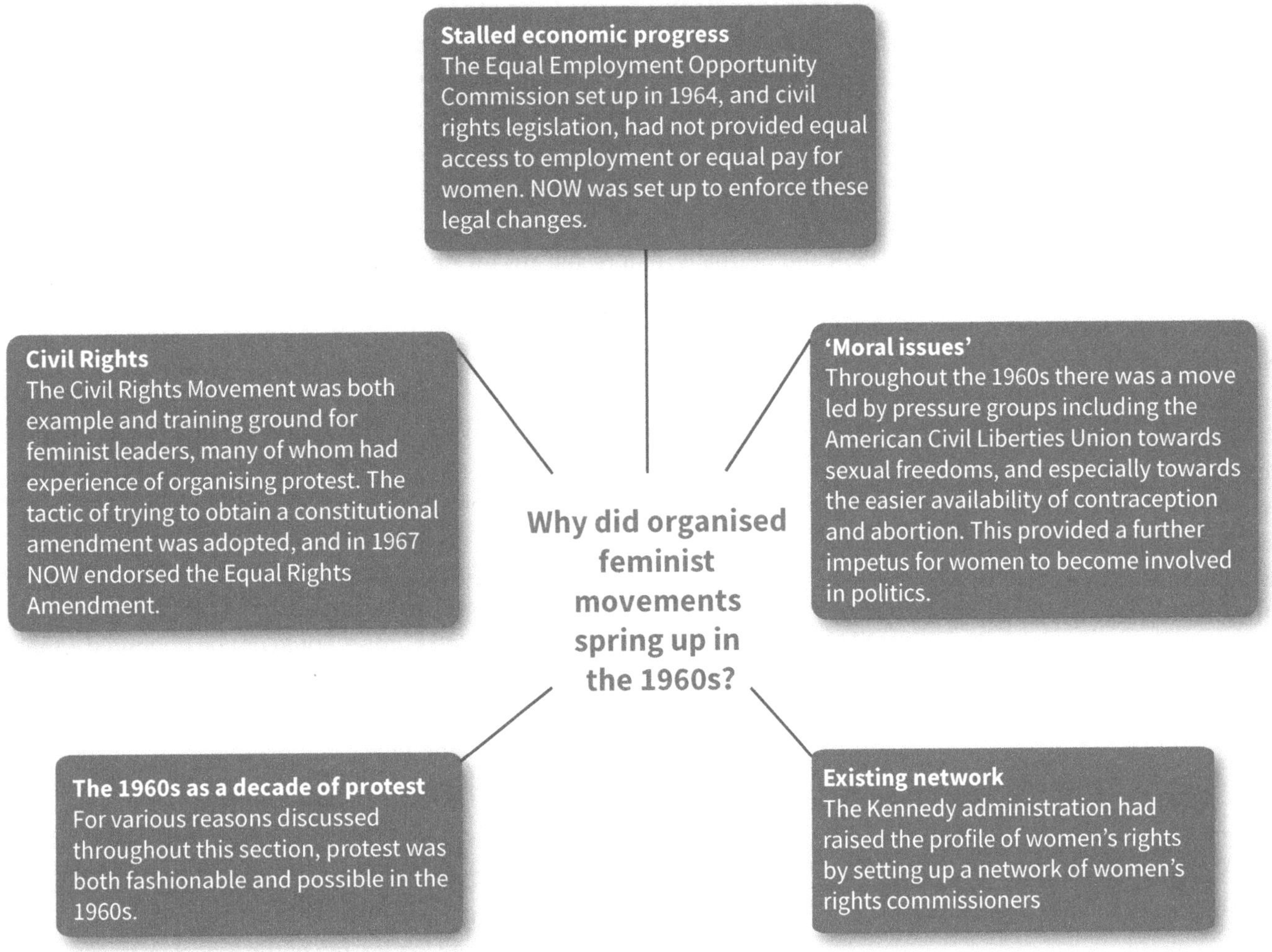

Stalled economic progress
The Equal Employment Opportunity Commission set up in 1964, and civil rights legislation, had not provided equal access to employment or equal pay for women. NOW was set up to enforce these legal changes.

Civil Rights
The Civil Rights Movement was both example and training ground for feminist leaders, many of whom had experience of organising protest. The tactic of trying to obtain a constitutional amendment was adopted, and in 1967 NOW endorsed the Equal Rights Amendment.

'Moral issues'
Throughout the 1960s there was a move led by pressure groups including the American Civil Liberties Union towards sexual freedoms, and especially towards the easier availability of contraception and abortion. This provided a further impetus for women to become involved in politics.

Why did organised feminist movements spring up in the 1960s?

The 1960s as a decade of protest
For various reasons discussed throughout this section, protest was both fashionable and possible in the 1960s.

Existing network
The Kennedy administration had raised the profile of women's rights by setting up a network of women's rights commissioners

Figure 4.9: Feminist movements in the 1960s.

as China came to take over some of the Soviet Union's leadership functions in the communist world. Table 4.5 summarises the differences between the sides.

The origins of the Cold War have been the subject of dispute among historians. It has been blamed on the Soviet leader Stalin, whose classically Russian foreign policy aim was to have an impenetrable barrier between the Russian western border and hostile European powers such as Germany. It has been blamed on American misunderstandings of Soviet motivation. It has been blamed on the deliberate overreaction of Americans to legitimate Soviet concerns. It has been blamed on Truman's failure to realise that Stalin had lied to Roosevelt with Roosevelt's full knowledge and complicity.

Truman's first overseas mission had been to attend the second victors' conference of 1945, in July and August at Potsdam. His problem there was that FDR had misrepresented the first, in February at Yalta. He had told Congress that the decisions made at Yalta 'ought to spell the end of the system of unilateral action,

ACTIVITY 4.11

In what ways were Americans united, and in what ways were they divided, from 1945–75? Make two lists. Use your lists to decide whether Americans were on the whole united or divided. Is it possible to come up with a single definition of 'American' for this period?

ACTIVITY 4.12

ACTIVITY 4.12

What methods of protest were used by the various protest groups of the 1960s and early 1970s? To what extent did different groups use different methods?

Key term

bipolar: in international relations, **polarity** is the identification of particular groups of countries that are aligned. During the early Cold War, most American politicians saw the world as bipolar, meaning that countries were either democratic, capitalist, individualistic and free or socialist, communist and unfree.

the exclusive alliances, the spheres of influence, the balances of power, and all the other expedients that have been tried for centuries and have always failed'. In fact, Yalta divided up Europe, producing a clear path for Stalin to create a sphere of influence for himself out of the countries of Eastern Europe. Stalin had perceived an impending conflict between capitalism and communism, and in that sense was more responsible than Truman for the build-up of tensions after 1945. He was not intent on provoking war, but in a long-term build-up of communist power, and in an age-old Russian goal of having some strongly defended states between the USSR and Germany, to forestall any further German invasions. The imposition of communist dictatorships in Eastern Europe was the most destabilising thing he did, but it had been fore-ordained at Yalta. Truman's problem was that he could hardly say so without accusing Roosevelt, his heroic predecessor, of lying.

The conference at Potsdam (Figure 4.10) came a month after the San Francisco Conference to establish the United Nations, at which the Soviet point of view was largely ignored. At Potsdam, Truman had been forced to tell Stalin about the impending atomic attack on Japan – Stalin had known about the existence of nuclear weapons for some time, and did not even bother to pretend to be surprised. At Potsdam, Truman was forced to concede that the plans made at Yalta for free and fair elections in liberated Europe would not be honoured – there would certainly be elections, but Stalin had no intention of allowing them to be free in the countries that the Russians had liberated. The Russians did not play any part in helping to reconstruct Germany, which was divided into four zones of

Country	Ideology	Economics	Geopolitical aims
USA (1945)	Democracy, freedom	Capitalist with small but growing welfare state	Domination of the western hemisphere (Monroe doctrine); leadership of the Free World
USSR (1949)	Marxist-Leninist Individuals work for the common good Controlled	Communist, centrally planned economy	Officially, to promote world socialism and spread the Revolution. Unofficially, to maintain client states in Eastern Europe as a barrier against German invasion
UK (1951)	Democracy, freedom	Capitalist with large welfare state	Successful decolonisation while retaining global influence
France (1964)	Democracy, freedom	Capitalist with very large welfare state	Initially, maintenance of French Empire. Ultimately, maintenance of global influence and European leadership
People's Republic of China [PRC] (1965)	Marxist-Maoist Individuals work for the common good Controlled	Communist, centrally organised economy	Initially, recognition as legitimate Chinese government. Then influence over Communist countries in East Asia, finally global leadership of Communism

Table 4.5: The nuclear powers during the Cold War. The date given is the date of acquisition of nuclear weapons.

occupation (the others held by Britain and France). Instead, Truman antagonised Stalin, perhaps by trying to hold him to agreements that he had not made at Yalta.

Figure 4.10: Clement Attlee, the new British Prime Minister, Harry Truman and Josef Stalin at Potsdam. Their facial expressions, and the body language of their aides, are interesting.

In the early years of the Cold War Truman had two main aims. The first was to prevent further expansion of the communist (Soviet) sphere of influence. The former British Prime Minister Winston Churchill had announced in a speech in Missouri, Truman's home, in 1946, that 'an Iron Curtain has descended across Europe'. American strategy was to prevent the Iron Curtain from moving any further west. This led to the formation of the **Truman Doctrine**, which stated that Americans would provide military support to democratic regimes, and to the Marshall Plan, which was the donation by Americans of billions of dollars of aid to countries in Europe in 1947–48. There was also a Point Four Plan to spend $400 million in Asia and Latin America in 1949. These were specific counter-measures to Stalin's tactic of sending money into Eastern European countries and allowing local communist parties to distribute it, while also sending in the Soviet army to 'oversee' elections – a tactic that delivered a number of communist governments. This attempt to prevent the expansion of communism is called containment. Truman's second aim, which was linked, was to reconstruct Western Europe as quickly as possible to prevent a further war. He was doing the same in Japan. The lessons of the First World War had been learnt.

John Lewis Gaddis, in *The Cold War*,[8] argued that it was a combination of all these factors, including Stalin's own paranoia, which led him to disbelieve any reassurance from Truman.

Key term

Truman Doctrine: Truman's statement that America would support free peoples resisting subjugation, by which he meant communist rule.

The Red Scare that Truman faced was the first cultural expression of the Cold War in the United States. There were other real features of this element of foreign policy. The permanent state of war led to a growth in presidential authority; there was, after all, a constant emergency. The military draft was continued, and dissenters were branded as unpatriotic, or traitors. Military spending was also an important factor. The military spending for the Second World War had decisively ended the Great Depression; now many members of the political and economic elite regarded Cold War military spending as a necessary means to forestall the return of depression. Moreover, the '**military-industrial complex**' (Eisenhower's term) had grown powerful, and the national security state actively resisted public accountability – especially when those who might carry out the scrutiny were so publicly suspected of communist sympathies. American patriotism developed along the lines of Cold War prestige, pride in the army and right-wing anti-socialism.

Berlin

All but one of the major points of conflict in the Cold War came at the points where the liberating armies had met at the end of the Second World War – Berlin, Korea and Vietnam. The other was in Cuba. In Berlin the first crisis was in 1948–49, and it centred on the decision of the Americans, French and British to combine their three zones of Germany, putting pressure on the Soviets to do the same and meet the commitment made at Yalta to reconstruct a united Germany. To nobody's great surprise, the Soviets refused to do so, continuing to administer their zone of Germany and passing up the chance to reduce their sphere of influence. The capital, Berlin, was inside the Soviet zone but had been divided like the rest of the country. Here was a western enclave 300 miles behind the Iron Curtain. Stalin tried to blockade it, hoping to secure a victory against the Americans. The blockade and associated American airlift lasted for nearly a year from June 1948–49, and was stopped only when Stalin had attained nuclear weapons, given Truman more problems to worry about. The Americans continued to use West Berlin as a shop window for both American protection and American capitalism. As long as West Berlin remained free, American protection seemed worthwhile. And as long as it remained prosperous and capitalist (and many resources were poured into it to ensure that it did), then the communists living across the city could be reminded of the superiority of capitalism. It was also a handy base for espionage. It was a combination of all of these factors that led to the erection of the Berlin Wall by the Soviets in 1961 (Figure 4.11).

By 1961 the USSR had come under pressure from the East German authorities to close the border between East and West Berlin. There were a number of reasons for doing this. Western spies used their freedom of access to and from the East with impunity. Eastern residents were moving West, attracted by the opulent lifestyle that the Americans and West Germans had ensured was on display in West Berlin, as part of their propaganda campaign against communism. In the weeks after a disastrous Vienna Summit in 1961, Khrushchev came to believe that Kennedy was weak and could be bullied. In early August 1961, Secretary of State Rusk and his French and British equivalents, meeting in Paris, decided that any action taken by the USSR in Berlin would be defensive in nature, and was not worth risking a war. Khrushchev's intelligence operation was excellent, and he knew about this; within a week, a barbed wire fence was erected in Berlin in the night of 12–13 August 1961, and became a solid wall over the following months. By 27 October the situation had degenerated and tanks faced each other across the Brandenburg Gate, the iconic central zone of Berlin that was just behind the Wall. Rusk told the American commander not to risk war over the Wall; Kennedy and Khrushchev meanwhile brokered a solution that saw the tanks retreating in turn, a few metres at a time. A wall, Kennedy said, 'is a hell of a lot better than a war'. West Berlin became even more a focal point of the Cold War; Kennedy expressed his solidarity in 1963 by saying that he was proud to be a Berliner, whose precarious situation was representative of that of the whole world.

Figure 4.11: The Berlin Wall divided Berlin in two. This is a view of the Wall in 1961 where it separated the iconic Brandenburg Gate, on the East German side, from the rest of the city.

Korea

In late 1940s Europe, a peaceful solution had been found. In Asia, that would prove less easy. To the horror of the Truman administration and US Congress, the capitalist leader of China, Chiang Kai-shek, had lost the civil war in his country to Mao Zedong, a communist. By the middle of 1949 the capitalist government had effective control only of the island of Taiwan; there were two Chinas. The communist China, the People's Republic, immediately set about joining the communist world. Mao had been a revolutionary leader in China for 20 years. He was happy to defer, to an extent, to the leader of the USSR, which had after all managed the first successful communist revolution. He also wanted to spread communism further.

The obvious place was in Korea. The USSR had liberated Korea from Japanese rule at the same time as the Americans; they had met at the 38th parallel, a line of latitude, and the country had been divided into two zones with different systems of government. By 1950, communist North Korea felt that it might be in a position to take over the whole country. Mao, Stalin and the North Korean leader Kim Il-sung met in Moscow in January 1950. We do not know exactly what transpired, although a best guess looks something like this: Stalin permitted Kim to invade the South, with Chinese assistance, as long as he, Stalin, and the USSR did not have to become directly involved. In America, meanwhile, the National Security Council (NSC) had issued a memorandum, NSC-68, which advocated a more active **containment** – now, communism should be actively contained everywhere, not just in Europe, and not just in opposition to the Soviet Union. The new secretary of state, Dean Acheson, mindful of this highly secret debate, had appeared to suggest that the Americans might be willing to leave Korea alone – after all, with China communist they no longer had an ally to protect in the Yellow Sea. Certainly, Kim expected that he would succeed.

The fighting in Korea was brutal. In Berlin, there was an uneasy stalemate – and nothing changed. In Korea, nothing changed despite the fighting. In June 1950 the North Koreans took the Americans by surprise and pushed them back so far that they nearly won; the Americans responded in force that autumn and nearly destroyed North Korea entirely. By 1951 the war had become a muddy stalemate in the rough vicinity of the original border. Truman had a public row with his commander, General MacArthur. As a result of this, Truman confirmed that nuclear weapons were to be for strategic use only, and were to be controlled directly by the civilian authorities – the president. He also confirmed that **rollback** – MacArthur's preferred alternative to containment – would not be acceptable. The Korean War would ultimately ruin the careers of both men: it was so unpopular that Truman was forced to accept that he would not be re-elected if he ran for the presidency in 1952.

War in Berlin was unthinkable. The European frontier, so neatly symbolised by Berlin, had become the front line between two different systems, and there was no doubt that any necessary means (which meant nuclear weapons) would be used to defend it. There was no such concern about Korea, where direct conflict between nuclear powers could be avoided. The Soviet Union was not opposed to the invasion of South Korea by the communist North, but nor was it actively involved. Truman pushed the United Nations into letting him lead a police action in Korea to contain the communist incursion there. In fact, American policy had been thrown into disarray after the defeat of the capitalist forces of Chiang Kai-shek in the Chinese civil war, which had broken out again after the Second World War. In response, Dean Acheson had made a vague pronouncement about a Pacific defence perimeter in the East China Sea. This seemed to include Japan but not Korea: after all, control of Korea would only really be of importance to the Americans should they wish to maintain open door access to mainland China, which was no longer an option.

The Korean War, when it came in 1950–53, cost millions of dollars and millions of lives. It was significant as it enabled Truman to articulate two important doctrines – that containment, rather than rollback (the eradication of communism in countries where it already existed) was the aim of US foreign policy, and that there were no such things as 'tactical' nuclear weapons, meaning that their use was so serious that it could only be authorised by the president in order directly to win a war. It was also significant as it established that the Cold War would not be entirely cold.

The arms race

The arms race is the name given to the process in which the USA and the USSR each attempted to have more, and better, nuclear weapons than the other. In technological terms, the initial atomic fission bombs of the 1940s gave way in the early 1950s to two-stage thermonuclear devices, which used a small fission trigger to control a fusion (hydrogen) bomb. H-bombs produce a far greater yield than A-bombs.

This in turn makes delivery easier. The need for a higher-yield bomb is in reality the need for a less cumbersome delivery system. The bombs dropped in Japan in 1945 needed the USAAF's largest bomber to drop them; by the 1950s, nuclear warheads could be placed onto missiles of varying ranges. By the middle of the 1960s, both sides had intercontinental ballistic missiles (ICBMs) that could travel halfway round the world's surface in half an hour. Both sides placed them in well-defended launch sites, often carved into mountainsides, and on submarines that patrolled the oceans.

The best way to deal with an A-bomb was clearly to shoot down the bomber carrying it; the best way to deal with short- and medium range missiles was to prevent them from being placed within range; the best way to deal with a missile that is within range, including an ICBM, is to prevent its being launched. Shooting missiles down is very difficult.

The logic of all this was deterrence. If both sides had nuclear weapons – it was obvious by the 1960s that both sides had so many nuclear weapons that they could destroy each other – then the situation of mutually assured destruction would apply. Any country thinking it was being fired upon would have half an hour to respond by firing back. So the arms race came to be about having sufficient nuclear weapons that nobody could ever fire them.

By the mid-1950s the situation in Europe was one of deadlock. Two armed camps faced each other – the North Atlantic Treaty Organisation (NATO) led by the USA and the Warsaw Pact, led by the USSR. In Asia, President Eisenhower and Secretary of State Dulles still had hope of assisting Chiang Kai-shek, by now marooned in Taiwan, in regaining control of the rest of China, and they practised their policy of 'New Look' **brinkmanship**, which involved repeatedly threatening to use nuclear weapons against the Chinese, to do so (Figure 4.12). Ultimately very little changed; Mao's communist China, while openly criticising the new, softer, regime of Khrushchev in the USSR, remained under its protection, and it was clear that any reconquest of mainland China would involve a messy operation with American boots on the ground. The South East Asian Treaty Organisation (SEATO) was a *bit* like NATO, except less acute; NATO was an absolute defensive alliance, meaning that an attack on West Germany was the exact equivalent of an attack on the United States, but in Southeast Asia the USA was not willing to be quite so

179

committed to its allies. It could not be; Eisenhower's New Look policy had focused on the creation of nuclear weapons as a cheaper alternative to maintaining a large standing army. Figure 4.13 explains this arms race and the logic of deterrence.

During the 1950s the arms race led Eisenhower to inaction against the Soviet Union, and aggression (which he called brinkmanship) against China. In 1956 it seemed as if Soviet attitudes were changing. Khrushchev had launched an extraordinary attack on the Stalinist system, and appeared to suggest that communist countries could leave the Warsaw Pact. When, in October 1956, Hungary tried to do just that, the eyes of the world were on America – which did not intervene. Nor did America intervene in the Suez Crisis. There was no appetite for war.

Ike's only real decision was over Hungary in 1956. America was supposed to be the leader of the democratic world, and the democratic revolutionaries of Hungary were asking for help. Eisenhower, less than a month away from a presidential election, could not do anything. To 'assist' Hungary would mean an invasion; it would endanger the situation in Germany; it would involve rollback rather than containment. Eisenhower also recognised that whatever Khrushchev had said in a supposedly secret meeting at 2 a.m., Hungary was of vital strategic interest to the Soviet Union as it formed part of the central European bulwark against further German aggression. So Eisenhower did nothing apart from complain. What could he do? He lacked the will and the resources to start a nuclear war, and the American army was not well placed to launch a conventional war. The USSR was just too dangerous; China was not.

Figure 4.12: Secretary of State John Foster Dulles, right, the architect of the policy of brinkmanship, seen here discussing American intervention in Guatemala in 1954 with President Eisenhower.

In China, Eisenhower's Secretary of State Dulles encouraged Chiang to threaten to reinvade the mainland. This caused the First Taiwan Strait Crisis, a year after the Korean War had ended, when the Republic of China (ROC: Chiang's capitalist nation, now called Taiwan) militarised the islands of Matsu and Kinmen in the Taiwan Strait, which seemed like an obvious prelude to a full-scale invasion of Mao's People's Republic of China (PRC). There was serious discussion within the US government about using nuclear weapons to defend ROC positions on the islands in the Strait in 1954–55 and again in 1958 when Mao shelled the islands: at this point, the USA installed missile bases to defend them. The major result of the policy of brinkmanship in the East China Sea was the build-up of US military power, on behalf of the South Korean and ROC governments, on the borders of communist states. In Korea, this was all about containment; in China, an aggressive policy of containment seemed to imply a threat.

With the arms race came strenuous efforts to avoid using nuclear weapons. This took two forms. The first was the creation of summit diplomacy, whereby representatives of the two powers met to discuss their problems, which often involved offers to limit the numbers of nuclear weapons each had. Many of the early summits were in Geneva; there was also an important summit in 1975 in Helsinki. Right at the start of the Cold War Truman had suggested to Stalin that the USSR abandon its nuclear programme in response for the USA doing the same. As the only man who has ever authorised the use of nuclear weapons, he did not wish to do so again. Stalin had refused – his nuclear programme was more advanced than Truman had known. In the early 1970s two important summits produced treaties designed to normalise relations and move towards the removal of some nuclear weapons: see Figure 4.13. This was part of the process of détente, which was established in the 1970s as a means of reducing the tension caused by the presence of nuclear weapons in the Cold War.

Speak like a historian

By 1959 [Eisenhower] was insisting gloomily that if war ever came "you might as well go out and shoot everyone you see and then shoot yourself." These comments seem completely at odds with Eisenhower's earlier assertion that the United States should fight wars with nuclear weapons "exactly as you would use a bullet or anything else." Now, he appeared to be saying, anyone foolish enough to fire a nuclear "bullet" at an enemy would also be aiming it at himself. Eisenhower … insisted that the United States prepare *only* for an all-out nuclear war.

This view alarmed even Eisenhower's closest advisers. They agreed that a war fought with nuclear weapons would be catastrophic, but they worried that the United States and its allies would never match the military manpower available to the Soviet Union, China, and their allies. To rule out nuclear use altogether would be to invite a non-nuclear war that the West could not win. The solution, most of them believed, was to find ways to fight a *limited* nuclear war; to devise strategies that would apply American technological superiority against the manpower advantage of the communist world.

Source: From J.L. Gaddis, *The Cold War*.[9]

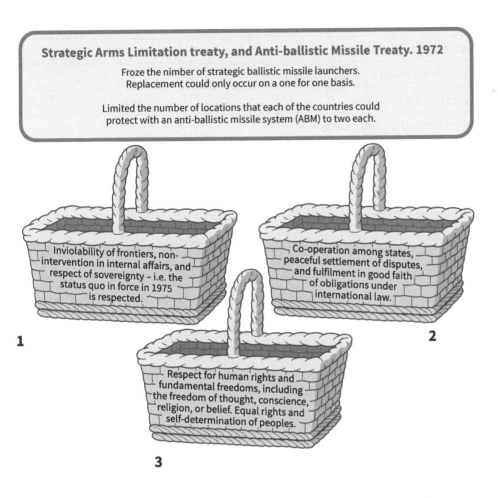

> **Strategic Arms Limitation treaty, and Anti-ballistic Missile Treaty. 1972**
>
> Froze the nimber of strategic ballistic missile launchers.
> Replacement could only occur on a one for one basis.
>
> Limited the number of locations that each of the countries could
> protect with an anti-ballistic missile system (ABM) to two each.

1 Inviolability of frontiers, non-intervention in internal affairs, and respect of sovereignty – i.e. the status quo in force in 1975 is respected.

2 Co-operation among states, peaceful settlement of disputes, and fulfilment in good faith of obligations under international law.

3 Respect for human rights and fundamental freedoms, including the freedom of thought, conscience, religion, or belief. Equal rights and self-determination of peoples.

Figure 4.13: SALT and Helsinki: détente in action. The idea of the Helsinki Accords being organised into baskets is how it was expressed at the time.

The second way in which the Superpowers sought to avoid nuclear conflict was by competing through other means. The space race was a good example of this. Both American and Soviet troops had sought German rocket scientists as they conquered Germany in 1945. The German V2 rocket was of the same basic design as the rockets that put a Soviet satellite – Sputnik I – into space in 1957, and which put Yuri Gagarin into space in 1961, the first man to leave Earth. This blow to American prestige inspired JFK to launch the Apollo missions that put Neil Armstrong – and 11 other Americans – on the Moon from 1969 to 1972. The Kitchen Debate between Nixon and Khrushchev was another example of this, when in 1959 Soviet and American leaders argued about which country had the better houses. As Nixon said, it was better to build better washing machines than better rockets – although he kept building rockets too. A couple of years later John Kennedy established the Peace Corps, which was an opportunity for young people to volunteer overseas doing good work and spreading democratic and capitalist ideas.

Latin America and Cuba

The logic of deterrence nearly failed in Latin America. Throughout this period, America attempted to fulfil its usual Monroe Doctrine assumption of pre-eminence in the western hemisphere. Thus Eisenhower intervened in Guatemala

1 January 1959	Revolution in Cuba. Fidel Castro became its leader.
3 January 1961	Eisenhower closed the US Embassy in Cuba.
17–19 April 1961	Bay of Pigs invasion backed by the CIA failed.
June 1961	Jupiter missiles placed in Turkey.
2 December 1961	Castro declared himself a communist.
15 October 1962	US spy planes flying over Cuba photographed what appeared to be nuclear missile installation sites. Kennedy placed the island under an 800-mile quarantine to prevent further missiles from arriving, and complained to Khrushchev.
22 October 1962	Kennedy went public with this information.
23 October 1962	As Soviet ships approached Cuba, Kennedy moved the quarantine to 500 miles and allowed the supply ship *Marucia* to approach Cuba.
26–27 October 1962	Exchange of letters between Kennedy and Khrushchev.
28 October 1962	Resolution of the crisis.

Table 4.6: Timeline of the Cuban Missile Crisis.

to safeguard the interests of the American United Fruit Company and Standard Oil, and Henry Kissinger, Nixon's chief diplomat, intervened in Chile to safeguard American oil interests in that country. The USSR left America to it, with the one exception of Cuba, where there was an infamous crisis the details of which are illustrated in Table 4.6.

The anti-American revolution in Cuba in 1959 had been successful; Fidel Castro, the revolutionary leader, was a socialist who became a fully-fledged communist in response to the American trade embargo that pushed him into trading with Khrushchev's USSR. President Eisenhower had prepared a plan for a counter-revolutionary invasion of Cuba, intending it to be inherited by Nixon. In the event, it was inherited by Kennedy, who at Nixon's insistence had known nothing of it.

The plan was a dubious one. It involved 1200 Cuban exiles – who had left the country after the revolution – being trained by the CIA to return to the country and regain control of the government. It relied upon a popular uprising in support of the rebels as they moved through Cuba. Kennedy changed the landing point to the Bay of Pigs, which was closer to the capital than the originally intended landing point of Trinidad, an area thought more likely to attract popular support for the rebels as they closed in on Havana. The invasion was an utter failure. There was no popular uprising, the fiction that America had nothing to do with it was barely worth maintaining, and Kennedy looked a fool. Castro, fearing for his regime's stability, declared himself a **Marxist-Leninist** at the end of the year in return for greater access to Soviet goods and trade.

Khrushchev, who had become convinced that Kennedy was weak, made a secret agreement with Castro to install nuclear missiles in Cuba, well within range of the American mainland. For 13 days in October 1962, at first secretly and then in public, there was a tense standoff. On more than one occasion nuclear weapons were nearly used, but they were not. The missiles were removed, more quietly;

so were the USA's missiles in Turkey and Italy, which had been pointing straight at Moscow.

The Cuban Missile Crisis ended with the establishment of the 'hotline' between Moscow and Washington. The leaders of these two great nations would no longer need to go through diplomats, but could speak to each other directly. In foreign policy terms this was absolutely new and revolutionary. This was the effect of nuclear weapons.

China: the end of the bipolar world

American relations with the Chinese government were officially excellent throughout this period; the problem was that there were two Chinese governments, and the one America recognised only controlled the island of Taiwan. The brinkmanship of the 1950s was replaced by acceptance; the People's Republic of China's acquisition of nuclear weapons in 1965, and its obvious involvement in Vietnam (just as it had been involved in Korea) meant that it could no longer be ignored. The North Vietnamese were a client state of the Chinese not the Soviets, and it was perhaps inevitable that Kissinger's diplomatic efforts to end the Vietnam War would involve his going to China. Nixon had long known that it would be important to engage with China; so did the Chinese communist leader Mao Zedong, who said in 1969, 'Think about this. We have the Soviet Union to the north and west, India to the south, and Japan to the east. If all our enemies were to unite, attacking us from the north, south, east and west, what do you think we should do? Think again. Beyond Japan is the USA. Didn't our ancestors counsel negotiating with faraway countries while fighting those that are near?'

For the Chinese had come into conflict with the Soviets. The border dispute that erupted into war in 1969 had been contained, but both Nixon and Mao were aware that there were now three major players in the world. China was not a Superpower, but it could be an irritant; it had (and has) far more resources along its long borders with the USSR, and the invasion and exploitation of Siberia is an obvious strategic goal for China. A shared ideology could not promote peace in the face of a shared border; Mao, moreover, thought that the Soviets had abandoned true communism following the death of Stalin and wished to assert global leadership for himself and for China. Richard Nixon trusted nobody but understood that negotiation might always be helpful. In the long term, his engagement with the Chinese helped to open up the Chinese market for American companies once again. In the short term, it made the USSR a little more careful in its own foreign policy.

The Vietnam War

The eastern part of the Indochinese peninsula had been French before the Second World War, and it was the French who gained control of it after that war. In 1946 there was an immediate war of independence launched by the communist nationalist Ho Chi Minh; this ended in 1954 with the partition of Vietnam, the crescent-shaped country on the east of the peninsula, between a socialist country in the North and a capitalist (and in theory democratic) country in the South. The French were unable to protect the new southern republic and asked the Americans for help. Eisenhower sent military advisers to provide that help, fearing that if

September 1964	Gulf of Tonkin incident: an American warship engaged with North Vietnamese forces. Congress allowed President Johnson to take all necessary measures to support the South Vietnamese.
March 1965	Operation Rolling Thunder, the military invasion of Vietnam, began in response to deteriorating South Vietnamese morale.
November 1967	General Westmoreland, the US commander, predicted victory within a year.
January 1968	After two years of stalemate, North Vietnamese forces launched an overwhelmingly successful attack, the Tet Offensive.
May 1968	As public opinion at home turned against him, Johnson asked for peace talks that would begin in Paris.
January 1969	New President Nixon announced a policy of 'Vietnamisation' – the withdrawal of American soldiers from positions in the war, which South Vietnamese troops would have to take over.
March 1969	Americans started bombing Cambodia to disrupt Viet Cong supply lines.
April 1970	Various revelations about poor American conduct in the war turned American public opinion even further against it.
February 1971	The Americans invaded Laos to disrupt Viet Cong supply lines.
June 1971	The *Pentagon Papers* were leaked – confidential documents suggesting the US had behaved dishonourably throughout the war.
October 1972	Henry Kissinger reached a peace agreement with his North Vietnamese opposite number.
December 1972	Nixon ordered a massive bombing raid on North Vietnam. The North Vietnamese stood firm.
January 1973	The Americans announced the peaceful withdrawal of their ground troops. The South Vietnamese, with American financial aid, continued the war, at first successfully.
December 1974–April 1975	Congress withdrew most of its financial support from South Vietnam, which fell.

Table 4.7: Timeline of the Vietnam War.

any country in Indochina were allowed to be communist, **domino theory** would prevail and the other countries around it would become communist too.

In his inaugural address in 1961, JFK promised to help the cause of freedom wherever it came up; clearly Ho Chi Minh was a threat to the free world. While he was a committed communist, he was no tool of the Soviet Union (although he would later accept Chinese weapons). Ho's sympathisers in South Vietnam – the Viet Cong – continued to destabilise that country, resulting in the assassination of President Diem in 1963. Kennedy continued to send American military advisers. In 1964, with 10 000 military advisers in the country, it was clear that America faced a choice. The military advisers could be withdrawn, leaving South Vietnam to its fate. Or the Americans could send in soldiers, launching another military invasion in eastern Asia and risking a confrontation with the PRC, and replacing the French as another imperial power. Lyndon Johnson campaigned in 1964 on a promise of peace; he won the presidency and it became clear that he had never intended to keep his promise. A timeline of what happened next is shown in Table 4.7.

The Americans lost the Vietnam War for a number of reasons:

- **Weaknesses of American troops**
  Most American troops were young draftees (average age 19) who had only to complete a single year of military service. They received inadequate training and never really gained enough experience to be effective. They were not trained properly for jungle warfare. They were undisciplined – supplies were often stolen and sold on by American quartermasters, and 'fragging' – killing their own gung-ho officers – became surprisingly common.

- **Strengths of Viet Cong and Viet Minh**
  In contrast, the Viet Cong (northern sympathisers in the South) and Viet Minh (northern army) were fighting in home terrain. Their guerrilla warfare worked well, and they could blend into the villages to avoid capture. Inexperienced American troops could not tell who their enemies were.

- **Loss of public confidence in America**
  The American death toll – nearly 60 000 – was such that most communities in America lost someone to the war. Photographs of the Tet Offensive of 1968, and of the My Lai Massacre (which happened in 1968 but only came to light later) eroded public support for the war as it was becoming obvious that Americans were neither winning nor acting well. The troops who were sent to Vietnam often did not want to fight, and the political will to fight was eroded at home.

The significance of the Vietnam War was to tell Americans that the self-conceit of America as the policeman of the world would have to end. Incidents like the My Lai Massacre, the obvious lack of integrity shown by the Johnson administration as shown in the Pentagon Papers, and images of villages and forest destroyed by napalm and Agent Orange, attacked America's status as a force for good. What went wrong? In his memoir *In Retrospect: The Tragedy and Lessons of Vietnam*, Robert McNamara recalls that the Americans approached Vietnam with:

'sparse knowledge, scant experience and simplistic assumptions … I had always been confident that every problem could be solved, but now I found myself confronting one – involving national pride and human life – that could not … We were wrong, terribly wrong.'[10]

Nixon and the end of the Vietnam War

Nixon was elected on a promise to obtain peace with honour in Vietnam. He began the American troop withdrawal early in his time in office. This was the policy of 'Vietnamisation' – an attempt to hand responsibility for the war over to the South Vietnamese forces. It was, after all, a Vietnamese civil war. At the same time as he began his troop withdrawals, Nixon also ordered the bombing of North Vietnam, Laos and Cambodia in an effort to help his South Vietnamese allies by destroying their opposition, and simultaneously Henry Kissinger began secret negotiations with the North Vietnamese. In 1970 Nixon announced the full-scale invasion of Cambodia. He had to do this because of the Ho Chi Minh Trail, the route through Cambodia that was the most direct route between North and South Vietnam. The Americans, of course, could not tell the difference between their allies, the Viet Cong (communist fighters in the South), the Viet Minh (the North Vietnamese army) and non-combatants. The Ho Chi Minh Trail was used to move men and weapons into South Vietnam. See Figure 4.14.

At the same time as Nixon was trying to bring the Vietnam War to an end, he was also negotiating with the Chinese. He and his national security adviser (later secretary of state) Henry Kissinger recognised that the assumptions of United States foreign policy since 1945 were no longer valid for three reasons:

1. China had become powerful enough that it needed to be dealt with independently of the USSR.
2. Ideologies, such as communism, are not fixed factors in international relations. They can change.
3. America had overextended itself (this gave rise to the Nixon Doctrine, which stated that America would no longer take responsibility for the defence of the entire free world).

In 1967, Nixon had written about the need to establish diplomatic relations with China. Kissinger started to make this happen in 1971, when he made a secret visit to Zhou Enlai, who was effectively Mao's deputy and was concerned with foreign affairs. This went well, and Nixon himself then visited Beijing in 1972. Nixon established friendly relations with China, which helped to calm the threat posed by Chinese nuclear weapons, and to stabilise the situation in Indochina even given the American defeat (which is what it clearly really was) in Vietnam. After China, Nixon went to Moscow. Kissinger had also been there, as part of his ongoing effort to pull together talks on nuclear weapon limitation. Brezhnev was keen to receive Nixon because he feared that the USA and China would become too close. Nixon had managed not just to calm American fears of nuclear-powered brinkmanship with China, but also to force the Soviets to the negotiating table.

The USA by 1975

In 1975 the USA was affluent, even in depression; it was internationally self-confident, even in defeat; it was more united than it had been before. Its political parties had realigned, with the party of Lincoln no longer being the party of black people, and the Democrats no longer being the party for which the South was solid.

There were more Americans than ever before – over 200 million of them. They were healthier than before, and older. For the first time, Gray Power – the 10% of the population at retirement age by 1975 – was really important. The idea of retirement communities in sunny areas such as Florida and southern California had taken hold. The affluent retired were politically active, diehard supporters of Medicare and social security, and beginning to mobilise against ageism and sexism. There were also younger people. The Baby Boomer generation – those born in the immediate aftermath of the Second World War – had grown up as a generation used to protest. They had come of age in the 1960s, fought in, or against, or avoided an unpopular war – and entered adulthood at a time when the economy was poor. Crucially, though, even the poor economy only really stopped the middle-class Baby Boomers from making more progress. It did not send them backwards. The generation that came after them did not have it quite as easy; the less affluent middle classes (who were really working class, but did not accept

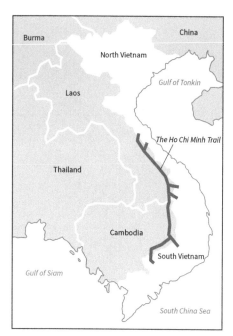

Figure 4.14: Vietnam has an unusual shape, which is why the most direct route from North to South is through Cambodia.

it) were less likely to go to college, and those who did had to pay more for their tuition.

What was society like in the 1970s? The radical protest of the 1960s burnt itself out to be replaced by the 'me' generation that was into self-help, psychotherapy and personal development. Health foods and fitness became popular – organic brown rice was the fashionable totem of the healthcare movement. Individuals searched for authenticity through New Age spirituality and organised religion. The consumer movement became politicised. Ralph Nader, the future presidential candidate, began to investigate poor standards and corruption in car manufacture, Congress, air travel and conservation. The Watergate scandal and the release of the *Pentagon Papers* showed that investigative journalism was strong. On the other side of the coin, *Rolling Stone magazine* became a respectable place for journalists to work.

 Thematic link: economy and society

The place of the USA as a Superpower

In late 1975, 15 000 Cuban troops, with Soviet support, intervened in the Angolan civil war on the side of the socialist MPLA and helped it to victory. The Americans did nothing to prevent it. Why not? Put simply, President Ford could not have got away with it. Vietnam, a country of very little strategic importance, had been allowed to become communist only after 50 000 American lives had been lost. There was no appetite for further foreign adventures in a country most Americans could not place accurately on a map.

Besides, America had quite enough to do. The situation in the Middle East was concerning. OPEC's decision to raise the price of oil had thrown the USA into a series of energy crises; it would be useful for the USA to find an ally in the region other than Israel, which could not be abandoned. The Chinese were, if not allies, and not even friends, then at least no longer enemies; ambassador George H. W. Bush had been sent to China essentially to wait for the ageing Mao to die and see what could be done thereafter. Relations with the USSR appeared to have been stabilised; the nuclear situation had become less dangerous and there seemed to be no further flashpoints likely to arise. The wall in Berlin seemed as if it would be there for a very long time. In the 1960s, America had had a buccaneering spirit and self-confidence – *Star Trek*'s Captain James T. Kirk was a thinly veiled portrait of JFK – but by the 1970s there were fewer certainties.

 Thematic link: world affairs

The limits of social cohesion

The self-help culture of Middle America was not the picture for everyone. There was an urban crisis, and very little money to deal with it. Slums caused crime; the cheap solution of urban renewal usually meant beautification, which just

ACTIVITY 4.13

Go back through the section on 'The USA and international relations' and write down any factor that appears to have created a change in American foreign policy.

meant taking housing out of city centres and moving the problems elsewhere. Suburban dwellers were doing a lot better, but there were still suburban homes, especially in the Sun Belt (those southern and south western states that stretch from Florida across to California) where there was not a lot of money to go around. In some parts of the country – those near the Mexican border – there were large numbers of Hispanic immigrants. Numbers had tripled since the 1960s. The borders were porous, and the infrastructure of Texas, New Mexico, Arizona and California not necessarily able to cope. The immigration of the 1960s and 1970s sowed seeds that would be reaped over the coming 50 years. Native Americans, meanwhile, benefited from an Indian Civil Rights Act (1968) but still suffered from worse unemployment, lower life expectancy, lower income and higher rates of alcoholism.

This was the period of the rise of the white ethnics. The 1970s saw the creation of bodies like the Italian American Civil Rights league and the Jewish Defence League, and a reassertion of Irish identity in response to the growing Troubles in Ireland. It was the end of the melting-pot narrative, and the decline of WASP culture and vision of national identity. In parts of the South that identity was reborn along with born-again religion. An evangelical awakening was under way in areas where, contrary to national trends, blue-collar workers still dominated, among the poor who lived in mining and agricultural towns.

These evangelicals entered politics. They were anti-establishment. They reacted against permissiveness, abortion and gay rights. They were overwhelmingly Republican. The first born-again president of the United States was Jimmy Carter, a Democrat; he was an exception. Over time evangelical religion became associated with an assertive foreign policy suggesting that America's role was to prepare the world for the second coming of Christ. It has also become associated with a mission to reconstruct America in preparation for that event.

New cultural developments, including the role of women and the position of African Americans

The real sexual revolution happened in the 1970s, not the 1980s. The divorce rate rose by 82% in the 1970s. There was a higher teenage pregnancy rate – so poor single-parent families (and rise in child poverty). *Roe v Wade* meant that abortion had become a touchstone issue, and the continued (but doomed) fight for an Equal Rights Amendment took feminists' time. Women had a role beyond that of wife and mother; however, it was still more difficult for women to gain promotion and be paid properly for it, and women's employment status was often more precarious than that of men. The poor economy of the 1970s was a great leveller; families that might have preferred to have a stay-at-home mother often could not afford to.

The urban crisis meant a crisis for black people – to the extent that 'urban' had become a code for 'black'. The white reaction to black rights had been of acceptance and entrenchment: acceptance of the inevitable changes in voting rights, and entrenchment economically. The typical scene was not the violence that surrounded the integration of schools in South Boston from 1973–75; it was a quiet white flight, and a massive increase of private schooling, especially in

Speak like a historian

'You may not have heard of Reconstructionists such as R.J. Rushdoony or Gary North. But individually and together they have influenced more American minds than Noam Chomsky, Gore Vidal and Howard Zinn combined. Since the 1970s, through hundreds of books and college classes, the doctrine of Reconstructionism has come to permeate not only the religious right, but mainstream churches as well. Evangelical Reconstructionists lined up behind Christian media mogul Pat Robertson in the 1970s, making him rich and powerful. In return, he gave them the power and confidence to launch politically charged movements such as the effort to overturn *Roe v Wade* ...

This push toward a theocracy and the infiltration of mainstream Protestantism by religious extremists was one of the biggest underreported political stories of the second half of the twentieth century ... Thousands of mainstream Methodist, Presbyterian, and other Protestant churches were pushed inexorably rightward, often without even realising it ... Other mainstream churches with more progressive leadership flinched and bowed to the radicals at every turn. They had to if they wanted to retain or gain members swept up in the evangelical movement. So what if the most fervent of these people ... vowed to reconstruct America to fit Leviticus?'

Source: Bageant J. *Deer Hunting with Jesus: Guns, Votes, Debt and Delusion in Redneck America*[11]

ACTIVITY 4.14

What, according to Bageant, was the impact of the evangelical revival of the 1970s?

faith communities in the South. All of this increased social segregation and urban decay, and when riots happened, they had very little effect as they did not happen in the suburbs.

Practice essay questions

1. To what extent do you agree that the Republican Party became stronger from 1945 to 1975?
2. 'Presidents became increasingly powerful from 1945 to 1975.' Assess the validity of this view.
3. To what extent do you agree that American foreign policy from 1945–75 represented a change from what had gone before it?
4. 'The Civil Rights Movement of the 1950s and 1960s secured progress for African Americans in the South only at the expense of those in the North.' Assess the validity of this view.
5. Using your understanding of the historical context, assess how convincing the arguments in the following three extracts are in relation to US foreign policy in the Cold War.

Extract A

'The effort to disengage from Vietnam was part of a wider reassessment of American foreign policy. Nixon and Dr Kissinger, his foreign-policy adviser and later Secretary of

State, recognized that the assumptions which had guided American diplomacy since 1945 were no longer valid. The bipolar post-war world on which the containment policy had been predicated had given way to a different configuration of power. Among the new international realities were the deepening hostility between the Soviet Union and China, the revival of Western Europe, and the re-emergence of Japan. Unlike their predecessors Nixon and Kissinger understood that this new kind of world required a more flexible diplomacy. Since enmities were not immutable, the United States ought not to become hypnotized by ideological differences … overt interventionism ought in future to be confined to areas where American national interests were at stake.

'This new approach to international affairs, subsequently known as the Nixon Doctrine, had dramatic and striking results.'

Source: Jones, M *The Limits of Liberty: 1607–1992.*[12]

Extract B

'In his brief, four hundred-word announcement of the opening to China, Nixon emphasized that the new relationship with the PRC* was "not directed against any other nation." But of course, Nixon and Kissinger saw the China initiative as a useful way to pressure the USSR…

'The White House did not want the opening to China to exacerbate tensions with Moscow. Nixon and Kissinger feared that it might move Russia to strike a relatively weak China with nuclear weapons in order to eliminate a two-front threat. Nor did Nixon and Kissinger believe that they could use detente with Moscow to directly pressure Peking:* it might recoil from improved relations with Washington and "reexamine its options with the Soviet Union." As Mao would later tell Nixon, we should not try to stand "on China's shoulders to reach Moscow."

'Difficulties between the two Communist superpowers, however, gave anything that the United States did with one or the other resonance in both nations' capitals.'

*PRC stands for People's Republic of China, and is the full name of the country we usually call China. Peking, which we would now call Beijing, is its capital.

Source: Dallek, R. *Nixon and Kissinger: Partners in Power.*[13]

Extract C

'In the summer of 1969 [a surprising conversation] occurred in Washington, where a mid-level Soviet embassy official posed a question… to a State Department counterpart: what might the American response be if the USSR were to attack Chinese nuclear facilities? The query could only have been made on instructions from Moscow, and … it had already been answered. Several days earlier, President Nixon had startled his Cabinet by announcing that the United States could not let China be 'smashed' in a Sino-Soviet war…

'It is unlikely that Mao had highly placed spies in Washington that summer, or that Nixon had them in Beijing: there was as yet little communication between them. What they did have, however, was a convergence of several interests. One, obviously, was concern about the Soviet Union, which appeared to both of them to be increasingly threatening. Its August, 1968, invasion of Czechoslovakia seemed to have been a ruthlessly successful

operation, an impression reinforced in November when Brezhnev claimed the right
to violate the sovereignty of *any* country in which an effort was under way to replace
Marxism-Leninism.'

Source: Gaddis, J.L *The Cold War*.[9]

Taking it further

Were Americans more united by 1975 than they had been in 1945?

Chapter summary

By the end of this chapter you should understand:

- the way in which the Solid South became Republican, not Democrat, in
  presidential elections, after significant liberal reforms
- the reasons why the American economy was secure by the 1970s
  despite a downturn, and the reasons for the exceptional growth in the
  economy in the preceding decades
- the effect of the Vietnam War on American foreign policy, and on
  Americans' ideas about themselves
- the reasons why the Civil Rights Movement achieved its aims in the
  South so completely, and the reasons why it was less successful in the
  North and for urban African Americans more generally.

Further reading

For more on the causes of the Cold War you might read:

Norman Friedman, in *The Fifty-Year War: Conflict and Strategy in the Cold War,*[14]
argues that Soviet strategy caused the Cold War.

In *The Sources of Soviet Conduct*[15] George F. Kennan, a state department analyst of
the time, argued that Soviet ideology had caused the conflict.

William A. Williams, in *The Tragedy of American Diplomacy,*[16] (1959), argued that it
was the overreaction of the Americans to legitimate Soviet concerns that caused
the war.

End notes

1. Davies G. *From Opportunity to Entitlement.* Lawrence: University Press of Kansas; 1996.

2. Bell, D. *The End of Ideology: On the Exhaustion of Political Ideas in the Fifties*: Cambridge: Harvard University Press; 1960.
Reprinted by permission of the publisher from THE END OF IDEOLOGY by Daniel Bell, pp. 393, 402-403, Cambridge, Mass.: Harvard University Press, Copyright © 1960, 1961, 1962, 1988, 2000 by Daniel Bell.

3. Scammon RM, Wattenberg BJ. *The Real Majority.* New York: Coward-McCann; 1970.

4. Thompson HS. *Fear and Loathing on the Campaign Trail '72.* San Francisco: Straight Arrow Books 1973

5. McGirr L. *Suburban Warriors: The Origins of the American New Right.* New Jersey: Princeton University Press; 2002.

6. Sugrue TJ. *The Origins of the Urban Crisis: Race and Inequality in Postwar Detroit.* New Jersey: Princeton University Press; 1996.

7. Buckley WF Jr. *Up from Liberalism.* Maryland: Rowman & Littlefield; 1961.

8. Gaddis JL. *The Cold War.* London: Allen Lane; 2005.

9. Gaddis JL. *The Cold War.* London: Allen Lane; 2005. p. 66.

10. McNamara R. *In Retrospect: The Tragedy and Lessons of Vietnam.* New York: Vintage; 1996.

11. Bageant J. *Deer Hunting with Jesus: Guns, Votes, Debt and Delusion in Redneck America.* New York: Random House; 2007. p. 167.

12. Jones M. *The Limits of Liberty: 1607–1992*: 2nd ed. Oxford: Oxford University Press; 1995. p. 558.

13. Dallek, R. *Nixon and Kissinger: Partners in Power.* Penguin; 2007. p. 300.

14. Friedman N. *The Fifty-Year War: Conflict and Strategy in the Cold War.* Annapolis MD: Naval Institute Press; 2007.

15. Kennan G. The Sources of Soviet Conduct. *Foreign Affairs Magazine.* 1947; 4(25).

16. Williams WA. *The Tragedy of American Diplomacy.* New York: Norton; 1959.

Glossary

A

Alphabet agencies — Alphabet agencies is the generic term given to the agencies FDR created to manage the various aspects of the New Deal. They are so called because they are often known by their initial letters. Examples include the CCC, PWA and TVA.

Amendment — An amendment is the only way in which the United States Constitution can be changed. Amendments are most commonly passed by two-thirds of the House, two-thirds of the Senate, and three-quarters of the states.

American dream — The American Dream is the idea popular in America that all Americans can, through hard work, achieve anything they want to.

American Exceptionalism — American Exceptionalism is the idea that because America has geographical, economic and political advantages, it has a responsibility to use those advantages well and (sometimes) to assume a position of global leadership.

Attorney General — The attorney general is the chief legal officer in a democratic government. In the USA, he is a member of the Cabinet.

B

Baby Boomer — The generation born in the years immediately following the Second World War, and which came of age in the 1960s, is known as the Baby Boomer generation because it was larger than the generation immediately before it. A lot of families had waited until the end of the Second World War to have children.

Brinkmanship — Eisenhower's secretary of state Dulles defined brinkmanship in this way: 'The ability to get to the verge without getting into war is the necessary art. If you cannot master it, you inevitably get into war. If you are scared to go to the brink, you are lost.'

C

Cabinet — The Cabinet is the group of departmental heads appointed by the US president. They are known as cabinet secretaries. Examples include the secretary of state and the secretary of the treasury.

Carpetbagger — Carpetbagger is a derogatory term for northerners who moved to the South during Reconstruction, stereotypically with their belongings held in a bag made of carpet, to seek political office or economic advantage in the defeated South.

Cold War — The Cold War is the name for the undeclared hostility and tension between communists and capitalists that began after the Second World War and ended in 1990. During the Cold War the USA assumed a position of leadership of the free, democratic, capitalist world.

Congress — Congress is the name for the American legislature. It consists of the House of Representatives, whose members (representatives) are elected by constituencies with roughly equal populations, and the Senate; there are two senators per state.

Containment — Containment is the idea that communism should not be allowed to spread to other countries. It is an important part of Cold War doctrine.

D

Declaration of Independence — The Declaration of Independence is the document written in 1776 in which the American colonies announced their intention to break away from the British Empire. Written largely by Thomas Jefferson, it argues that people have rights and should not be subject to tyranny.

Deficit — A deficit is the amount by which a country overspends in a year. When a country is in deficit, its debt increases.

Democracy — Democracy is a political system run by the people, for the people, and of the people. It involves regular elections, and some protection for the rights of minorities.

Dixiecrat — A Dixiecrat is the name given to a southern Democrat who did not accept the need for civil rights legislation. An example is Strom Thurmond of South Carolina.

Domino theory — Domino theory is the idea that if a country became communist, other nearby countries might also 'fall' to communism, like dominoes.

E

Executive order — An executive order is when the president uses his power as head of the executive branch to make things happen, not by ordering people as their president, but by ordering them as their boss.

F

Federal government — The federal government is the central government of the United States, as distinct from the state governments. Its head is the president.

Freedom Rides — Freedom Rides began in the 1950s; civil rights activists rode on buses in defiance of segregation rules. They aimed to attract publicity by being arrested.

Fundamentalism — Fundamentalism is a belief in the literal truth of the Bible. It has become increasingly common in the USA since the 1970s.

G

Gross domestic product (GDP) — GDP is a measure of the total amount produced by a country in a year. The higher the GDP, the wealthier the country.

H

House of Representatives — The House of Representatives is part of the Congress of the United States. It contains representatives elected by districts throughout the country. Its members are sometimes called congressmen (or congresswomen).

I

Impeachment — Impeachment is the process by which high-ranking American officials, including presidents, may be removed. The House of Representatives is entitled to impeach, which means sending the impeached official to the Senate for a trial on charges specified by the House.

Inaugural address — By tradition, the incoming president makes a speech at the inauguration ceremony in which the new president's agenda is set out. Some of these addresses – Franklin Roosevelt's first and John F. Kennedy's – have become iconic.

Isolationism — Isolationism is the foreign policy doctrine of refusing to engage in world affairs except when absolutely necessary, refusing positions of world leadership.

K

Keynesianism — Keynesianism is the economic theory that originated in the 1930s that governments should lead spending programmes during a Depression in order to stimulate recovery. It is named after the British economist John Maynard Keynes.

L

Lend-lease — Lend-lease is the practice adopted by FDR during the Second World War of giving military, economic and food aid to America's allies in return for the right to future military bases.

Liberalism — Liberalism is an ideology that emphasises freedom from restraint by government: people should be allowed to do what they want. It has also come to be used in an American context to indicate a belief in change in society.

M

Manifest destiny — Manifest destiny is the idea that America was and is fated to dominate the continent of North America, the western hemisphere and the world. It drove expansion in the 19th century.

McCarthyism McCarthyism is named after Senator Joseph McCarthy, Republican of Wisconsin, who made his name as an anti-communist campaigner. From the moment in February 1950 when McCarthy claimed that he had a list of 205 communists working in the State Department, the anti-communist movement was associated with him. Throughout his career, McCarthyism did not uncover a single actual spy.

Medicaid Medicaid is a Great Society policy that provides free healthcare for low-income individuals and families.

Medicare Medicare is a key Great Society policy, originally proposed by Truman but then passed by LBJ. It provides free medical insurance for the elderly; Truman received the first Medicare card in 1965.

Middle America Middle America is a term used to describe conservative rural and suburban Americans, associated by Richard Nixon with being in the 'silent majority'. Middle America is the home of old-fashioned values and patriotism. It is a highly contentious term.

Midterm elections Midterm, or off-year, elections, are Congressional elections held in years when there is no presidential election.

Military-industrial complex President Eisenhower coined the term 'military-industrial complex' to indicate his belief that, by the end of his presidency, a large part of the American economy depended on military production.

Modernism Modernism is the philosophical explanation of the way in which culture changed in the modern age, taking off in America in the 1920s. It involves ideas of self-consciousness, aesthetics and celebrity.

Monroe Doctrine The Monroe Doctrine, named after James Monroe, the fifth president, is the idea that America should be the pre-eminent power in the western hemisphere, and that European powers should not interfere there.

N

Native American Native Americans were the inhabitants of the USA before the phase of European settlement began in the 16th century. There were many different Native American tribes, many of whose names survive in the names of states such as Massachusetts, Connecticut and the Dakotas.

New Deal The New Deal is the name for FDR's efforts to restructure and support the failing American economy in the 1930s. Historians are divided on whether there was one New Deal or three separate New Deals. In modern American thought the New Deal is seen as a cornerstone of liberal politics.

New South The New South is the term used to describe the South from the 1970s, in the post-segregation era.

P

Polarity Polarity, in international relations, is the identification of particular groups of countries that are aligned. During the early Cold War, most American politicians saw the world as bipolar, meaning that countries were either democratic, capitalist, individualistic and free or socialist, communist and unfree.

Populism Populism is a political movement that grew up in the last years of the 19th century. It emphasised support for farmers and bimetallism. It came to be associated with the Democratic politician William Jennings Bryan.

President The president of the United States of America is the head of state and the head of the executive branch of government, elected every four years.

Progressivism Progressivism is a political doctrine of the early 20th century. It was concerned with modern social developments and rights for workers. The idea of progressive politics still remains part of American discourse. It became associated with Theodore Roosevelt.

R

Red Scare — A Red Scare is a cultural and political reaction to fear of domestic or foreign communism. Red Scares occurred in the USA in the 1920s and 1940s to 1950s.

Rights — Rights are specific guarantees given by governments to people. An example is the right to freedom of speech, which is guaranteed by the 1st Amendment to the US Constitution.

Rollback — Rollback is the opposite of containment, and is the doctrine favoured by General MacArthur during the Korean War that communist countries should be invaded to bring down their communist governments.

S

Scalawag — Scalawag is a derogatory term applied by white southerners after the Civil War to other white southerners who cooperated with northern Republicans during Reconstruction.

Secretary of state — The secretary of state is the most senior member of the US Cabinet. US secretaries of state are in charge of foreign affairs and diplomatic relations.

Segregation — Segregation is the deliberate separation of black from white people in public and private areas.

Senate — The Senate is a branch of the US Congress. It contains two senators from every state.

Silent majority — The silent majority was Nixon's term for those Americans who did not protest against the Vietnam War, and who exhibited conservative values without feeling moved to demonstrate them publicly.

Spoils system — The spoils system is the convention by which presidents (and governors) who have won an election appoint their own friends (or donors) to profitable positions in the bureaucracy, following the ancient maxim of 'to the victor, the spoils'.

State capacity — State capacity is a term used by political scientists that has recently been adopted by historians. It refers to the bureaucratic or logistical ability of governments to exercise power and to get things done. It is a measure of the potential effectiveness of a government.

States' Rights — States' Rights refers to the political doctrine that states should set their own social legislation. In practice, the term is often used as a shorthand for legislation designed to promote white interests at the expense of black people.

Superpower — The USA and the USSR were Superpowers during the Cold War, as they dominated other countries through their political, economic and military power.

Supreme Court — The Supreme Court is the group of nine justices who head the American judiciary. They have the right to declare laws passed by Congress or by states, and actions of the president or state governors, as unconstitutional.

T

Tariff — A tariff is a tax placed upon the importation or exportation of goods. Higher tariffs are usually seen as good for industrialists, and lower tariffs as good for consumers.

V

Veto — The president is entitled to veto legislation, which prevents it from becoming law. The president can be overridden by a vote of two-thirds of both the House and the Senate.

W

Watergate — The Watergate Hotel is a plush hotel and office complex in Washington, famous as the site of the burglary that ultimately brought down Richard Nixon.

White House — The White House is the building in Washington that functions as the president's residence and office. It was built in 1800.

Bibliography

Chapter 1:

Benedict ML. *A Compromise of Principle: Congressional Republicans and Reconstruction, 1863–1869*. New York: WW Norton & Co; 1974.

Blight D. *Race and Reunion: the Civil War in American Memory*. Harvard: Harvard University Press; 2002.

Clemens E. *The People's Lobby: Organizational Innovation and the Rise of Interest Group Politics in the US, 1890-1925*. Chicago: Chicago University Press; 1997.

Fitzgerald M. *Splendid Failure: Postwar Reconstruction in the American South. Chicago*: Chicago University Press; 2007.

Foner E. *Reconstruction: America's Unfinished Revolution*. New York: Harper & Row; 1988.

Ingraham Colonel P. *Adventures of Buffalo Bill from Boyhood to Manhood. Deeds of Daring, Scenes of Thrilling, Peril, and Romantic Incidents In the Early Life of W. F. Cody, the Monarch of Bordermen.* Beadle's Boy's Library of Sport, Story and Adventure, 1(1): New York: Beadle and Adams; 1882.

Novak W. The Myth of the 'Weak' American State. American Historical Review. 2008; 113 (June): 752–2.

Richardson HC. *West from Appomattox: The Reconstruction of America after the Civil War*. New Haven: Yale University Press; 2007.

Rubin SA. *A Shattered Nation: the Rise and Fall of the Confederacy, 1861–1868*. Chapel Hill: University of North Carolina Press; 2005.

Scaturro FJ. *President Grant Reconsidered*: Lanham, MD; 1998.

Simpson BD. *Let Us Have Peace: Ulysses S. Grant and the Politics of War and Reconstruction, 1861–1868*. Chapel Hill, 1991.

Smith JE. *Grant*. New York: Simon & Schuster; 2001.

Stampp K. *The Era of Reconstruction*. New York: Alfred A. Knopf; 1965.

Summers MW. *The Gilded Age, or the Hazard of New Functions*. New York: Prentice Hall; 1997.

Summers MW. *The Ordeal of the Reunion: A New History of Reconstruction*. Chapel Hill: University of North Carolina Press; 2014.

Vann Woodward, C. *The Strange Career of Jim Crow. New York: Oxford University Press;* 1955.

Chapter 2:

Archer R. *Why is There No Labor Party in the United States? New Jersey*: Princeton University Press; 2007.

Baum LF. *The Wonderful Wizard of Oz. Chicago*: George M Hill; 1900.

Beckert S. *The Monied Metropolis: New York City and the Consolidation of the American Bourgeoisie, 1850–1896. New York*: Cambridge University Press, 2001.

Chandler AD. *The Visible Hand: The Managerial Revolution in American Business. Cambridge*: Harvard University Press; 1977.

Hofstadter R. *The Age of Reform: From Bryan to FDR*. New York: Knopf; 1955.

Ignatiev N. *How the Irish Became White. New York: Routledge; 2008.*

Johnston RP. *The Radical Middle Class: Populist Democracy and the Question of*

Capitalism in Progressive Era Portland, Oregon. New Jersey: Princeton University Press; 2003.

Lloyd HD. *Wealth Against Commonwealth. New York: Harper & Brothers;* 1894.

Livingston J. *Origins of the Federal Reserve System: Money, Class and Corporate Capitalism, 1890–1913. New York*: Cornell University Press; 1986.

Postel C. *The Populist Vision. New York*: Oxford University Press; 2007.

Reynolds D. *America – Empire of Liberty: a New History. London:* Allen Lane; 2009.

Tyrrell I. *Transnational Nation: the United States in Global Perspective Since 1789. Basingstoke*: Palgrave Macmillan; 2007.

Veblen TB. *The Theory of the Leisure Class. New York: Dover Publications;* 1899.

Chapter 3:

Badger AJ. *The New Deal: The Depression Years 1933-1940.* Basingstoke: Palgrave Macmillan; 1989.

Bernstein B. *The New Deal: The Conservative Achievements of Liberal Reform. London*: Chatto & Windus; 1970.

Brinkley A. The End of Reform: New Deal Liberalism in Recession and War. New York: Vintage; 1995.

Cohen L. Encountering Mass Culture at the Grassroots: The Experience of Chicago Workers in the 1920s. *American Quarterly* March. 1989: 41(1).

Degler C. *The New Deal. Chicago*: Quadrangle; 1970.

Dumenil L. *Modern Temper: American Culture and Society in the 1920s. New York*: Hill and Wang; 1995.

Hacker L. *Short History of the New Deal*. New York: Crofts and Co; 1935.

Hamby AL. *The New Deal: Analysis and Interpretation. New York*: Weybright and Talley; 1969.

Hayward S. *The Age of Reagan: The Fall of the Old Liberal Order 1964–1980. Roseville, CA*: Prima Publishing; 2001.

Katznelson I. *Fear Itself: The New Deal and the Origins of Our Time. New York*: WW Norton and Company 2014.

Leuchtenburg, W. *Franklin D. Roosevelt and the New Deal, 1932–1940*. New York: Harper Collins; 1963.

Murphy M. Bootlegging Mothers and Drinking Daughters: Gender and Prohibition in Butte, Montana. *American Quarterly*. 1994; 46(2).

Stone O, Kuznick P. *The Untold History of the United States. London*: Ebury Press; 2013.

Chapter 4:

Bageant J. *Deer Hunting with Jesus*: Guns, Votes, Debt and Delusion in Redneck America. New York: Random House; 2007.

Bell, D. *The End of Ideology: On the Exhaustion of Political Ideas in the Fifties*: Cambridge: Harvard University Press; 1960.

Buckley WF Jr. *Up from Liberalism*. Maryland: Rowman & Littlefield; 1961.

Dallek R. *Nixon and Kissinger: Partners in Power*. London: Penguin; 2007.

Davies G. *From Opportunity to Entitlement. Lawrence*: University Press of Kansas; 1996.

Friedman N. *The Fifty-Year War: Conflict and Strategy in the Cold War. Annapolis MD*: Naval Institute Press; 2007.

Gaddis JL. *The Cold War. London*: Allen Lane; 2005.

Harrington M. *The Other America: Poverty in the United States*. New York: Macmillan; 1962.

Jones M. *The Limits of Liberty: 1607–1992*: 2nd ed. Oxford: Oxford University Press; 1995.

Kennan G. The Sources of Soviet Conduct. *Foreign Affairs Magazine*. 1947; 4(25).

McGirr L. *Suburban Warriors: The Origins of the American New Right. New Jersey*: Princeton University Press; 2002.

McNamara R. *In Retrospect*: The Tragedy and Lessons of Vietnam. New York: Vintage; 1996.

Scammon s, Wattenberg BJ. *The Real Majority. New York*: Coward-McCann; 1970.

Sugrue TJ. *The Origins of the Urban Crisis: Race and Inequality in Postwar Detroit. New Jersey*: Princeton University Press; 2005.

Williams WA. *The Tragedy of American Diplomacy. New York*: Norton; 1959.

Thompson HS. *Fear and Loathing on the Campaign Trail '72. San Franciso*: Straight Arrow Books; 1973.

Acknowledgements

The authors and publishers acknowledge the following sources of copyright material and are grateful for the permissions granted. While every effort has been made, it has not always been possible to identify the sources of all the material used, or to trace all copyright holders. If any omissions are brought to our notice, we will be happy to include the appropriate acknowledgements on reprinting.

The publisher would like to thank the following for permission to reproduce their photographs (numbers refer to figure numbers, unless otherwise stated):

0.3 Alamy Images: Niday Picture Library (tl). **Chapter 1 opener TopFoto:** The Granger Collection, New York. **1.1 Shutterstock:** Everett Historical. **Table 1.1 Shutterstock:** Everett Historical. **Table 1.1 Alamy Images:** World History Archive. **Table 1.1 TopFoto:** Topham Picturepoint. **1.3 Alamy Images:** North Wind Picture Archives. **1.4 Shutterstock:** Everett Historical. **1.5 Alamy Images:** Everett Collection Historical. **1.8 Alamy Images:** Shawshots. **Chapter 2 opener Alamy Images:** PF-(bygone1). **2.1 Alamy Images:** Everett Collection Historical. **2.3 Mary Evans Picture Library: 2.4 Corbis: 2.5 Alamy Images:** GL Archive. **2.10 Shutterstock:** Everett Historical. **Chapter 3 opener Alamy Images:** Everett Collection Historical. **3.1 Alamy Images:** GL Archive. **3.2 Shutterstock:** Everett Historical. **3.3 Corbis: 3.5 Rex Features:** Courtesy Everett Collection. **3.8 Alamy Images:** Glasshouse Images. **3.10 and 3.11 Rex Features:** Courtesy Everett Collection. **Chapter 4 opener Alamy Images:** PF-(aircraft). **4.1 Rex Features:** Courtesy Everett Collection. **4.2 TopFoto:** Granger Collection. **4.3 Rex Features:** Nara Archives. **4.4 Getty Images:** Fotosearch / Stringer. **4.6 Getty Images:** Don Cravens/The LIFE Images Collection. **4.7 TopFoto:** The Granger Collection, New York. **4.8 Rex Features:** Sipa Press. **4.10 Rex Features:** Nara Archives. **4.11 TopFoto:** The Granger Collection. **4.12 Alamy Images:** Everett Collection Historical.

The publisher would like to thank the following for permission to reproduce extracts from their texts:

Extract Chapter 1 from Foner E. *Reconstruction: America's Unfinished Revolution*. New York: Harper & Row 1988; **Extract Chapter 1** from THE ORDEAL OF THE REUNION: A NEW HISTORY OF RECONSTRUCTION by Mark Wahlgren Summers. Copyright © 2014 The University of North Carolina Press. Used by permission of the publisher www.uncpress.unc.edu; **Extract Chapter 1** from Richardson HC. West from Appomattox: The Reconstruction of America after the Civil War. New Haven: Yale University Press; 2007; **Extract Chapter 2** from The Populist Vision by Charles Postel, Oxford University Press, USA (0100). "By permission of Oxford University Press, USA"; **Extract Chapter 2** from Reynolds D. America – Empire of Liberty: a New History. London: Allen Lane; 2009; Extract **Chapter 2** from Hofstadter R. The Age of Reform: From Bryan to FDR. New York: Knopf; 1955; **Extract Chapter 3** from Stone O, Kuznick P. The Untold History of the United States. London: Ebury Press; 2013; **Extract Chapter 3** from Murphy, Mary. "Bootlegging Mothers and Drinking Daughters: Gender and Prohibition in Butte, Montana". Volumn 46: Issue 2 1994, American Quarterly. Reprinted with permission of John Hopkins University Press; **Extract Chapter 3** from Cohen, Lizabeth. "Encountering Mass Culture at the Grassroots: The Experience of Chicago Workers in the 1920s". Volumn 41: Issue 1 1989, American Quarterly. Reprinted with permission of John Hopkins University Press. **Extract Chapter 3** from Dumenil L. Modern Temper: American Culture and Society in the 1920s. New York: Hill and Wang; 1995; **Extract Chapter 4** Reprinted by permission of the publisher from THE END OF IDEOLOGY by Daniel Bell, pp. 393, 402-403, Cambridge, Mass.: Harvard University Press, Copyright © 1960, 1961, 1962, 1988, 2000 by Daniel Bell; **Extract Chapter 4** from Gaddis JL. The Cold War. London: Allen Lane; 2005; **Extract Chapter 4** from Bageant J. Deer Hunting with Jesus: Guns, Votes, Debt and Delusion in Redneck America. New York: Random House; 2007. **Extract Chapter 4** from Jones M. The Limits of Liberty: 1607–1992: 2nd ed. Oxford: Oxford University Press; 1995; **Extract Chapter 4** from Dallek R. Nixon and Kissinger: Partners in Power. London: Penguin; 2007

Index

Lightning Source UK Ltd.
Milton Keynes UK
UKOW07f0626200516

274637UK00008B/31/P